WINGS OVER MEIR

The Story of the Potteries Aerodrome

WILLIAM COOKE

AMBERLEY

First published 2010

Amberley Publishing
Cirencester Road, Chalford,
Stroud, Gloucestershire, GL6 8PE

www.amberley-books.com

British Library Cataloguing in Publication Data.
A catalogue record for this book is available
from the British Library.

ISBN 978-1-4456-0135-9

Typeset in 10pt on 12pt Sabon.
Typesetting and Origination by Amberley Publishing.
Printed in the UK.

Contents

Acknowledgements

I should like to express my gratitude to the following for their help in providing information and for allowing me to quote freely from letters, memoirs, and books: the Air Historical Branch (RAF), the late Squadron Leader Dennis Armitage and Mrs Margaret Armitage, Maurice Bann, BBC Radio Stoke, Peter Berry, Reg Bott, Catherine Bradley (sister of John Cedric Moores), Ian Carter, the late Nicholas Cartlidge, Judy Chilvers (niece of Amy Johnson), Ralph Cooper, Wing Commander Bob Doe, Dame Margaret Drabble, Frank Goff, the late Alex Henshaw, Guy Jefferson, Stephanie Caplan-Jerromes, the Libraries, Museums and Information Committee, the *London Gazette*, Macclesfield Historical Aviation Society, Errol Martyn, Meir Library, the late Dr Gordon Mitchell, the National Archives, Newcastle-under-Lyme Library, the New Zealand Fighter Pilots Museum, Robert Owen (official historian of No. 617 Squadron), RAF ACOS (Manning), the Royal Air Force Museum, the late Vic Reynolds, John Shipman, Roger Lycett-Smith, Stoke-on-Trent City Library and Archive, Charles Strasser, Dean Sumner, the Battle of Britain London Monument website and the Shoreham Aircraft Museum, Irene Turner (Biddulph & District Genealogy & Historical Society), Janette Tyreman, Squadron Leader Brian Waite (for an extract from the archives of No. 609 Squadron), Heather Wareing (sister of Bill Astell), Carolyn Wood, Alistair Wright, and Geoffrey Wright.

Wing Commander Ken Rees spoke to me about The Great Escape and kindly allowed me to use an extract from *Lie in the Dark and Listen* (ISBN 9781904943419, Grub Street Publishing). Eric Clutton let me ransack his memory and also gave permission for the use of extracts from *An Aeroplane Called FRED*. Passages from *Shot Down in Flames* by Geoffrey Page and *Flying In, Walking Out* by Edward Sniders are reprinted by permission of Grub Street and Pen and Sword Ltd respectively. Martin Tideswell (Deputy Editor of the *Sentinel*) generously allowed me to quote from numerous editorials, letters, news reports, and articles.

Photographs and other illustrations are used courtesy of the Aldershot Military Museum (for the image of Samuel Cody), John Ash, Maurice Bann, Bill Bond and the Battle of Britain Historical Society, the Borough Museum and

Art Gallery, Newcastle-under-Lyme, Eric Clutton, Tony Eyre, Stephen Frakes, John Godwin/Staffordshire Arts & Museum Service, Robert Hale Ltd (for the portrait of Dolly Shepherd from her book *When the 'Chute Went Up*), the late Alex Henshaw, David Lam, John Lowe (for the photo of Vic Reynolds), Tony Price, RAF/106G/UK/646, frame 4200 11 August 1945 English Heritage (NMR) RAF Photography (for the aerial view of Meir Aerodrome) , Ken Rees, Earl Rogers, the Rootes Archive now held at the Coventry Transport Museum, Staffordshire Sentinel News & Media Ltd, Trounce/Wikimedia Common (for the image of the Schneider Trophy edited by Eric Menneteau), and Brian Waite. The portrait of Trevor Oldfield is used courtesy of the aviation artist Geoff Nutkins and the pictures of Eric Lock courtesy of the *Shropshire Magazine*. The photograph of the Queen's Vase is used by kind permission of the Royal Collection © 2010 Her Majesty Queen Elizabeth II.

Harry Carson, Mrs S. Boughey, and Jim Eardley were instrumental in identifying the crash site of Pilot Officer Sankey's plane after more than sixty years. Tony Chadwick, Joan Harrison, Joan Rothery, and Janette Tyreman all read the manuscript before publication and made valuable suggestions. My thanks, too, to the staff of the Learning Resource Centre at Stoke-on-Trent College, who were always ready to help with technical problems. Finally, I should like to express a general debt to all the books referred to in the selected bibliography.

1

When the Balloon Went Up

The 'leap for life' from 10,000 feet certainly brought out the crowds in the Potteries on 30 August 1890. At 5.30 p.m. that Saturday, Port Vale Football Ground (from where the ascent was to take place) was packed, with thousands more outside the gates and on many hills in North Staffordshire, all hoping for a glimpse of the intrepid aeronaut. 'Professor' Higgins, sometime London cab driver and keeper of a licensed house at Crewe, intended to fly by balloon to Stoke and then 'drop in' on the County Cricket Ground (now the site of Staffordshire University) where a match with the Australians was in progress. It was to be a spectacle that none of those watching would ever forget.

Although parachuting was a century old, it was still primitive and hazardous. Higgins sat on a trapeze bar, the limp parachute attached to the balloon by a cord that would snap when he jumped. However, just as he was leaving the ground, the parachute broke loose, and the 'professor' sailed upwards with it hanging beneath him 'like an open and inverted umbrella'. The 'leap for life' was about to become literally true.

Higgins knew that his best chance of survival was to gain as much height as possible and he soon became a faint speck in the clear sky. Over the furnaces at Etruria he decided that the critical moment had arrived – and dropped into the open parachute. Momentarily he blacked out, but an eye-witness saw 'man and parachute twirl over two or three times before the air got under the parachute'. When he came to, Higgins found that he had fallen about 6,000 feet and that almost miraculously he 'was hanging all in a heap from the parachute, which was inflated and coming down steadily'.

With his legs twisted in the guiding ropes, he missed the cricket ground, where his appearance had stopped play, and landed with one knee pulled up against his chin in Station Road, opposite the statue of Josiah Wedgwood. Badly bruised and shaken but otherwise unharmed, the 'hero of the clouds' returned to Cobridge by cab and was met by the Port Vale Band and a huge throng cheering him mightily.

A reporter subsequently interviewed him and asked if it was not time for him to retire. Higgins pooh-poohed the idea. The journalist then asked:

'Do you think parachuting serves any purpose? Will it lead to any useful end?' Higgins replied:

'I think it will be used for war purposes.' The journalist remained sceptical, but wished him success, for 'he was one of those men who rise in the world'. 'Yes, I get up above my fellow-men, don't I?' responded the 'professor' with a smile. Within a year he was killed in a balloon accident over Leeds.

*

Balloons, though rare, had been seen before in the area. As early as 4 January 1785, one carrying a Mr Harper ascended just after mid-day from the tennis court in Coleshill Street, Birmingham, watched by one of the largest crowds ever to assemble in the town. Mr Harper then drifted over Staffordshire, and at Trentham, the seat of Earl Gower, he descended sufficiently to address one of the workmen in the park with his speaking trumpet. 'How far is it to Birmingham?' he enquired. 'Forty miles, master,' came the reply, 'but you are going the wrong road.' He eventually came down at about 2 p.m. at Millstone Green, near Newcastle-under-Lyme, his car being extremely damaged by hedges and trees on his descent. Mr Harper (and his balloon) left by carriage for Lichfield the same evening, and the following morning he arrived back at his starting-point in triumph, his carriage drawn through the streets by the citizens themselves. It was just three months after the first ever balloon ascent in England.

The first ascent in Stoke-on-Trent took place on Tuesday, 3 October 1826, when 'a vast concourse of persons' assembled at the enclosure in Shelton where the process of inflation was being carried out. Many more watched from windows, rooftops, and adjoining streets, roads and fields.

At 3.30 p.m. a pilot balloon was released to ascertain the probable direction of the flight, and then the well-known aeronaut Charles Green entered the car. At the last minute a gentleman who had previously agreed to accompany him had had cold feet and it seemed that he would have to travel alone. Suddenly, however, the band struck up 'Fly Not Yet!' and the Reverend Dr Benjamin Vale, the somewhat eccentric rector of Longton, offered to go along and took a seat in the car to much applause. The ropes were then detached and 'the splendid machine rose in the most graceful and majestic style' to the music of the band and the acclaim of the assembly.

For about twenty minutes the balloon was visible before being lost in cloud. The two voyagers travelled for nearly an hour at an altitude of two miles and covered nearly twenty-five miles, sailing over Blythe Marsh Bridge, Cellarhead, Werrington Windmill, Consall Woods, Ipstones, and Kingsley. As their descent began, Dr Vale noted that 'what appeared narrow straight lines hardly distinguishable turned out to be the King's highway; what appeared to be a mushroom turned out to be a haystack; and what appeared to be a solitary bush turned out to be a plantation or wood.' They finally came safely to earth on the Staffordshire Moorlands, but not before their grapple had caught in two walls, dragging parts of them to the ground.

So sublime had been the spectacle of the launch that Mr Green was invited to give a repeat performance in Newcastle-under-Lyme, which he undertook on Thursday, 19 October, from a walled paddock near Hassell Street. This time, however, as a contemporary report makes clear, things did not go quite so smoothly. A strong wind buffeting the balloon led to an ascent that was abrupt, premature, and distinctly hazardous:

> At this time all the weights attached to the balloon, together with the ballast, were in the car and could not be less than 16 cwt; but this enormous weight, together with the united assistance of about fifty men, was unavailing in keeping her steady, and she went with violence against a tree, which unfortunately happened to be near. A rent of about 14 inches square, near the equator of the balloon, was the fatal consequence, through which the gas began to escape with great rapidity. At this critical juncture, the intrepidity of the aeronaut was strikingly manifested – the ascent must be made then or not at all that day; for the ascending power was becoming less and less every moment, and any attempt at repair and renovation with gas was out of the question.
>
> Mr Green, with that coolness and courage which in so peculiar a way fit him for his profession, determined to ascend. The ropes were immediately cut from the iron weights – the grapple was thrown into the car – and Mr Green took his seat. But before the machine was entirely liberated, a gust of wind forced her to one end of the enclosure, and in spite of the exertion of the assistants, the balloon rolled over the high brick wall which bounds the enclosure, whilst Mr Green and the car remained on the inner side of the wall. In this dangerous situation it remained a short time, but on Mr Green insisting on the men quitting their hold of the ropes, the car was instantly pulled over the wall, and after Mr Green had thrown out two bags of sand, she began to ascend and proceeded over the town, taking a westwardly direction.

For the immense crowd still flocking into the town, the news that Mr Green had already gone was an enormous disappointment, though when the circumstances were explained this changed to sympathy and a fervent desire for his safety.

Meanwhile, Mr Green had discovered that because of the hurried ascent the valve cord was out of reach, and his first task was to use a rope hanging from the neck of the balloon to climb high enough to reach it. Having achieved this, he sought a convenient place to descend and settled on Ravensmoor Common, near Nantwich. His grapple took hold in a hedge, and two men who were close by threw themselves on the rope to secure it. A chaise and four then speedily transported Mr Green to Nantwich where a number of its leading citizens invited him to dine. He finally returned to Newcastle at 6.30 p.m., where he was greeted 'with the loudest acclamation' before taking supper at the Castle Hotel.

To make up for the general disappointment, Mr Green put on a second demonstration a week later. On Thursday, 26 October, Newcastle began to fill rapidly, well before the launch hour. At 2 p.m. Lord Francis Gower, his Lady, and the most distinguished families of the neighbourhood arrived to occupy the enclosure, while thousands of others crowded the surrounding open spaces. At 3 p.m. the pilot balloon was dispatched, and Mr Green's balloon ascended a short distance with cords still attached to give the spectators a good view. Then Mr P. E. Wedgwood, who was to share 'the perils of the enterprise', took his seat in the car. The final ceremony – the presentation of the flags – was performed by the nobles present, who committed the banners to the charge of the aeronauts and wished them a safe and pleasant excursion.

The balloon then rose without a hitch to the cheers and applause of the excited throng. It remained in sight for a good half-hour before it passed over Trentham, where the aeronauts, having drunk the health of the Sovereign, toasted the noble owner of the mansion below them. The duo then reached Stone before a fresh current of air whisked them nearly due east to within a few miles of Uttoxeter. At Abbot's Bromley Mr Green began the descent, and the machine skimmed along the surface of the earth for a mile and a half, the grapple trailing along the ground the whole way until it finally took hold in a ploughed field where a safe landing was made. A chaise then returned them to Newcastle, where they were received with great enthusiasm by its residents.

*

Dr Vale had been fascinated by his first flight, but had to wait more than twenty years to repeat the experience. Then, in 1847, John Hampton arrived in the area to make two ascents with his Royal Irish Balloon *Erin-Go-Bragh*. The first ascent took place on Monday, 14 June, from Whieldon's Grove, Stoke. Although the balloon was capable of carrying six people, Mr Hampton was accompanied only by Mr G. W. Filcher of Shelton, because of a shortage of gas, which also delayed the start by two hours. Despite this, and the unfavourable weather, thousands upon thousands of spectators had turned up, and most of the hills for miles around were thronged with eager-eyed visitors.

Just after 7 p.m. the balloon at last sailed majestically away, moving onward and upward at some speed, the aeronauts acknowledging the shouts of delight by waving their hats. Within minutes the balloon had become a mere speck in the sky before being lost to sight. High above, Mr Filcher had a bird's-eye view of the Potteries that appeared 'like a vast smoking cauldron', the flames and the fumes of various iron-furnaces aiding the illusion. All was soon left behind, however, as the balloon reached an altitude of three miles and travelled for three-quarters of an hour before descending without accident at Meg Lane, to the east of Macclesfield.

As he had had to disappoint several intending passengers, Mr Hampton decided to mount a second flight a month later from the same venue. At 7 p.m. on Monday, 12 July 1847, the trip began with Dr Vale, Captain Ross, and Mr Sheppard accompanying the aeronaut. Initially all went well:

> The ascent was splendid – never was one more beautiful. Majestically the balloon rose from the earth, and rose higher, and higher, and higher, but so gradually that it scarcely seemed to move, and the current of air in which it floated was so gentle that it appeared to hover almost directly over the spot it had left. In a few minutes it entered a fleecy cloud, and then one more dense, by which it was entirely concealed from the gaze of the admiring spectators.
>
> Suddenly it reappeared *below* the cloud, which occasioned some surprise; but its seemingly rapid increase of size betokening a rapid descent changed surprise into alarm for the safety of the aeronauts. The ballast was seen being poured out of the car to check the descent, but when the large bulk of the balloon collapsed and shrunk into the form of a parachute, alarm was succeeded by intense feelings of apprehension. The pouring out of the ballast had little if any perceptible effect in checking the velocity of the descent, and appearances threatened a shock when the car touched *terra firma* that should dash its occupants almost to pieces. Providentially the danger, though great, was less imminent than it appeared to be, and the descent was accomplished in safety in a small open space near the Flint Tavern, Flint Street, Longton, within a quarter of a mile from Dr Vale's residence, the balloon having travelled scarcely two miles. The worthy Doctor was the only one of the party who sustained injury from the concussion. The accident is attributed by Mr Hampton to the rapid condensation of the gas.

Although Dr Vale referred only to 'a few bruises' that he had suffered, his friend Samuel Taylor recorded that he 'was taken out of the car more dead than alive'. Whatever the case, he did recover though he never took to the skies again.

*

On Wednesday, 25 July 1888, the Duke of Sutherland opened Queen's Park in Longton – the first public park in the Potteries – and among the many and varied attractions on offer was a 'grand balloon ascent' by Captain Moreton, which took place on three days of the extended event.

So popular were such aerial displays that thereafter balloon flights and parachute drops became a regular feature at the annual fêtes held in the newly created parks. In 1890, at Clough Hall Park, Kidsgrove, the famous tightrope walker Blondin topped the bill, but Miss De Voy (the 'celebrated parachutist') was not far behind, while at Queen's Park the services of 'the great parachutist' Charles Baldwin had been obtained 'at enormous cost'. Soon, to maintain the element of novelty, there were double descents, then parachute races, and finally 'great balloon races' in which three balloons were released simultaneously. Visitors with a good head for heights could also apply to be taken up. As in previous years, however, not everything went according to plan for aeronaut, parachutist or passenger.

In 1902 Captain Henry Spencer was at Longton and determined to go up in spite of what he described as 'the roughest weather in which I have ever ascended'. He was accompanied by Councillor Clement Meigh, the honorary secretary of the park fête, and the Misses Eva Hamilton and Alma Beaumont, who were to make a double parachute descent. The trip was to prove a traumatic experience for three of them.

The balloon ascended to 6,000 feet, and Miss Hamilton released herself and descended safely, landing in a farmer's field at Cocknage. With less weight on board, the balloon rapidly shot upwards to between 12,000 and 15,000 feet and began drifting over Trentham towards Stone. Captain Spencer immediately started to take measures to regulate their progress:

> He went to the valve rope, pulled it, found it would not act and climbed up to the valve. He reached the mouth of the balloon where the gas partially overcame him, and the two occupants of the car were horrified to see him fall backwards. The instinct of self-preservation caused him, however, to catch one foot in a rope of the netting, and he remained suspended until almost black in the face and foaming at the mouth. To the cries of the terrified occupants of the car he made no response, and Miss Beaumont eventually climbed up to him, reaching him just as he was recovering consciousness. With great difficulty the Captain was then got inside the car.

The balloon finally came to earth at Wolseley Bridge, between Rugeley and Colwich, being torn in the process by coming into contact with the tops of trees. When interviewed, Councillor Meigh declared: 'Not if anyone would place a thousand pounds in my hand as a gift would I go up in a balloon again.'

There were no such alarms at Hanley a few weeks later, except those suffered by the aeronauts when they saw a multitude of people trying to get as near as possible to their balloons with pipes and cigarettes in their mouths. Among the crowd were some notable visitors, including the exiled Grand Duke Michael of Russia, a cousin of the Tsar, who was renting Keele Hall. With his wife, the Countess of Torby, and his children, he was enjoying a typical English summer fête.

As usual, the parachutists – billed as the Spencer sisters – were regarded with awe as they took their seats. Viola (whose real name was Edith Maud Cook) was dressed in a neat costume of blue velvet, Elsa in a green outfit of similar material. Both landed safely, the latter in a yard close by (though she nearly fell into a pot kiln) and Viola in Broad Street. They were driven back to the park where

Stanley Spencer was offering a flight to any of the councillors present. However, after Councillor Meigh's experience at Longton, there were no takers.

Captain Spencer eventually ascended at 7 p.m. with Mr T. H. Greatbatch and a *Sentinel* representative, both of whom tried to ignore the somewhat ironical handshakes and farewells of their friends as they were about to depart. The order to 'let go' was given, and the crowd lining the railings seemed to slip below them. 'God save the King! Success to the Hanley Show!' sang out Captain Spencer to much cheering from the spectators.

The *Sentinel* representative subsequently gave his impressions of his maiden flight and of the townscape seen from an entirely new perspective:

There was no suggestion of motion, but the Park, with its white beflagged marquees, its lake, and its thousands of people suddenly seemed to fall away from us, and it was really most difficult to imagine that we were leaving them and not they were leaving us. We could hear shouts, cheers, and a curious humming roar, with the occasional puffing of a train. Shelton church, looking like an inkpot with the tower for a dipping well, and the deep marl-hole off Regent Road were landmarks which were easily recognised. Then, looking over towards Etruria, we could see the blast forges pouring forth huge pillars of grey smoke, and the whistle of a loop line train came up to us, recalling the familiar penny wooden whistle of our youth. The factory chimneys as we looked down upon them presented the appearance of black circular spots, this impression being conveyed presumably through our being immediately

A balloon ascends
from Hanley Park,
c. 1908.

above them and our seeing the black interior of the shafts. Rows and rows of houses in regular outline and a patch of whitened yard which we guessed to be the cattle market came under our notice and then a feeling of intense cold came over me. Worldly objects became fainter, and looking round we saw a light mist enveloping the balloon. We were in the utmost solitude and in the strangest silence.

After an hour and a quarter, Captain Spencer opened the valve to allow the gas to escape. Suddenly hedges, fields, houses, pools, trees, and roads seemed to jump up at them. They paid out 300 feet of guide rope, and a number of red-faced panting youths raced after them, tugging at the rope and being immediately bowled over by the momentum of the balloon. 'Hang on tight!' shouted the skipper as they came down the last few hundred feet and then with a terrific jolt crashed into a potato field near Dilhorne. According to the *Sentinel* man, 'It was one of the most thrilling yet one of the most enjoyable experiences I ever had.' Next time, though, he made a mental note to wear an overcoat.

*

Ever on the lookout for variety, the committee behind the Hanley Horticultural Society's Show dispensed with a parachutist in 1904 in favour of 'the newest and most sensational machine yet perfected by an Englishman' – Spencer's Great Airship, 'with motor, propeller and rudder – the latest development of aerial navigation'. Watched by an immense crowd on Wednesday, 6 July, the huge cigar-shaped craft, filled with 40,000 cubic feet of coal-gas, made the first flight by an airship from any part of North Staffordshire, eventually alighting safely near Alton Towers.

On the following evening, when Captain Spencer offered a flight to any of the 30,000 spectators, Harold Hales was the only person to come forward. Hales (who claimed to be the original of Denry Machin in Arnold Bennett's *The Card*) sold motor cars in Market Place, Burslem, and had long wished to make an ascent. Now he seized his opportunity. 'I believe that I am entitled to claim that I was the first paying passenger by airship in Great Britain who went any distance and rose to 1,000 feet,' he later recalled. At 8.30 that July evening, he joined Captain Spencer in the basket and began to ascend, while a reporter begged him for any instructions as to the disposal of his worldly goods.

The airship rose swiftly and had soon left the park far behind, as Hales recounted in his autobiography:

South by east we travelled, the lilac evening creeping all around us.
 'That's Blythe Bridge,' I said. 'What height are we now?'
 '3,000 feet,' said Spencer. 'Time we were getting down.'

'What's that place there?' I asked.

'That's Leigh,' he said, 'and farther on Creswell. Stand by. I'm going to pull the cord.'

As he spoke he switched off the motor and I shall never forget that moment as long as I live. I had never realised what utter peace could be like. Now as we drifted through the stillness of the dusk there was not one single sound. We seemed to be lost in a sea of quiet.

The anchor was slung overboard, and Hales was watching it leap downwards when he was dragged forcefully into the bottom of the basket. At once they crashed into the branches of a large oak tree, the now partially deflated balloon fluttering lamely above. 'Below us was the ground,' he reported,

> a good 30 feet away. For a few moments we remained stationary. Then came another terrible crack and I felt myself upside down, head over heels, holding on for dear life. The airship had broken into two, and we were hanging suspended in mid air, held only by the cords which secured the basket to the balloon.

Farm labourers rushed to help, and cautiously the two airmen climbed down to safety. Then they solemnly shook hands. Unlike Councillor Meigh, Hales could hardly wait to go up again.

For the parachutists, too, life could be just as exhilarating as they had close encounters with canals, sewage farms, chimneys, and even speeding trains. In 1890, Charles Baldwin had landed not back in the park at Longton but in a tree in New Park Wood. In 1901, after a drop over Hanley, Daisy Sinclair went crashing through a window of Mr Green's pottery works at Fenton. In June 1906, Dolly Shepherd in her descent at Longton was lucky to alight safely in a field on Trentham Road after her parachute struck a telephone wire. The following month another descent left the whole crowd aghast. The celebrated Spencer family had returned to Hanley with their balloon *Carnation*, piloted by Captain Percival Spencer, and a smaller parachute balloon in the charge of Captain Henry Spencer. Together with Miss Viola Spencer, the latter was to make a double parachute descent.

On Wednesday, 4 July, the balloon quickly soared to 2,500 feet and the two parachutists were clearly visible as they prepared to plunge into space. Viola went first, her companion following a few moments later, but it was the lady who became the focus of attention:

> Through the field glasses it appeared as though the material of which the parachute was made tore as it broke away from the side of the balloon. The parachute fell some little distance before her headlong course earthwards was arrested, and then, as the folds of the parachute bulged out by reason

Edith Maud Cook
(aka Viola Spencer).

of the resistance of the air, the watchers were startled to observe that an enormous rent had developed in the cloth. Practically one third of the parachute seemed to have been torn away, and the jagged edges of the rent could be clearly seen fluttering about.

Miss Spencer's parachute descended with alarming rapidity, and it was feared that an accident would be inevitable. Exactly three minutes from the time when the balloon commenced its ascent, she had reached the earth again. She alighted on a shraff heap close to the Cauldon Works [today the site of Stoke-on-Trent College], within a few yards of the Park and happily quite unhurt. The balloon in which the parachutists had ascended turned turtle soon after they had left it, and swooping downward in rapid flight damaged several chimney pots in Guilford Street, where it fell.

This 'rather exciting descent' was too much for the fête committee. Thereafter no more parachute jumps were booked at Hanley.

*

The balloons still appeared, however, and the following year Harold Hales enjoyed his longest trip so far. With Captain Sidney Spencer, he ascended from Hanley Park at 4.45 p.m. on Wednesday, 3 July 1907, and soon they were passing over Burslem and Mow Cop, and later over Congleton and Macclesfield. As they approached Manchester and started to descend, the exciting part of the journey began which caused wonderment on the ground and left destruction in their wake:

The trail rope came into touch and caught every obstacle it came across, and as it liberated itself each time it gave violent jerks to the car, precipitating the occupants into each other's arms. The rope seemed to be infused with an impish spirit and find a joy in coiling itself round the chimney pots, which it would pluck up and toss into the air with a gaiety as if she would say, to use a current localism, 'Up she goes', and as the fragments descended the people ran out of their houses, the dogs barked, and in one case a horse stampeded. A curious sensation was felt as the rope passed along a corrugated iron fence, and in this it lodged, but only to pull part of the fence down. It trailed through a mill pool and became entangled in the ventilation on the roof of one of the mills themselves. As they sailed over the roofs of some houses, the irrepressible Mr Hales shouted to an alarmed lady at the back of one, 'Get the kettle on, mother, we're coming for tea.' The roofs were cleared, but only for the rope to land on the top of some telegraph wires, several of which were broken.

The car suddenly lurched to the ground just before a large reservoir and was surrounded by mill hands who held it down until more gas had escaped. Young Mancunians in their hundreds also thronged the area to feast their eyes on the now half-empty balloon, still majestic though in ruins. The trip had lasted 2 hours and 35 minutes and was the farthest voyage that had yet been made from Hanley Park.

It was as nothing, however, compared to the new world record of 703 miles recently established by Captain Auguste Gaudron. In 1908, the famous aeronaut exhibited his record-breaking craft (billed as 'Britain's Biggest

Longton fête announces the advent of Britain's biggest balloon.

Balloon') at the Longton fêtes. He also brought with him two parachutists whose descent turned out to be the most sensational yet – indeed, it entered the annals of parachuting history.

Even before the publicised jump took place, a correspondent to the *Staffordshire Sentinel* accused the fête committee of 'sensation mongering' by endangering the lives of female parachutists and called for the display to be abandoned. It seemed that his prayers had been answered when, on Monday, 9 June, the jump from the mammoth balloon had to be cancelled owing to the turbulent conditions. Then the following evening a mishap prevented the use of the large balloon and a smaller one had to be prepared. By 8 p.m., however, it was ready, the weather was tranquil, and an expectant crowd of 10,000 people had turned up to watch.

Anxious not to disappoint again, Gaudron decided to make this a dual drop featuring two young ladies on his team. The first was Dolly Shepherd, unfazed by her previous experience at Longton. She was a former waitress at Alexandra Palace, where one day she overheard the flamboyant American showman and aeronaut 'Colonel' Samuel Cody talking to Gaudron. He was lamenting the fact that he had grazed his wife's scalp the previous evening while shooting an egg from the top of her head and so would have to cancel his show. Dolly immediately volunteered to take her place – and went through with it even though she discovered at the last moment that Cody performed the

Dolly Shepherd.

shot blindfolded! Gaudron then took an interest in her and asked if she would like to make a jump – which she did after only thirty minutes' instruction. Renowned for her courage, Dolly had since become 'the parachute queen' and was thrilling crowds throughout Britain with her act.

Described as 'a tall and bonny girl of twenty-two years', Dolly was accompanied by Louie May, 'a fine-looking girl of twenty', who was making her first jump. They took up positions on either side of the balloon, each sitting in a sling underneath a crossbar onto which they held. Their parachutes were mechanically attached to the side of the balloon, and when all was ready they began their ascent to 4,000 feet, from which height they intended to jump.

At the crucial moment, however, Louie was unable to free her parachute. Frantically she tugged and tugged at her release cord until it cut into her hand – to no avail. All the while the balloon was rising to greater altitudes, and the two girls gradually lost sight of the park, drifting in a south-easterly direction towards Meir. On the ground anxiety spread, and it was rumoured that one of the pair had fainted. Gaudron guessed the real reason and was worried that the girls would begin to suffer from exposure. He summoned a cab and ordered its driver to 'follow that balloon'.

At a height of 11,000 feet, the two young parachutists were entering a black mass of cloud, ignorant of what lay beneath them. By this time the balloon had travelled over and beyond Meir and was heading towards Uttoxeter. Louie, unnerved, begged her friend not to leave her, and the latter reassured her that whatever happened they would see it through together. Dolly could see her companion looking like a ghost in the mist, her face ashen, her body chilled to the bone. She prided herself on being 'like a mother' to the other girls and now took matters in hand. Firstly she decided that Louie should be brought across so that they could share the one sling – a dangerous enough manoeuvre in itself, as can be seen from an interview Dolly gave to a representative of the *Uttoxeter Advertiser* some weeks later:

'I saw Miss May in difficulties. I called to her to throw me the rope and she did so. I then advised her to unfasten her belt and other things connecting her to the trapeze, and I pulled her towards me by the rope. She was parallel with me. She then jumped, catching her feet around my waist, and her hands clasped me around the neck.'

'You were two miles high at that time?'

'Yes,' she added with a smile.

Then they hesitated, deliberating as to whether they should leave the balloon or not, but with darkness setting in they concluded that they had no alternative but to trust their double weight to the single parachute.

Simultaneously, they uttered a short prayer before Louie said: 'Now we must go; it's either life or death for us.' She again locked her legs around her friend and clasped her around the neck, and then the release cord was pulled. In seconds they had hurtled through the terrifying void for more than 500 feet and nothing had happened. Louie cried out and tightened her grip. Dolly could hear the silk rustling above them – was it struggling to take shape or had it collapsed completely? Then she felt the parachute partially open, and they steadied, their breakneck fall checked. Suddenly – *wonderfully* – the canopy billowed fully above them, but as they descended it was obvious that they were still falling too quickly. Approaching the ground at speed, they passed over a road, cleared a hedge and thumped heavily into a field, narrowly missing a scythe stuck in the soil. As they lay there, numb and exhausted, both girls began to laugh uncontrollably.

Louie was able to get up and walk, but Dolly had lost the use of her legs altogether, which was hardly surprising if the account in the *Staffordshire Sentinel* is to be believed: 'Miss Shepherd was at the bottom and came to the ground first. In accordance with the usual custom she raised her legs so as to fall with her back on the ground, while Miss May came down upon her.' Mr Hollins, the gentleman farmer on whose land at Leigh they were, was soon on the scene and ordered a bed and restoratives – hot milk and brandy – to be immediately prepared for her at his home. After a doctor had arrived and diagnosed 'concussion of the spine and pelvis', several villagers gently carried her to Fields Farm on a stretcher, where she remained in bed for some time. She had certainly created a stir: the farm was beset by reporters, and a columnist for the *Sentinel* rightly predicted that the fête committee would scarce venture to put this particular item on their programme again in the near future. The Vicar of Trentham, the Reverend Edmund Pigott, went further: he called for parachuting to be banned.

Despite her predicament, an eye-witness pronounced Dolly 'as lively as a cricket', and during her press interview she made light of her injuries in a characteristically forthright manner:

> 'They say you injured your spine, Miss Shepherd,' queried the reporter.
> 'Fiddlesticks,' was the answer. 'Not a word of truth in it. Look here, I can stand!' and she walked a short distance. 'It is my legs only, and they are getting along splendidly. Why I shall be marching up to Uttoxeter some day soon.'

She also dismissed reports that she was about to embark on a lecture tour as 'nonsense'. In due course, as a result of some primitive electric shock treatment (and more of Mr Hollins' restoratives), she made a complete recovery and returned to her perilous occupation eight weeks later. Though she never saw Louie again, the two girls had achieved the first tandem parachute jump and mid-air rescue ever recorded.

2
A Flying Start

The episode was the talk of the Potteries as it was no doubt among local schoolchildren. One of them, thirteen-year-old Reginald Mitchell, may well have seen the balloon, as he lived within walking distance of the park. Even this incident, however, was soon eclipsed by the momentous events that followed. Four months later, on 16 October 1908, Samuel Cody made the first flight in an aeroplane in the British Isles when he flew at a speed of 25 mph for about 1,400 feet at Farnborough in Hampshire. After thirty seconds the biplane, which he had built for the British Army, crashed to earth, though Cody emerged unscathed from the wreckage. Less than a year afterwards, on 25 July 1909, Louis Blériot amazed the world and won the *Daily Mail* prize of £1,000 (then a small fortune) by making the first flight across the English Channel in a heavier-than-air machine. Although his monoplane looked to one spectator 'like some monstrous prehistoric bird', it did in fact herald the dawn of a new modern age.

Both Cody and Blériot had designed and constructed their own aircraft, as had Arthur Phillips of Market Drayton, a friend of the Wright Brothers who had made the first ever flight in an aeroplane a few years earlier. On Christmas Eve 1908, he patented his 'British Matchless Flying Machine' – the world's first vertical take-off plane. Mr Phillips used to try out his propeller-driven machine on the Market Drayton Cricket Club Ground. As a precaution he always attached it to a rope beforehand to stop it from going too far! This was not a problem for the Mitchell brothers, whose model planes of their own design were easily contained within the garden of their Normacot home.

Another *Daily Mail* prize – a whopping £10,000 (today worth several hundred thousand pounds) – had been on offer since 1906 to whoever made the first flight from London to Manchester (a distance of 183 miles) in less than twenty-four hours. Two stops only, for rest and refuelling, were allowed. In 1910, it resulted in a 'sensational and thrilling contest' between an Englishman and a Frenchman that sent a frisson of excitement through many parts of Staffordshire and gave hundreds of people their first ever glimpse of an aircraft – in this case the Farman biplane that both men were flying.

Claude Grahame-White, one of the first Englishmen to qualify as a pilot, had already tried for the prize on 21 April. His second stopping-point for taking on petrol was to have been a field at Baldwin's Gate, Whitmore, but as it happened this was not used as he was forced down at Lichfield after 117 miles. There his plane was blown over by the wind and he had to abandon the attempt. It had been a glorious failure.

He was back in action within days. A rival, Monsieur Louis Paulhan, left London on 27 April at 5.20 p.m., descending at Lichfield where he refuelled and spent the night. Informed of his departure, Grahame-White set off an hour later in hot pursuit, but baffled by darkness had to land at Roade in Northamptonshire, about 80 miles from the start. In a desperate attempt to catch up, he took off at 2.45 a.m. the next day, his path lit by car headlights, and at great risk flew through the dark – making the first ever night flight in England. It was in vain, however, for he was forced down again, this time near Tamworth, just as Paulhan was leaving Lichfield at 4.09 a.m. Despite the early hour, many hundreds of people had congregated there and on Cannock Chase to witness his departure, and many hundreds more lined his flying route (which followed the railway line) to cheer and wave madly as he went by.

Heading towards Crewe, Paulhan flew rapidly across North Staffordshire at 800 feet, clearly visible in the early morning light for fully four miles. Spectators at Norton Bridge and Standon had a magnificent view as he cruised overhead, returning their waves. (One Norton Bridge resident was so delighted that the aviator had flown over his home that he had a plaque made to commemorate the fact and fixed it to his house for all to see.) Paulhan finally reached Manchester at 5.32 a.m. to an ecstatic welcome, having achieved the journey in just over 12 hours; 4 hours and 12 minutes of which were spent in the air. It had been the greatest cross-country race the world had then seen. The cheque was subsequently presented to Paulhan by the French ambassador at the Savoy Hotel in London.

The London to Manchester air race, April 1910.

A few months afterwards, North Staffordshire's first 'flying machine' arrived in the Potteries courtesy of Harold Hales, who had attended the first great aviation show at Rheims in 1909, where he met Blériot, Paulhan, and other leading aviators of the day. He returned home 'a man inspired'. First of all he designed and patented a machine that would revolutionise air travel, according to the *Staffordshire Sentinel*: 'The greatest merit of the invention is that it will allow the monoplane to rise from the ground vertically, and will permit it to hover above any given spot as desired.' Unlike Arthur Phillips' machine, this invention never got beyond the model stage for lack of funds, though when Hales saw the later autogiros he knew he was on the right track.

He then decided to become 'the first private owner of an aeroplane in this country' and bought a second-hand Antoinette for £150. He put it on static display in an 'aeroplane tent' at the Burslem and Hanley fêtes in June 1910, and recouped half of his outlay by making a small charge for admission. It was just as well, for when he took it to Keele Racecourse for a trial flight the following month it was not a conspicuous success. That Sunday, watched by a respectful crowd, Hales sat in the cockpit and adjusted his goggles. The only instructions he knew were that he had to pull the joy stick towards him if he wished to ascend.

As he taxied along, the 50-hp engine buzzed furiously and castor-oil sprayed everywhere. Undaunted, he pulled the joy-stick and the plane – like a gigantic dragonfly – lifted into the air to a height of about 50 feet. Almost immediately, the machine swayed and then crashed to earth in a steep dive. The flight had lasted exactly 23 seconds. Remarkably, Hales escaped serious injury, though the plane did not. He had the wreckage carted to a nearby barn where it was left overnight. When he returned the next morning, he found that cows had eaten the wings. So ended what is regarded as the first such flight in North Staffordshire.

Harold Hales sits in his aeroplane at Burslem Park in June 1910.

With other aircraft falling out of the skies and killing their pilots (parachutes were not generally used in planes until the late 1920s), there was questioning in some quarters as to whether the conquest of the air was not being achieved at too great a human sacrifice. The latest casualty that July (and the first Briton to be killed in an aeroplane accident) was Charles Rolls, who had made the first non-stop two-way crossing of the English Channel shortly before his death. He was, in the words of the *Weekly Sentinel*, 'the most brilliant of the little band of British airmen', and unlike many pioneer aviators now long forgotten, his name would live on by virtue of the partnership he had entered into with Henry Royce. Another early aircraft designer claimed to have the answer to the carnage. Mr J. H. Walker, a Stoke cabinet-maker, had invented an aeroplane that, when the engine stopped, would come down gradually, its 'curved planes acting as a parachute'. During the Wakes, he exhibited the machine at Hanley, and when funds allowed he intended to install the driving power and then take it for a trial flight on the Stoke Football Ground.

Some of those daredevil pilots so often in the news could now be seen close up at the early flying exhibitions they gave in the area, the very first being the 'Grand Aviation Exhibition' (that featured two aircraft) at the Longton Park fêtes of 1911. A ring used on previous occasions for horse leaping had been enlarged and transformed into an aerodrome, and a vast crowd collected around the barriers during the afternoon and evening of Monday, 5 June, to watch the mechanics at work on a Short-Wright biplane.

About 7 p.m., one of the pilots, Charles Favre, clambered into the seat and began driving the plane up and down the ring. It was obvious, however, that something was wrong, and the crowd, which had remained good-humoured till then, began to grow fidgety. One individual, with 'the strident voice of a fish hawker', offered various suggestions 'as to the fit and proper treatment of aeroplanes and the ultimate destination of aviators'. Then he began offering odds against either machine flying, gradually increasing the price as the time went on. He was smugness itself when it was announced that the biplane would not fly because of engine trouble.

All the while the other pilot, Clement Greswell, clad in brown overalls, had been lying on the grass, smoking and smiling quietly to himself. He was a former pupil of Grahame-White's and had recently caused a sensation by flying over the Oxford and Cambridge boat race. At long last, when the sun had set, he slowly got up and casually strolled into the hangar that contained his Blériot monoplane. There he struggled into his flying suit, while his assistants wheeled out the dainty little machine and positioned it close to the railings at the end of the aerodrome to allow as much room as possible. Still unhurried, Greswell climbed into the seat, shouted a few final instructions and then started the engine.

Immediately there was a storm of hats – straw boaters, caps, bowlers, with one glossy silk topper sailing high above the others – as the great blast caused by the propeller blew off the headgear of everyone behind the plane. A mad scramble to retrieve the items followed, much to the amusement of the rest of the crowd. But the monoplane was already embarking on its journey, rapidly gathering speed over the grass and then suddenly soaring into the air. For a moment the crowd gasped. Then, beside itself with excitement, it broke through the barriers and swarmed all over the aerodrome, cheering wildly all the time the plane was airborne.

Greswell reached a height of 500 feet and then, travelling at 50-60 mph, made three wide circuits of the park. Unable to return to the aerodrome because of the crowd, the pilot swooped gracefully to earth in a meadow on the far side of the Florence Colliery sidings, where the plane was lodged at a neighbouring farmhouse for the night. The 'bookie' had lost a packet. Next day all flying was cancelled owing to a gusting wind.

*

The first Circuit of Great Britain was one of the major air races of 1911 and gave the plane-spotters of North Staffordshire another memorable opportunity. The race was to cover more than a thousand miles for another £10,000 prize, and a maximum flying time of 24 hours had been allowed. On the afternoon of Saturday, 22 July, nineteen of the thirty entrants set off from Brooklands Aerodrome in Surrey on a triangular course that would cover most parts of Great Britain.

It was reckoned that the leaders might pass over Whitmore on the Tuesday morning, and a large number of people from the Potteries travelled there, only to be disappointed. Nothing happened, and by late afternoon the crowds began to return home. Suddenly, and quite unexpectedly, at about 6.30 p.m., a Blériot monoplane was seen at Rode Heath. It travelled right over Wolstanton golf links, Etruria Wood, the centre of Hanley, and then Stoke. At some places, the approach of the airman was announced by the sounding of the fire-alarm; at others, a cry of 'the flyers' brought people rushing out of doors. In the twinkling of an eye the streets were alive with folk gazing at the sky.

Staff at the telephone exchange in Hanley had an excellent view as the plane was so low. Nearby a reporter happened to be sitting in the open air and recorded the unsettling effect on himself and others around him at seeing an aeroplane for the very first time in their lives. Initially, he became aware of the sound of an engine he couldn't quite place. Then, out of the blue, came the monoplane:

I don't know whether everybody else's sensations are different from mine on first seeing an aeroplane. I am inclined to think they are somewhat similar from conversations I have had with others. I had a feeling somewhat of exhilaration, coupled with a kind of wondering awe. 'Hail to thee blithe spirit! Bird thou never wert.' Well did Shelley's lines seem to apply to this new creation of the air. The whole atmosphere seemed to be throbbing and pulsating with energy, and when the aeroplane had flown beyond our ken we felt disinclined to sit and read. We wanted to do something.

With the planes now scattered far and wide around the country as a result of breakdowns, accidents, adverse weather, and navigational problems, this was the only one to pass over the Potteries. Yet it was the most notable, for although they did not know it, the crowds were watching the eventual winner – André Beaumont (the racing name of the French naval lieutenant Jean Conneau) – who had either been carried off course by the wind or had mistaken the railway line he was following. Next day in his Blériot monoplane he completed the course in a flying time of 22 hours and 28 minutes, at an average speed of 45 mph, just over an hour ahead of his main rival and fellow Frenchman Jules Vedrines, with whom he had been neck and neck for much of the race.

With many of the other competitors now out of the race, attention focused on two remaining British aviators, 'Jimmy' Valentine and Samuel Cody, who were striving to complete the course despite the terrible flying conditions. Valentine passed over Madeley at 6.30 a.m. on Monday, 31 July, on his way to Bristol and an eventual third place. Cody, recently naturalised, had once toured the Midlands in his Wild West show *The Klondyke Nugget* (in which he appeared four times in the Potteries); now he was flying over the area and creating a sensation wherever he went. Early on the morning of Wednesday, 2 August, shouts heralding his approach emptied every bed in the village of Woore, and Cody dropped low over the church tower to exchange a few pleasantries with the crowd. He finally finished the circuit on the last day of the race, Saturday, 5 August, only the fourth contestant to complete. By his epic flight, he somehow managed to steal the thunder of the first three pilots home.

Such races (which later inspired the film *Those Magnificent Men in their Flying Machines*) brought to the awareness of the general public that long-distance flying was becoming feasible, though few believed that it would ever have any practical application.

*

In April 1913, Newcastle-under-Lyme and the Potteries enjoyed their first ever visit by a reigning sovereign when King George V and Queen Mary made a tour of the area. Newcastle was described as 'a blaze of colour' for the occasion, and a special attraction during this royal week was a flying display on the

Samuel Cody.

Butts, given by 'the great Australian airman' Sydney Pickles. Exhibitions of 'passenger carrying, bomb dropping, and fancy flying' were promised, as well as 'flying at dusk, guided by rockets'. For good measure the pilot also intended to try to beat his Midlands' height record of 7,500 feet.

Pickles was obviously a born showman and made his presence felt by flying low over Hanley, Stoke, and Newcastle. He also put on an impromptu display for the royal couple as they were driving to the area from Crewe Hall, where they had stayed overnight. At Madeley on 22 April, Pickles' monoplane was seen soaring over the countryside to the left of the motorcade before it passed directly over the royal car, then swerved round to cross the procession once more. For some time afterwards Pickles continued his 'fancy flying', at one point causing much excitement by gliding with the engine cut off to within a few feet of a coppice. He then fell in behind the cars, which he followed all the way to Newcastle. Among his claims to fame, he thereafter boasted that he had been the first Australian to fly before the King.

Three weeks later, the fête committee of Longton Park proudly announced the appearance of a famous pilot of their own – the glamorous Gustav Hamel ('the most daring aviator in the world'). Hamel had twice flown in the Potteries the previous year, at the Stoke Football Ground (24 October 1912) and at Hanley Park (4 November 1912). The reappearance of the twenty-four-year-old proved to be an irresistible attraction, and the attendance that June exceeded all previous years despite the usual poor weather. On the Monday afternoon there was a strong breeze and rain, but the celebrated airman lived up to his reputation of flying if it were at all possible. At 4 p.m., an hour behind schedule, several thousand sightseers around the sports ring cheered as the monoplane was finally wheeled out of the large marquee that housed it. Hamel at once took his seat, the propeller began to whirl, and with a wave of his hand the pilot set off, racing for about 30 yards on the turf before the plane soared into the air. At a height of about 500 feet, Hamel circled the enclosure twice and then came in to land, to much applause. Given the conditions, the onlookers were perfectly happy to have seen any flying at all.

He made a second brief flight at 5 p.m. and then called it a day, but during the afternoon and evening of Whit Tuesday he managed to make three 'very fine' flights in spite of the still unfavourable conditions. The first at 3.20 p.m. lasted only five minutes, but a height of 1,000 feet was reached. After being photographed with the fête officials and surrounded by girls seeking his autograph, Hamel took off again at 5.30 p.m., waving his arm to those below to acknowledge their delighted cheers. Against a clear blue sky the monoplane swept through the air 'like a gigantic stork with far outstretching wings and legs streaming out at right angles'. This time he flew for ten minutes – 'minutes brimful of excitement and interest' – before deftly landing back in the park.

Suddenly, at sunset, the wind slackened, and Hamel's final ascent into the picturesque evening sky was to captivate his audience:

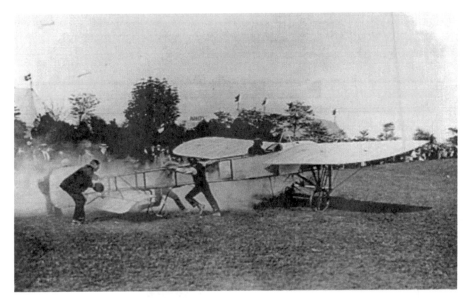

Gustav Hamel prepares to take off at Longton Park on 12 May 1913.

Gustav Hamel soars into the air on his first flight.

The machine was far overhead to the north, and then all of a sudden its size increased with amazing rapidity. The spectators held their breath, for the machine planed down till it seemed to pass just a few yards over the heads of the people, and many, no doubt, imagined the flight was coming to a sudden if not a ghastly termination. The aviator waved his hand reassuringly, and instead of alighting or dashing into the sports ring, he soared gaily ahead, turned towards the setting sun and flew straight over Cocknage, demonstrating his perfect mastery over his wonderful piece of mechanism by surprisingly rapid manoeuvres, now over Normacot, now over Florence, and then over in the direction of Blythe Bridge. Over Fenton he hovered, and then made an inspection of Stoke and its vicinage, circling the town and causing no little surprise and commotion, especially in the neighbourhood of Warrington's field.

To those in the aviation ground the machine was a mere grey speck in the dark grey sky. After thirteen minutes had elapsed those whose eyes could no longer behold it thought the aviator had quitted the scene of his successes for good, but he soon removed this impression, for, turning to the right, he began to become a more prominent object in a clear space of sky in the north, and steadily made back on his homeward way, and when seventeen minutes had sped by, the throbbing of the Gnome engine was heard. This steadily increased in volume as did the aeroplane in size, and then its pilot became visible. Going to the north-east he gave an admirable example of descent by a series of circles, huge masses of smoke being emitted from the engine exhaust pipe, and then, making for the sports ring with a beautiful volplane, reached the centre, the machine travelling some distance up the field. The end of this brilliant twenty minutes' flight was heralded with an outburst of joyful cheering which made the welkin ring.

Within a quarter of an hour of his descent, Hamel and his sister left on their home journey to London in their powerful 60-hp motor car. Crowds had invaded the flying ground and lined the roadway leading to the main entrance to the park to catch a final glimpse and cheer them on their way. 'The memory of their brief visit,' recorded the *Staffordshire Sentinel*, 'will not soon be forgotten.'

No one could easily forget the colourful Samuel Cody either. Once regarded almost as a figure of fun, the forty-six-year-old grandfather had become a national treasure, the 'best-loved showman of flight', the 'father of British aviation'. On 7 August 1913, his hydroplane broke up in the air over Farnborough and he hurtled to his death. Though a civilian, he was accorded a full military funeral, with 100,000 people lining the route of the cortège. The entire body of the Royal Flying Corps (RFC) was in the funeral procession and was followed by a thousand soldiers from every unit at Aldershot. He was buried at Thorn Hill cemetery, the first Wild West cowboy to be interred among some of the country's greatest military heroes.

There was to be no such funeral for Gustav Hamel, who had been booked to reappear at Longton in June 1914. A week before the fête he disappeared on a flight over the Channel. A last-minute stand-in was found in the person of the twenty-one-year-old Lord Carbery, who had recently taken part in that year's Schneider Trophy Race. His aircraft – a Morane-Saulnier monoplane – arrived by train, as did its pilot. On the first afternoon, with the weather ideal for flying, the tramway company brought large contingents from all parts of the district. An hour or so before the first show, the pilot himself appeared, and the plane was immediately pushed out of its marquee and final adjustments made.

At 3 p.m., with a vast crowd encircling the enclosure, he took his seat to a round of applause. The next minute he was off, rising beautifully into the air in the direction of Trentham, and then turning towards Cocknage before returning via Florence at a height of about 1,000 feet. Once it had been sufficient for pilots merely to fly; now they had to perform – and the noble lord did not disappoint:

Once more the aviator encircled the park, and when over in the vicinity of Florence he looped the loop in magnificent style and then turned back 'on

Lord Carbery.

the wing' and performed another loop, finishing the figure with a splendid spiral descent which his manager said was the best he had ever given.

At 7 p.m. he made his final flight of the day, which was generally reckoned his best:

> Whereas in the afternoon he had risen to an altitude of about 1,000 feet, on the last occasion he at times flew much lower and in several instances he rushed but a few feet above the crowd, which caused some sensation. He also confined himself more to the flying ground and gave two splendid exhibitions of looping the loop when directly over the heads of the people.

On his return to the park, the young pilot was mobbed and had difficulty in making his way to the committee tent. A total of 25,000 people had passed through the turnstiles that day, and the receipts had exceeded £700 – more than ever before – which was 'ample evidence of the enthusiasm the public had for flying'.

Another innovation this year was the chance of accompanying the pilot, and on the first evening several people (including two ladies) had taken flights and even looped the loop with him. All agreed that it had been 'simply a dream'. One motorist waxed lyrical about 'the ecstasy of riding the air, a thousand feet above, at 40 or 45 mph, without fear of police trap, contemptuous of speed limits'. For the last flight of all, on the Tuesday evening, a reporter was invited to 'go up'. He later recorded his experience:

Climbing gingerly along the tail portion, I ensconced myself behind the pilot, feeling my way with trepidation among the network of wires. There was no room to sprawl about and I subsided eventually into a semi-doubled up position, with my knees guarding his Lordship's body on either side. My head just showed over the framework.

We started off beautifully, making towards Lightwood, and then we swung round over the Florence Colliery and Dresden. When just above the colliery we made a sharp turn, the machine being on its side in the course of the operation. I looked down into the belching chimneys and thought it would not exactly be pleasant to tumble into one of them. We then had a circle round the park [and] I recall peeping over the plane and watching the crowd, who appeared like a lot of ants. I also thought the park lake would be a desirable place to jump into if anything happened.

Then something did happen. The engine stopped:

The propeller seemed to be taking a rest for a second or so, and we went into a horrible drop. It was the only unpleasant experience of the trip, causing a sensation somewhat familiar to people who have been on the 'Figure 8'. We had three of these drops, each appearing worse than the previous one. I thought at the time Lord Carbery was playing tricks on me, but I understood afterwards that it was the spiral dive.

After enjoying a short cross-country flight over Trentham, they returned to the park for one final thrill:

We were right over the park enclosure and the machine's nose was turned downwards almost perpendicularly. I could see the crowds scattering as we shot down, describing what is known as the 'nose-dive'. At this, as at every other period of the journey, the airman had the machine under perfect control, and after a short circuit of the park at a comparatively low altitude, we descended in a field whence we started.

Already the planes were becoming so fast that they could no longer land back in the park for fear of running into the crowd. Soon they would outgrow these makeshift aerodromes altogether. For the moment, however, the two-day fête had been a spectacularly joyous success.

*

If Gustav Hamel was unable to return, at least his favourite monoplane could. For three days, from Thursday, 2 July 1914, it was flown by Frank Goodden in the Hartshill Road Fields, Stoke, where he gave a sensational display of looping the loop and upside-down flying. Passenger flights were again on offer and could be booked through Mr F. Etches, manager of the Copeland Arms.

One spectator with no thought of taking part in the demonstration was the *Sentinel*'s Mr H. N. Heywood. But when the pilot invited him for a flight, he could not resist and found himself walking towards the machine with 'a dim consciousness that [his] knees were performing an involuntary "bone solo".' He was 'packed into a small hole' right behind the aviator and then, with a terse *Allez!* the French mechanic started the propeller and there was a wind that nearly blew him out. It was, however, already too late for any second thoughts, for immediately they were racing furiously across the field and then gliding into the air over the houses and tramway:

We circled round and round, mounting higher and higher. A slight veil of mist enfolded the machine, but higher still we soared until we were in clearer air again. At eight hundred feet I looked overboard – phew! – and directly beneath us were what appeared to be six pennies nicely laid out in two rows of three each. They were the huge metal upright cylinders in some works near Stoke Workhouse, and the workhouse buildings were a little toy, dark and sombre, set in a bright green landscape.[...]

Flying in a wide circle we passed over Newcastle and the outskirts of Stoke and Hanley. Occasionally we met gusts of wind, and the machine bobbed and swayed like a cork in the current, with a sensation like that of being in a small boat on a choppy sea. It was gloriously invigorating, the purer, rarefied atmosphere giving additional pleasure. Then we commenced the descent, which brought an entirely new type of thrill. Sailing out almost to Trent Vale, Mr Goodden turned back to face the breeze. With tilted tail the machine made a terrific dash to earth, and the passenger felt as if at least some of his internal mechanism was trying to climb out. But it was only momentary. The machine swung round again in another circle, and the crowd merged from black indefinite spots into hand-waving, shouting people. In another few seconds we had skimmed a hedge and were lightly floating inches from the ground. The machine landed without any perceptible bump, and I was being handed out by smiling mechanics.

Sadly, this was to be the last such exhibition in the area for some years. A month later Britain was at war.

3

Night of the Zeppelin

No doubt the imagination of Reginald Mitchell was being fired by such aerial displays, some of which he probably witnessed. In the later film of his life he was portrayed as a dreamy romantic deriving inspiration from watching seagulls fly around an isolated cliff-top on the coast. It is much more likely that his early inspiration came from watching the monoplanes of Gustav Hamel or Lord Carbery in a crowded park at the heart of the Potteries.

Frank Goodden's demonstration was held not far from Mitchell's workplace, and it is tempting to imagine Goodden (who went on to co-design the SE-5, one of the most successful fighters of the First World War) being watched by the future designer of the Spitfire. Then nineteen, Mitchell was three years into a five-year engineering apprenticeship with Kerr, Stuart & Co., railway locomotive builders in Fenton, where he worked in the engine sheds and then the drawing office. There, in his own words, he gained 'a thorough and practical training [...] very largely responsible for any success I might have achieved.' After the outbreak of war, he twice tried to enlist, but it appears that his employers blocked his call-up by informing the authorities that he was in a reserved occupation.

The park fêtes continued into the early years of the conflict with their more traditional offerings of military bands, horse-leaping competitions, floral exhibitions, and sports matches. But with men and machines wanted elsewhere, all flying disappeared from the scene. Then, in 1916, as the war news became ever grimmer, the fêtes themselves ceased for the duration.

Zeppelin raids had also become more prevalent, and at the end of January 1916 six counties (including Staffordshire) had been attacked by nine airships. Tipton, Wednesbury and Walsall were all bombed by the L-21 whose captain believed he was over Liverpool. In total sixty-one people died in the raids, including children, with many more injured. A notable casualty was Julia Slater, the Mayoress of Walsall, who was wounded as she rode on a tram and died a few weeks later. It was reported that one of the Zeppelins had dropped the message 'We will be back later.' It was no idle threat.

At 1 a.m., on the night of 27 November 1916, it was the turn of North Staffordshire when the L-21 attacked Kidsgrove, Goldenhill, Tunstall, and Chesterton. However, 'the raid was marvellously ineffective for the amount

An insurance company offers protection against damage caused by Zeppelins.

of explosives expanded', with many of the 100 bombs falling harmlessly on rural areas. Chesterton suffered the most, with one man wounded and several houses destroyed. There, according to the *Staffordshire Sentinel*, 'the population turned out into the streets en masse, many in their night attire, and obtained a good view of the raider, which was clearly visible in the star-lit night.' At dawn, while trying to make good its escape, the Zeppelin was shot down in flames over the North Sea by Flight Lieutenant Egbert Cadbury and other pilots of the RFC. Its entire crew perished.

Another pilot in the news locally was Lieutenant Thomas Seaman Green, the elder son of Councillor T. S. Green of Burslem. He had been educated at King William's College on the Isle of Man, where he shone as an athlete and won the Chili Cup for shooting two years running. On the outbreak of war, he had enlisted in the 5th North Staffordshire Regiment, but transferred in January 1916 to the RFC. From June of that year, he served as a front-line pilot with No. 3 Squadron and was soon its acting Flight-Commander. Success came quickly. He shot down five enemy planes and an observation balloon, and was recommended for the Military Cross. Sir Douglas Haig, Commander-in-Chief of the British Expeditionary Force, personally commended him for his work.

In October 1916, when the famous German ace Oswald Boelcke was killed after colliding with another plane during a dog-fight, Green was the officer selected to fly 17,000 yards unescorted over the enemy lines and drop a wreath. The card read: 'To the memory of Captain Boelcke, a brave and chivalrous foe. From the British Royal Flying Corps.' Only a few months afterwards, on 13 February 1917, Green was himself killed in single combat with five enemy aircraft. His body was recovered and later interred at Heilly station cemetery, at Méricourt l'Abbé. He was twenty-two. His younger brother, Wilfred Barrat Green, had just joined the air service and would become a highly decorated ace in the remaining years of the conflict. Later still, he would play a significant part in the activities of the North Staffordshire Aero Club at Meir.

Mitchell would have read these newspaper stories with interest, especially the report of the raid on Kidsgrove, which was close to his birthplace. (A recurring theme in his later speeches was the importance of the defence of the realm from air attack.) In 1917, with German aircraft carrying out their first bombing raids on London, he made a transition from locomotives to aeroplanes by joining the Supermarine Aviation Works in Southampton, returning to Stoke-on-Trent a year later to marry Florence Dayson at Caverswall church. In the same year, aeroplanes returned briefly to the Potteries as part of a huge fund-raising enterprise.

To help meet the colossal costs of the conflict, it had become necessary to raise £25 million each week by the sale of War Bonds. Market Drayton

Thomas Seaman Green.

put on an 'Aeroplane Week' with an aeroplane as a bank; a similar week at Lichfield set out to raise £25,000 – the cost of ten new aircraft. However, Stoke-on-Trent's 'Tank Bank Week' was on a much more substantial scale, with an initial target of £500,000. The focus of attention was naturally on the tank, the latest and weirdest instrument of war that had recently spread terror and panic among the enemy at Cambrai. Leading that attack had been Major Gerald Huntbach, the only son of the coroner for Hanley.

'Old Bill' (as the fund-raising tank was known) arrived on Monday, 7 January 1918, lumbering up from Hanley Railway Goods Yard to the town's Market Square, which had been gaily bedecked with flags and bunting. It drew enormous crowds. The boys of Clarence Street School, assembled near the Grand Theatre, had an excellent view and gave 'three lusty rounds of cheering', though the 'great concourse of people' on Crown Bank and in the Square watched in silence, 'lost in wonder and admiration for this amazing machine of war'. All were careful to observe the warnings of the police to 'stand back' as it approached. Later, purchasers of War Bonds and War Savings Certificates could take their receipts to the tank and present them at one of its portholes. Post Office officials inside would stamp them with the date and the words 'British Tanks', before returning them as a souvenir of the occasion.

On most days special events were arranged to maintain interest, and on the Thursday the promised appearance of aeroplanes was enough to bring out another vast crowd. Three aircraft were flown in from a Midlands aerodrome by Captains Wood and McArthur and Lieutenant Openshaw, who between them flew over each of the six towns and Newcastle. The show put on over the tank held all present spellbound:

> The airman who visited Hanley provided the crowd with thrills galore and saluted 'Old Bill' with a fine display of skill and daring. He came very low in performing a marvellous nosedive and in the course of his operations dropped a despatch for Lieutenant Brocklehurst, Officer Commanding the Tank. The crowd, including a host of schoolchildren, alternately held their breath and cheered as the past master of his craft looped the loop and vaulted about; and after an extraordinary display lasting several minutes he passed out of sight in the direction of Longton.

Over each of the towns the airmen dropped thousands of souvenir cardboard discs, on the outer edge of which were printed the words 'Dropped from the sky by British aeroplanes' and in the inner circle 'Put all your money in the Potteries' Tank and so do your bit for your country.' Such exhortations seemed to work. On Saturday, 12 January, as the tank departed, it was announced that the revised target of £1 million had been triumphantly surpassed. Ten months later, after four harrowing years, the 'war to end all wars' was over.

4

A Genius with a Magic Wand

Determined to carve out a postwar career in flying, some pilots travelled the country, giving demonstrations and offering joyrides. Any open space would suffice – for a week in August 1919 three aeroplanes used the beach at Rhyl. A month later 'A Great Aviation Week' under the auspices of the Berkshire Aviation Company brought to Wolstanton a flyer who was destined to become the most famous showman of all. From 15 to 21 September, Alan Cobham was at Porthill Meadow, where he attracted a large number of spectators and many passengers, eager to accompany him in his Avro three-seater biplane at a guinea a time. The churches, though, were less than thrilled at the prospect of Sunday flying and organised a protest that was signed by 550 people.

Undeterred by the churches' wrath, the Berkshire Aviation Circus (as it had been renamed) returned to Porthill a year later with Captains O. P. Jones and A. L. Robinson and two Avros. From Tuesday 26 October to Tuesday 9 November 1920, they gave exhibitions of 'looping, spinning, and falling leaf' in addition to the lucrative joyrides, now on offer for 12s 6d. The first day was considered the best opening day they had had so far on their tour, with many passengers and many more paying for admission to the ground. The latter were entitled to participate in a periodical draw for a free flight, and on the first Tuesday alone twenty had secured trips for only a few pennies, the successful competitors including boys as young as ten. An extra attraction for 5 November was a firework display and the chance to 'see the Potteries from the air by night'. Certainly the company's advertisements exhorting the Potters to *Get off the Earth* were being heeded – so much so that their visit had to be extended until 14 November.

Flying meanwhile had all but disappeared from the postwar programmes of the park fêtes. One exception occurred in 1922, when joyrides were given by Captain W. G. Pudney at Longton, which 'created a lively interest'. The advertisements also publicised a 'parachute descent from an aeroplane', though whether this actually took place is not recorded. In 1922 it would really have been a novelty, for war-time pilots like Captain Pudney had flown without parachutes and the RAF continued to do so. So too did the pilots who took part in that year's Schneider Trophy Race. By now Mitchell's prodigious talents had been recognised by Supermarine and, at the age of twenty-five, he had become their chief designer and engineer. Against the odds, it was his plane that won the race with an average speed of 145.7 mph, thus denying the Italians a third consecutive victory.

*

One of the first people in Stoke-on-Trent to travel for any distance in an aeroplane was Councillor George Barber, a cinema pioneer, whose trip took place on the morning of 8 June 1923 when he travelled from Manchester to London, en route to France. On the way he took cinematographic pictures of important places, including 'How Stoke-on-Trent Borough Looks from Above', which he intended to show on his screens.

Not one to miss a trick, he advertised his flight in the local press and announced that he would also be dropping numbered tickets, some of which would win the finder £1 and 10s prizes (the winning numbers to be shown at his Palace and Regent picture houses the following week). Things did not go quite as he had hoped, however. During the flight over the Potteries the pilot descended to about 100 feet, but owing to the buffeting of the wind there were fears that the film shot would be 'somewhat shaky'. As to the 4,000 tickets scattered over the side, the strong wind carried them for miles, some turning up at Brindley Ford, Biddulph Moor, and even as far away as Rudyard Lake. Councillor Barber had to abandon his trip at Croydon because of the gale and returned to Tunstall by train. Nevertheless, he had doubtless increased his box-office takings for the coming week. He had also become one of the first ever people to drop advertising material from an aeroplane.

*

In May 1927, Charles Lindbergh made the first solo non-stop flight across the Atlantic. Overnight he became an international superstar. In September, after a series of reverses, Mitchell regained the Schneider Trophy for Britain, his S.5 achieving a new world speed record. Outside aviation circles, he remained relatively unknown.

In February 1928, he returned to the Potteries to distribute prizes to engineering students at Fenton Town Hall. Some of them were from the Fenton Technical School, where he himself had been a student and then a lecturer only eleven years before. The following evening he was principal guest at the tenth annual festival of the Stoke-on-Trent Association of Engineers. Its president, Mr W. E. Swale, welcomed him as 'a master of his craft and a creative genius of the highest order', and said that he felt something akin to awe at the privilege of sitting next to a man who had made it possible to attain a speed of 281 mph.

In a much-applauded speech, Mitchell referred to the winning of the Schneider Trophy and sought to answer the voice of the sceptics:

> I have heard the question asked: 'How is it that so much money and energy are spent in producing a machine with the object of driving an airman through the air faster than he wishes to go?' In the first place, it is a good thing for England to be kept to the forefront in international trials, events of a sporting nature. But apart from the sporting side, I speak with experience when I say that a great deal of knowledge is gained from the designing and construction of such craft, and this knowledge is applicable to the improvements of other types of aircraft, such as are used by the Royal Air Force. The design of these Service aircraft, in fact, has been very much improved as a result of these contests. For this reason alone these sporting events are worth continuing. I hope I shall be given the opportunity of designing and constructing a machine to defend the title next year.

*

Flying returned to the district for a fortnight from 2 to 14 May 1928, when the Cornwall Aviation Company offered residents the chance to 'see your homes from above'. The company had been formed in 1924 by two ex-Servicemen and offered not only passenger flights but a special show each Sunday that would include spinning, looping, and walking the wings in mid-air – the only display of its kind in the country according to its advertisements.

Based in a field called Windy Arbour off Cocknage Road in Longton, the plane attracted thousands of people, an increasing number of whom wanted to fly. After several days without incident, however, a mishap occurred on Sunday, 6 May, that curtailed activities for some time. About 100 people had already been taken up by 4 p.m. when the pilot, Mr S. Summerfield, took off with his final two passengers before the show began. Almost immediately the Avro developed engine trouble. The plane was then close to the huge tip at the Florence Colliery, but Mr Summerfield managed to turn parallel to it and glide down to safety, though he was forced to land on a rough uneven stretch that caused the undercarriage to collapse. The plane then had to be dismantled in order to convey it back to the field where the company's mechanics were soon working busily on it. The wing-walking had to wait for another day.

During the above visit, the *Staffordshire Sentinel* began to champion the idea of an aerodrome for the recently designated City of Stoke-on-Trent. An editorial began: 'It will not be long before the development of civil flying compels municipalities to decide what they intend to do in the matter of suitable landing grounds.' Manchester had been quick off the mark, being granted a licence for the first municipal aerodrome that April, and other towns and cities throughout the country were preparing to follow suit. Having listed them, the *Sentinel* asked:

When will Stoke-on-Trent be added to this list? Large open spaces, admittedly, are not plentiful, but useful work might be done by a City Council committee in exploring the possibilities in the outlying parts of the area. A little foresight and timely action might make all the difference between the selection of Stoke-on-Trent as an air station and its being given the go-by.

Two months later, on the eve of a council meeting, the newspaper returned rather impatiently to the theme, concluding: 'Far-seeing men realise that, as civil flying becomes more common, those cities that can offer aerodrome facilities will have a great advantage over more backward areas. The city that establishes for itself a place in a national chain of air stations will gain not merely in prestige, but eventually in commercial prosperity.' A correspondent to the newspaper – a Hanley airman – could not have agreed more: 'England is behind Germany and America, and Stoke-on-Trent will soon be behind England unless the problem of setting aside ground for an aerodrome is faced – and faced now.' The Council may well have been swayed by such arguments, for at its meeting the next day the possibility of providing an aerodrome was raised for the first time and preliminary steps were taken to investigate possible sites.

Members of the newly formed North Staffordshire Aero Club had already been in touch with a company that was just being formed, later known as National Flying Services Ltd. At the request of the club, the prospective Managing Director, Lieutenant-Colonel I. A. Edwards, visited the area and inspected possible sites at Trentham, Wetley Common, Weston Coyney, and elsewhere. He was most taken with the site at Meir, and, as a result, was introduced to members of the Council's Aerodrome Sub-Committee. Following further advice from an Air Ministry official, Meir was chosen as the most suitable site for development in February 1929. At a meeting at the beginning of June, the City Council decided to purchase 154 acres there for £11,850, hoping that the site would be taken over and run by National Flying Services, which would meet the whole of the costs associated with the provision of hangars and other accommodation. The Lord Mayor seemed to catch the mood of the time when he said: 'We do not want to be behind other places with regard to flying. Who can say how long it will be before aircraft are as common as motor cars?'

Lieutenant-Colonel Edwards' vision of what the 'Air Age' would mean for Stoke-on-Trent was set out in an article he published in the *Sentinel*. For the present, he felt that 'a system of air taxis' would meet the needs of North Staffordshire and be more convenient and economical than a regular air service. 'This can be done,' he went on,

without making a demand for a subsidy from the people of the Potteries. Furthermore, if this is done we shall be able to offer to flying clubs not only quarters but also qualified instructors and mechanics – in fact, a complete flying and social organisation. To private owners of aeroplanes we shall be able to offer properly equipped landing grounds complete with everything making for efficient services. Under these circumstances, I cannot imagine Stoke-on-Trent and other progressive provincial centres not going 'all out' for a real and complete flying service.

The overall cost to the Corporation would be around £18,000, which included the purchase of the land and the work deemed necessary on it (clearing hedges, filling in ditches and providing a wooden fence around the whole of the site). The Council was warned that they should not expect the aerodrome to pay from the start, although National Flying Services would immediately pay a fixed rent of £200 a year and an increasing percentage of the income derived from the management of the ground. A dissenting voice was raised at one council meeting when Mr G. B. Rogers questioned whether they were justified in incurring the expenditure at a time when people were hard pressed to pay their rates, but the general feeling was one of optimism. Alderman H. Leese said that for the first year about £800 would be added to the rates, but landing fees would increase every year and in about twelve years the Corporation would have recouped all its money. Much now depended on the inspection of the site to confirm that it would meet the requirements of civil aviation.

On 14 June 1929, Captain Neville Stack, the chief pilot of National Flying Services, arrived by air in a Cirrus Moth from London to assess the site. His visit caused something of a stir, for he was a distinguished flyer who had recently taken part in the prestigious King's Cup Air Race. He was received by Captains J. L. Mayer and H. B. Elwell of the aero club and various civic employees, including the City Surveyor. The omens were good. Captain Stack said that the site compared very favourably with others, and that provided plenty of men were put on the work of levelling the ground, it was probable that 'towards the end of the year there would be civil flying in North Staffordshire'.

He announced that at first there would be two planes at Meir, one for the members, the other for joyrides and taxi services. A staff of two instructors, two ground engineers, and engineering and clerical assistants would be stationed at the airfield by the company. The social side of the club would be in the hands of the committee, though flying displays, open to the public, would be held periodically. The air park, he foresaw, would be an important link in the chain of aerodromes as it was on the chief flying route from Glasgow and the north to London and the Continent.

*

No one, it seemed, was now immune from the flying bug. That June the Prime Minister, Ramsay MacDonald, had taken to the air – flying from the north of Scotland to London – the first time a Prime Minister of this country had flown. In September, when the Mayor of Newcastle-under-Lyme, Mr R. Beresford, flew with his wife from Croydon to Paris to celebrate their silver wedding, he was dubbed the 'flying Mayor' by the *Evening Sentinel*, and the occasion deemed sufficiently novel for a news item with a photograph of the passengers awaiting their flight.

The same story mentioned that the Lord Mayor of Stoke-on-Trent, Alderman W. T. Leason, had been initiated into air travel a few months earlier, having been piloted for a short trip by Sir Alan Cobham, the recently knighted pioneer of long-distance aviation, who had made a return visit to the area. The item concluded on a very positive note with reference to future developments in the area: 'The personal tests made by both [...] will sharpen that interest in the movement for the formation of a North Staffordshire Light Aero Club. The club will use the aerodrome to be laid out at Meir. Somewhere about 150 members are needed to run the club successfully and it ought not to be difficult to obtain them. The Mayor and Mayoress of Newcastle intend to join and do everything possible to induce others to follow their example.'

Much of the credit for this popularisation of flying belongs to Sir Alan, who possessed an almost missionary zeal in stimulating interest in aviation among all sections of society – especially children. In 1929 he toured Britain with his Municipal Aerodrome Campaign, aimed at persuading local authorities to establish their own aerodromes, and everywhere he went he was inundated with requests for flights. From 25 to 27 June he had been at Crewe, where civic dignitaries from Stoke-on-Trent (including Alderman Leason) were invited to join him in his airliner 'Youth of Britain' and sample the delights of flying.

Eighty-eight schoolchildren were also lucky enough to be taken up, twenty-two of them from Stoke. It was a breathtaking, unforgettable experience (for adult, child or Mayor), since most people had still never seen a plane, let alone travelled in one. Thousands of future pilots, including many of those who fought in the Battle of Britain, would trace their love of flying back to a trip they made as a youngster with the famous airman. Such was the enthusiasm that greeted him in Cheshire that his agent, Mr Murray de Monti, predicted that 'Crewe will soon be on the aerial map'.

*

Another fillip to Stoke's own aerial ambitions must have been given by the euphoria generated by an event that took place that September, only days after the Mayor of Newcastle's departure. For if he was flying to Paris, it seemed that the rest of the country was making for Portsmouth, Gosport, Southsea, and Hayling Island. Two hundred and fifty special trains ran from Waterloo and Victoria, and roads were crowded with all types of motor vehicle, from the modest two-seater to the huge charabanc. Southsea's population doubled overnight, and hotels and boarding-houses were so packed that visitors slept on the floor or in the bath. Schools and drill halls were thrown open during the night, but many people still had to camp on the beach.

The Schneider Trophy Race of 1929 had become the focus of the nation's attention, and in an age before television it was necessary to turn up to see it. An estimated million and a half spectators did just that, among them, from the Potteries, the parents and brothers of Reginald Mitchell, once more the designer of the British entries. Elsewhere in the crowd was a young woman who had given up her typing job the day before – Amy Johnson – and amid thousands of excited schoolboys was Neil Wheeler, who went on to fly the Spitfire and would one day play an important role in honouring Mitchell in Stoke-on-Trent.

The Schneider Trophy, one of the most coveted international awards, was presented to the nation whose seaplane flew fastest over a number of laps round a closed circuit. The first contest, held in Monaco in 1913, had been won by a Frenchman with a speed of 45.75 mph. Subsequently America, Great Britain, and Italy had all taken the trophy before they had all suffered setbacks. No country had yet achieved the three consecutive wins that would ensure retention of the trophy for all time, but the competitive nature of the event was inspiring ever faster aircraft.

At Venice in 1927, Mitchell's S.5 had won the previous race with a new world record of 281.66 mph. Six weeks later, the Italians had snatched back the record with a speed of 297.76 mph. For these old adversaries – the only remaining teams in that year's race – the stakes were high. Mussolini had commanded the Italian flyers to 'bring the trophy back to Italy', but Mitchell was determined to retain it. On 3 September, he published an article in the *Evening Sentinel* entitled 'Why Britain must win the Schneider Trophy.' In it he wrote of the national prestige and commercial interests at stake. He also looked into the future: 'In 30 years' time, we shall probably regard today's speeds as the tottering pace of a child.' The more immediate future also seemed to be a concern. Although Germany had not entered the competition, he stated that 'it [would] be wise to keep a watchful eye on German progress in the air'. Ten years on to the day, Britain and Germany were again at war.

On the afternoon of Saturday, 7 September, the stage was set for an epic encounter. Conditions were almost perfect – a cloudless turquoise-blue sky and water that shimmered like an emerald sheet of silk. The Solent was crammed with boats of every description – yachts, launches, motor boats, and even floating grandstands. The Prince of Wales and Ramsay MacDonald watched from the deck of the aircraft carrier HMS *Argus*, while General Balbo, the Italian Secretary of State for Air, looked on from an Italian battleship. Loud-speakers gave up-to-the-minute commentaries for the excited crowds thronging the shores, the most favoured spots being the turning-points on the course, for it was here that a race could be won or lost. Shortly after 2 p.m., as the band on the pier played *Ole Man River*, the booming of a gun gave the signal for the race to start. As one, thousands of field glasses were raised to eager eyes.

The contestants took off at 15-minute intervals on the seven-lap course. Flying Officer 'Dick' Waghorn had drawn first place and received an enormous

Reginald Mitchell (extreme right) oversees work on the S.6 by searchlight on the eve of the race.

cheer as his blue and white craft passed the starting boat, flying low and fast. For the first time Mitchell's plane – the S.6 – had been fitted with a Rolls-Royce engine. Until that moment its speed had been a closely guarded secret; after its first lap it was announced over the loudspeakers to a collective gasp – 324 mph, then the greatest speed ever officially recorded.

Just as Waghorn was completing his third lap, Tommaso dal Molin, Italy's crack pilot, set off in his red Macchi M.52R and flashed past the crowds like a streak of blood through the sky, the S.6 closely behind. As Molin entered the 'straight' to finish his initial lap, Waghorn overtook him, provoking a mighty roar from the spectators massed on the pier. Molin's speed had been a disappointing 286 mph, but at least he managed to complete the course (achieving second place), unlike his two compatriots who were forced down with engine trouble.

All three British entries finished, though Flying Officer R. L. R. Atcherley was disqualified for failing to round one of the pylons. Waghorn himself, on what he believed to be his last lap, was distraught when his engine cut out and he too was forced down on the water. But when a jubilant rescue launch reached him, he was told that he had already completed the course and won with an average speed of 328.63 mph – a sensational new record. Waghorn became an instant celebrity, a public idol. Within days the King had conferred the Air Force Cross on him, and his model was on display at Madame Tussaud's. As usual, Mitchell preferred to merge into the background.

However, on Friday, 27 September, he was given a hero's welcome when he returned to Stoke-on-Trent for a luncheon at the North Stafford Hotel as guest of honour of the local Chamber of Commerce. Accompanied by his wife and parents, Mitchell listened as the Lord Mayor recalled how in his early days their guest had

Souvenir programme of the celebrated race.

almost become an architect in the Surveyor's department; now, young as he was, he had become 'the world's leading aircraft designer'. Alderman Leason also praised Mitchell's wisdom in his choice of engines and (to laughter) said that he had noted with some surprise that their distinguished guest had not arrived in a Rolls-Royce.

Sir Francis Joseph, president of the Chamber of Commerce, then went on to recall how the science of aviation had of necessity developed rapidly during the dark days of war:

> We saw the German planes coming over in numbers, which we were unable to stop at that time, perform their work of destruction, both in the City of London and elsewhere. And then the genius of this race, as always, concentrated on the problem and won for us, even at the close of the war, the supremacy of the air, due to our inventive genius and the high craftsmanship of British workmen – which is still supreme – and the undaunted courage of our young men. Since those days there has been great progress in aviation, and our distinguished guest today, young as he is, has played a notable part.

Addressing Mitchell directly, he then declared:

> You are one of those men who make miracles come true. It is an age when miracles are coming true. You are a genius with a magic wand, with an alert

brain and with applied science, who says that all things are possible. Three hundred and twenty-eight miles [per hour] today. What is it going to be in ten years' time and twenty or thirty years' time?

Rising to respond amid prolonged applause, Mitchell paid tribute to the hundreds of people involved in the preparation and research for the race, to the bravery and brilliant flying of the pilots, and to the Rolls-Royce Company, which 'had established itself as the finest designers of aero engines in the world'. He again stressed the significance of such competitions: 'The Schneider Cup race must not be looked upon as purely a sporting event. Just as this county, through the medium of North Staffordshire, has established itself as the producer of the finest china in the world, so the British aircraft industry is striving finally to establish its supremacy.' Such contests had a profound effect not only on foreign trade but also on 'the improvements of our service aircraft and on the development of civil aviation'. The importance of keeping their machines up to a pitch of perfection was paramount, he said, 'particularly seeing we are a country so open to attack by air.'

He concluded by noting with satisfaction that Stoke-on-Trent was considering the question of a municipal aerodrome and said that it was a step in the right direction: 'I am a firm believer in the future of civil aviation and believe it will play a very great part in the future.' He must in fact have been delighted at the prospect of an aerodrome at Meir. It was his wife's home town and only a few minutes away from his own former home at Normacot.

Principal guests at the North Staffordshire Chamber of Commerce luncheon held on 27 September 1929 include (standing, left to right) Herbert Mitchell, W. H. Good, Sir Francis Joseph, R. J. Mitchell, the Lord Mayor (Alderman W. T. Leason), A. H. C. Wenger, Sidney Dodd, and (seated, left to right) Lady Joseph, Mrs R. J. Mitchell, the Lady Mayoress, and Mrs Herbert Mitchell.

5

Open for Business

Captain Stack's prediction of civil flying at Meir by the year's end proved over-optimistic. It was not until 22 January 1930 that Lieutenant-Colonel Edwards, together with Major F. R. Williams, his Chief Engineer, visited the site to discuss final plans for the aerodrome's lay-out and equipment. Accompanying them were a number of civic officials, including the City Surveyor and the Town Planning Assistant. Mr B. C. Harrison, secretary of the aero club, was also present.

After spending two hours inspecting the area, both executives were enthusiastic about its potential. Trees needed to be felled, hedges levelled, and drainage work carried out, but they emphasised the fact that the contours of the land in its rough state did not greatly matter so long as its general trend was level. Major Williams was moved to comment that he did not remember ever having seen a better site, if one took into consideration the large quantity of ground.

On reaching a field near to the main road and almost opposite the pumping station, they were struck by its suitability for the headquarters of the airport. A provisional plan was therefore conceived to site the main offices, hangars, and staff accommodation there, near to a principal entrance to be built on the Longton-Uttoxeter Road. As such work would prove too lengthy and costly to embark on straight away, this section was earmarked for future development after the aerodrome was a going concern. In the meantime, about 100 acres further to the south were mapped out for immediate development so that temporary hangars could be erected as soon as the necessary financial arrangements had been completed. 'To set to work now on the permanent entrance, centre and hangars would mean twelve or eighteen months' work before we were ready,' Major Williams concluded. 'As it is, I see no reason why the first planes should not be flying from the aerodrome in the spring.'

Planes were certainly flying by April – not at Meir, but at Trentham, where the North British Aviation Company had installed three Avros and two pilots to provide joyrides and occasional displays over an 11-day period. A 'plain flight unadorned with loops and twists or any of the more hectic forms of flying' could be had for 5s, and it was announced that the mayor had already put his name down to fly again.

As usual, a reporter turned up on the first day and found Flying Officer Flesson sitting at a typewriter in a bell-tent in a large field near to Trentham station. The latter said 'Good Morning', finished typing his letter, and then took the plane up with the journalist tucked in the seat behind him. The *Sentinel* man marvelled at the minimum of fuss that now prevailed:

> Flying isn't what it used to be! Time was when an airman said elaborate farewells, made his will, dressed himself in special clothing and gave interviews to the Press before every flight.
>
> Nowadays he puts a muffler over his plus-four suit, climbs into the plane, says 'contact' (whatever that means) to a man in grimy overalls who swings the propeller, and then goes flipping casually into the air, much as one would go out on the bicycle to fetch the milk.

The pair sailed nonchalantly over the golf course, Trentham Park, the Michelin works and Stoke church before heading for Northcliffe House, the new home of the *Sentinel*. Despite the fact that everything from the air was veiled in yellow-grey from the Potteries' smoke, they were able to spot the building as it was one of the few white ones. On their return the pilot twice looped the loop before landing with another gratified customer. 'A bump-bump and the plane is back on the earth again,' wrote the reporter. 'It is all over. But what a feeling of exhilaration as you climb out of the cockpit with your head clear and your skin glowing with reaction.'

*

By 6 May, when Captain Mayer and Mr Harrison of the aero club flew in to inspect the Meir site, it was evident that real progress had been made. This was just in time for the aerodrome to feature significantly in the Josiah Wedgwood Bicentenary Celebration – a week-long programme 'on a colossal and unprecedented scale'. It was opened on Monday, 19 May 1930, by Princess Mary, Countess of Harewood, who received a tumultuous reception on her arrival at Stoke station. She proceeded through massive crowds thronging the gaily-decorated streets (in which Wedgwood blue figured prominently) to the King's Hall, where she opened the exhibition of modern pottery and was presented with an exquisite coffee set by Mr Henry Johnson on behalf of the British Pottery Manufacturers' Federation.

The Princess was then driven to Hanley Museum to open an exhibition of historical pottery, to which the Queen had contributed from her Wedgwood collection at Windsor. Afterwards she attended the first performance of the Bicentenary Pageant in Hanley Park, which told the story of North Staffordshire and its industries in a series of living pictures. 'The Pageant is a spectacular triumph, the like of which North Staffordshire has never seen before,' enthused the *Sentinel*. It was no exaggeration. There were 5,000 performers, an orchestra of 100, and 500 in the chorus. A covered auditorium was provided for 3,000 spectators. There were so many colourful and historic costumes that when an official saw a group of disreputable-looking people at the gates of the park, he told them to move on. 'Mister, we're in the Chartist riots!' came the unexpected reply.

The following day, designated 'Transport Day' in the Festival programme, celebrated the evolution of transport from the time of Josiah Wedgwood to the present – from pack horse to the aeroplane. It brought more distinguished guests to the city, including Sir Josiah Stamp, president of the London Midland and Scottish Railway; Sir Ralph Wedgwood, a direct descendant of Josiah and Chief General Manager of the London and North Eastern Railway; Sir Herbert Austin, the well-known motor manufacturer; and Monsieur Marcel Michelin, representing the tyre company that had recently come to the district. Joining them at the Lord Mayor's luncheon was Miss Molly Brown, the sixteen-year-old Railway Queen from Preston, who wore a crimson cloak lined with ermine.

For the first time the aerodrome came into its own to stage 'the most important aviation event that had been held in North Staffordshire'. Despite the cold weather, quite a crowd had gathered there to watch the arrival of famous figures who were to take part in an air pageant over Stoke-on-Trent. They included Captain Norman Blackburn, Director of the Blackburn Aircraft Company; Flight Lieutenant 'Dasher' Blake, his chief test pilot; Charles Shearing, who for a number of years had been a pilot on the Transcontinental American Air Mail; Captain Andrews, who had been chosen by the Spanish government to train their Service pilots; and Captain Worrall, DSC, chief instructor of the Yorkshire Aero Club, who had flown with Sir Alan Cobham around Africa. Numerous members of the Lancashire and North Staffordshire Aero Clubs also arrived during the day in a variety of planes – Bluebirds, Avians, and Moths.

However, the star of the show was undoubtedly Lady Bailey, whose epic flight from London to Cape Town and back in 1928 had been hailed by the press as the greatest solo effort ever accomplished. She had been glad to come and had accepted Sir Francis Joseph's invitation with alacrity. 'How splendid of you to include aviation in the Transport Day,' she wrote. 'It needs all the propaganda it can get, as we are just about eight years behind the trend of commercial aviation in some of the countries of Europe and America.' It was fitting for her to be asked on this particular day to inaugurate the aerodrome, which she did in a brief ceremony. She congratulated Stoke on the enterprise it had shown in taking up this most modern form of transport, and said it was splendid to see such an excellent choice of site for the aerodrome. 'I very much hope,' she said, 'that the North Staffordshire Aero Club may prosper and bring help, amusement, and sport to this district.' George Barber, who had become Lord Mayor of Stoke-on-Trent, then presented her with a fruit dish as a memento of the occasion.

The Lord Mayor (Alderman George Barber) welcomes Lady Bailey to Meir Aerodrome on 20 May 1930.

After the ceremony, the Lord Mayors of Stoke and Newcastle were delighted to be taken up for a flight by Captain Mayer, who led a formation of five planes carrying Lady Bailey and several other visitors on a tour of his native city. It was then the turn of Flight Lieutenant Tommy Rose to go through his repertoire. A veteran of the air battles over the Western Front, where he had scored nine victories and been awarded a Distinguished Flying Cross (DFC), he was regarded as one of the best pilots in the world. As soon as the others were out of sight, he took up an Avro and performed twists, turns, rolls, and loops that brought him ever closer to the ground. He was given a hearty cheer when he finally landed safely. 'Dasher' Blake then took over and gave an amazing display of upward spins, slow rolls, and inverted flying, a loudspeaker van giving a running commentary on the various moves to help the spectators. Meir had seen nothing like it – and there was much more to follow during the day.

When the flying party returned, the Lord Mayor described the experience as 'splendid' and said: 'We encircled the whole of the city and went over every town. At times we were doing 140 mph, and a speed like that makes the city seem a very tiny place.' Lady Bailey had also greatly enjoyed the tour and, like several guests, expressed surprise at the 'glorious scenery' on view. Captain Blackburn then brought this stage of the proceedings to an end as Lady Bailey was promised elsewhere. Speaking into the loud-speaker, he paid tribute to their distinguished guest and to the aerodrome:

Civil aviation is making great advances nowadays and I think we all appreciate that no small thanks is due to the women for these advances.

[Cries of *hear! hear!*] Lady Bailey with her great flights, especially her flight to the Cape, has shown that the small engine and the small plane are reliable and safe. We have also to thank Amy Johnson who is making her very courageous flight [to Australia] under all kinds of adverse circumstances. I think in future that the people of Stoke-on-Trent will have every reason to think as much of the City Fathers of today as they do of Josiah Wedgwood, because the City Fathers have given them this fine aerodrome.

Lady Bailey and the other visitors then left for an official reception at Stoke Town Hall, after which she reopened the Modern Pottery Exhibition. As the week progressed, other famous visitors followed in her footsteps, though a notable absentee was Arnold Bennett, who had to deny rumours that he was slighting his native city. On 'Industrial Day', 22 May, Sir Oliver Lodge, the Penkull-born physicist and pioneer of radio-telegraphy, was an honoured guest. On the same day, not long after the giant British airship R-100 had passed unexpectedly over Hanley, another unexpected visitor – a tall thin man carrying a green hat – joined the *6d* queue for the pottery exhibition at the King's Hall. It was only when he was recognised as the eminent playwright George Bernard Shaw that he was quickly ushered inside.

*

Barely a month later Captain J. R. King, on behalf of National Flying Services, became the first pilot to begin commercial flying at Meir. For a fortnight, from 15 to 29 June, a Desouter monoplane was available for hire as a 'saloon air taxi', with short flights around the aerodrome also on offer. Apart from the pilot, the plane could accommodate two passengers who were assured that they could wear their ordinary clothes and would be able to converse with the same ease as when motoring.

The purpose of the visit was to make the people of the Potteries 'air-minded' – and it succeeded. Captain King, an ex-RFC pilot with twenty years' flying under his harness, was kept busy from day one, when 200 people took flights. His oldest passenger was a lady of seventy-one, his youngest a four-year-old child who flew with his father. According to the local press, the interest aroused by the flights was 'astonishing', and during the fortnight thousands of people visited the aerodrome simply to view the yellow and black Desouter at close quarters and watch the trips of those fortunate enough to be able to afford them. So dense was the milling crowd that the pilot experienced some anxious moments when taking off and landing.

On the very last day the Desouter met with a slight mishap when part of the undercarriage gave way as it touched down, the plane finishing up at an acute angle. No one was injured, and Captain King attributed the accident to the strain imposed on the undercarriage by the constant landings and take-offs.

FLIGHTS
FROM
5/-

Two passengers fly
in company with
the Pilot.
Perfect Comfort.
Unrestricted View.

Don't miss a Flight
in the Latest National Flying Service's
SALOON AIR TAXI
AT THE
Stoke Municipal Aerodrome
MEIR (near Longton)

Daily From TO-MORROW
(Sunday, June 15th to
Sunday, June 29th)
'Buses to and from Aerodrome.
NATIONAL FLYING SERVICES, LTD.,
Grand Buildings, Trafalgar Sq., London, W.C.2.

The aerodrome opens
for business on Sunday,
15 June 1930.

Over the two weeks he had piloted more than 1,000 people on what was for
most their first ever flight.

Captain King was the first pilot to have any lengthy experience of using the
airfield, and his opinion of it at this stage is therefore of genuine interest. In an
interview with the *Sentinel*, he said:

> Your aerodrome will develop into a very convenient and suitable, if not ideal,
> centre for commercial flying activities. Of course, the ideal of every airman
> is a flat 'drome without boundaries, and though the Stoke-on-Trent site does
> not conform to this, it will become highly efficient in time and the nature of
> its situation gives it other advantages not obtainable on a level aerodrome.
>
> I refer to the favourable air-currents which abound. They are set up by
> the surrounding high ground, which breaks up the air. They are very helpful
> to pilots, who can take off very easily with their aid. However, I might add
> that these conditions are only known to an experienced pilot, and a beginner
> would not be able to take advantage of them at all.
>
> The ground surface is not perfect in its present state by any means, and
> when you consider that one day alone I made 120 flights you will realise the
> strain placed on my plane, in continually landing and taking off.

He went on to say that as a result of a very favourable report he had made
to National Flying Services, the firm was to speed up its operations, and an
inspection had been made that week with regard to erecting hangars. Until
an air taxi station was established at Meir, arrangements could be made at

any time to pick up passengers and fly them to any part of the country or to the Continent. Moreover, dual control machines were to be sent down in the near future to establish the flying school there. 'I believe there are thirty-four members of the aero club,' he continued, 'and I am confident that this number will be doubled immediately actual flying commences.'

Captain King returned to Meir on the two following Sundays, 6 and 13 July, to provide air trips for those who had been disappointed as a result of his mishap. A week later, on Monday 21 July, the whole of Staffordshire was stunned by the sudden death of one of its most popular figures, Rosemary Ednam. Lady Ednam, the thirty-seven-year-old only daughter of the fourth Duke of Sutherland, had spent most of her early life at Trentham and had replaced her mother, Millicent, as president of the North Staffordshire Cripples Aid Society, for which she had worked tirelessly in fund-raising activities.

That Monday she was flying back to England from Le Touquet, where she had been staying with her husband, Viscount Ednam, who was ill. The air taxi, a single-engine Junkers F13, flew into a gale over Kent and seemed to disintegrate in the air. The four passengers were flung to their deaths and the two pilots died on impact. (The second pilot was Charles Shearing who two months earlier had attended the inauguration of Meir Aerodrome.) 'Seldom has the public of Staffordshire been so painfully shocked,' stated the *Sentinel,* as messages of sympathy began to flood in, including those from King George V and Queen Mary, and the Prince of Wales, all close friends of the family. Indeed, Prince Edward had fallen in love with Lady Ednam before her marriage and proposed in 1918, but the match was apparently opposed by his father and came to nothing.

At the funeral at Himley Hall, near Dudley, there were more than 100 magnificent floral tributes, among them a wreath of roses from the Prince of Wales and a card that read 'With Love, from E. P. [Edward, Prince]'. Another wreath was from the former Prime Minister Stanley Baldwin. One beautiful tribute was inscribed 'a token of deepest respect and loyal affection from the old estate servants at Trentham and Lilleshall'. A large floral cross of crimson roses and asparagus ferns came from the committee of the Orthopaedic Hospital 'in grateful memory of our president'. A more lasting memorial to her was to be the £20,000 extension then being made to the Hospital at Hartshill, the opening of which would incidentally provide another memorable moment in the history of the City Aerodrome.

In August, Amy Johnson, who had become the first woman to fly solo from England to Australia, returned home to a rapturous welcome. Only a handful of people had been at Croydon to watch her depart in May; now the airport was besieged as London went 'frantic with joy', with over 100,000 people thronging the twelve-mile route to her hotel. She was met by Lord Thomson, the Air Minister, and in her luggage she had a letter of congratulation from the King, scores of gifts from Australian admirers, and hundreds of marriage proposals. Flowers and fruit were named after her, a song was composed to celebrate her homecoming, and Amy, 'wonderful Amy', was mobbed wherever she went. A nationwide tour was hastily arranged, but that autumn, owing to the intense media attention, she fell ill and a scheduled visit to Stoke-on-Trent on 10 October did not take place.

At Meir so great was the enthusiasm for joyrides that National Flying Services put on an additional week from 4 to 10 August, and made a further return visit at the end of their summer tour from 25 to 28 September. Some in the area, however, were less keen. The Council had already received letters from several nearby churches protesting against the Sunday flights that were taking place, and the attention of National Flying Services was drawn to the problem of noise disturbing the devotions of the faithful.

By then the first hangar had been erected close to the main road. It measured 75 by 90 feet, and was of a steel framework and asbestos fireproof sheets. It contained a suite of offices and was to be illuminated by six gas lamps of 600 candle-power each. The company was also considering building a clubhouse for the proposed flying school, although lessons had had to be postponed until the following spring as the ground was not yet in a fit state. For the time being, therefore, Dr Stanley Glass, a Norton doctor who was one of the first private owners of an aeroplane in North Staffordshire, had to have lessons in his Blackburn Bluebird at Manchester Airport. At Meir the flying season was over.

On the evening of 4 October, Britain's million-pound R-101 – the world's largest airship – set off on her maiden flight from England to India. A year earlier, when it had been due to pass over the Midlands on a test flight, the Potteries was said to be 'agog with anticipatory excitement', though in the event the airship flew over South Staffordshire and so many were disappointed. In the debate that was then current, sceptics believed that the newfangled aeroplane would never replace the airship, and the R-101 was the visible manifestation of that confidence.

However, early next morning the giant airship nosedived into a hillside near Beauvais in northern France and erupted into a fireball. Of the fifty-four men on board, only six survived the inferno. Lord Thomson, the Secretary of State for Air, and Air Vice-Marshal Sir Sefton Brancker, Director of Civil Aviation, were among the dead, as were many leading engineers in the airship industry. Graphic images imprinted the horror on the public consciousness. Suddenly, and dramatically, the debate was over. The future belonged to the aeroplane.

*

In March 1931, Arnold Bennett died at his London home aged sixty-three, and in the 'Five Towns' flags flew at half-mast. Although he had been a great traveller and a yacht owner, there is no evidence that he had ever flown in an aeroplane, unlike his school friend Harold Hales. His final journey was in a third-class railway carriage, when his brother Frank transported his ashes back to the Potteries to be interred in the family grave at Burslem cemetery.

Another death that touched the nation was that of Schneider Race winner 'Dick' Waghorn ('the Wizard of the Air') who was killed after baling out in May. A thousand mourners followed his coffin to the grave. His loss, if anything, intensified the fascination of man, woman, and child with all things aeronautical. The League of Nations might try to get the bomber banned; others, it seemed, wished to uninvent the aeroplane. But aviation had come to stay. The momentum was unstoppable.

Nowhere, it seemed, was this more apparent than at Meir Aerodrome. National Flying Services had arranged for gliding exhibitions to take place at all of their airfields, and early that month, during the weekend of 2 and 3 May, 'Professor' C. H. Lowe-Wylde, the leading authority on auto-towed gliding in the country, gave demonstrations of this new method of launching a glider by towing it behind a car. Hundreds of people turned up, including visitors from the Manchester, Nottingham, and Wrexham Gliding Clubs. North Staffordshire had recently established a gliding club of its own under the chairmanship of Mr F. Northall, and had begun its New Year programme a few months earlier at Barlaston Downs. Its members too turned up in force to lend support and take part in the exhibition. Also there was a *Sentinel* reporter to record the scene and describe this latest aerial novelty for his readers: 'The glider itself is not unlike a dainty aeroplane in structure, and its controls are very similar to the orthodox flying machine. From the manner in which it circled slowly round and swooped here and there as the pilot willed, however, it reminded me of a huge bat.'

Lowe-Wylde declared himself highly satisfied with the first day's outcome: 'On Saturday my longest flight was one of four minutes and thirty-three seconds,' he said. 'I climbed to about 800 feet. The conditions were wonderful.' After the demonstration, members of the gliding clubs took flights, as did members of the public, a particularly keen interest being shown by the women present, many of whom went up in the glider. Then it was the turn of the reporter. After a two-minute flight with Lowe-Wylde, he pronounced the experience 'genuinely thrilling', and went on: 'Imagine riding on the pillion of a motor cycle travelling at 60 mph down a very steep hill, and you have a slight idea of the thrill of being a passenger in a glider as it swoops towards the ground.'

Future prospects for the City Aerodrome seemed as bright as the weather. When asked if it would be possible to start a flying school there, Captain King, who was co-operating with Lowe-Wylde, replied that until the on-going work had finished, the Air Ministry would not issue a licence for instructional purposes. That, he said, was the only cause of delay. It was, however, obvious to everyone (including Sir Alan Cobham who flew in on an inspection visit on 7 May) that the work was proceeding apace and that an ample stretch of ground had already been cleared. In addition, the aerodrome hangar now housed the Blackburn Bluebird biplane of the first private owner (Dr Glass) to make permanent use of the facilities.

'Professor' C. H. Lowe-Wylde gives the first demonstration of gliding in North Staffordshire and South Cheshire at The Cloud, Congleton, on Sunday, 14 September 1930.

Hot on the heels of Lowe-Wylde came Captain Charles Barnard and what was described as 'the world's first air circus', part of a tour of 150 towns to demonstrate the great advances made in aviation. On 18 May, the *Sentinel* announced the forthcoming visit of this celebrity pilot and reported that he would be flying his monoplane *The Spider*, in which he had made record flights to India and Cape Town. The Fokker aeroplane was ideal for joy-riding, comfortably holding twelve passengers in its roomy cabin, and on offer, courtesy of the newspaper, were twenty free flights for those readers who could complete an 'aerial limerick' most successfully. In addition, an outstanding opportunity was being offered to a local boy to win one of the 100 flying scholarships that were being offered by Captain Barnard in connection with the tour. The winner would be taught to fly free of cost at the local flying club and would be helped to take up aviation as a career.

Two days later, on Wednesday, 20 May, Captain Barnard and his wife landed at Meir shortly after 11.15 a.m. to be accorded a civic reception by a party headed by the Lord Mayor and Lady Mayoress, Mr and Mrs H. J. Colclough. Captain Barnard paid tribute to the airfield, saying he was surprised to find what a fine and spacious site the city had for its aerodrome, adding that 'after it had been properly levelled and drained, it would certainly be one of the best in the country.'

During his two-day visit he put on a spectacular air pageant, featuring exhibitions of looping, rolling, inverted flying, and 'crazy' flying by Captains Ayre and Crossley in their Spartan light aeroplane. This was followed by a breathtaking display of wing-walking and a parachute descent by John Tranum,

CAPT. C. D. BARNARD'S

AIR PAGEANT

STOKE'S MUNICIPAL AIR PARK
Near LONGTON
WEDNESDAY and THURSDAY, MAY 20th and 21st, 11 a.m.

The "Autogiro."   "Daily Mail" Aviation Lesson.
Parachute Descents.   Aerobatics.
Broadcast Programme and Music.
Flying Thrills all day.

PASSENGER FLIGHTS WITH CAPT. BARNARD.

Admission 1/-   Children 6d.   Motors 1/-

The first 'flying circus' comes to Meir.

who held the world record with 1,200 'live drops' from aircraft. The 'windmill' plane, the Cierva autogiro, was then in action, demonstrating its remarkable powers of vertical ascent with Wing Commander Reginald Brie at the controls.

During the afternoons, the *Daily Mail* aviation lesson was given over a powerful loudspeaker, the special broadcast equipment being in communication with the plane in the air demonstrating the points in the lesson. Many of the children present were seen taking notes, which perhaps inspired the *Sentinel* to give its readers this glimpse into the future: 'To the generation now at school, air travel will become as normal a means of transport as railways, steamships, and motor cars, and the generation that follows will take to flying as a duck takes to water.'

Certainly the citizens of the Potteries were taking to the air as to the manner born, with flying lessons or passenger flights on offer at 5s a time. The civic representatives had been invited on the first flight on the Wednesday morning and voted the experience 'wonderful'. Next day, in brilliant sunshine, the twenty prize-winners reported to the *Sentinel* tent at the aerodrome and were taken up. Mrs Ada Woodings described her first joyride as 'magnificent' and said that she had not been nervous at all. Mr George Howell enjoyed seeing the Stoke City Football Ground from the air and said he had never imagined that air travel could be so comfortable. Although cotton wool had been provided, none of the passengers had plugged their ears. Miss Lena Bateman agreed: 'It was really fine. It was very steady indeed and in my mind as comfortable as a motor car.' Mrs W. Allen was equally sold on the experience: 'It was wonderfully clear and I was able to recognise Florence Colliery and the district round about Longton police station. The train at Meir looked like little painted matchboxes. It was altogether thrilling – I would not have missed it for anything.' Mr W. E. Fryer said simply, 'I only wish I could have stayed up all day.'

Captain Charles Barnard and his wife (centre left) are greeted by the Lord Mayor (Mr H. J. Colclough), Lady Mayoress, and other visitors on 20 May 1931.

Visitors watch the autogiro in flight at Meir.

6

Of Royal Descents

A few weeks later, on 1 July 1931, the stage was set for the arrival of another eminent visitor, who was to make an informal two-day tour of local industries. There was to be only one public ceremony performed during the visit, but this would mark an important stage in the history of the aerodrome. A large party of city councillors and their wives were joined by VIPs and other distinguished guests, including the heads of aerodromes from Leeds, Hull, Nottingham, and Blackpool, who had flown in especially for the occasion. Among a number of well-known pilots was Colonel 'the Master of Sempill', one of the country's most distinguished pioneer aviators, who had flown his Puss Moth from London.

A *Sentinel* reporter at the airfield recorded his impressions:

The scene while officials and civic dignitaries were assembling was one of brightness and animation, sunlight flashing on the graceful wings of the planes as, from all quarters of the sky, they approached, circled, swooped, and touched surface before taxiing to their allocated stations. The presence of many prominent flying men added special significance to one of the most effective aerial rallies ever staged in the district – a happy and appropriate augury for the future success of the aerodrome.

Scarcely five minutes after their scheduled time of arrival, two glittering aircraft were seen heading straight for the cleared space in which the Lord Mayor's party had taken up their stand, close to the Union Jack that floated from a flag-post erected in front of the hangar. The planes circled, slowing and losing height, until the leader – G–ABDB, a slim silver Moth with a bold star on the side of its fuselage – grazed the grass and glided smoothly to within a few yards of the table behind which stood the hosts.

Twenty-eight-year-old Prince George, the Duke of Kent and youngest son of King George V, was warmly greeted as he emerged from the aircraft on what was his first visit to North Staffordshire. After extending an official welcome, the Lord Mayor said:

I have very great pleasure indeed in asking your Royal Highness to perform the ceremony of formally opening this aerodrome. We have been informed that it is one of the finest existing in the country. I am afraid I am not a competent judge of that, but we are only too ready to believe that it is so, and I have now the utmost satisfaction in requesting you formally to open the aerodrome.

To much applause, Prince George, who was himself a qualified pilot, duly obliged, saying:

It gives me great pleasure to come here today and open this aerodrome. I am sure it is going to be of great benefit to your city, and that it is a very good thing that Stoke-on-Trent should have an airport. I have much pleasure in declaring the aerodrome open.

Afterwards he made a short tour of the airfield, pausing to inspect the aeroplanes lined up on the edge of the landing ground and to chat to the pilots who had flown in to honour his presence and the occasion.

During his stay, the Prince visited representative pottery factories in each of the 'Five Towns', and was presented with an elegant coffee set at the Copeland-Spode works in Stoke. Later he inspected a silk mill at Leek, dropped in on the Staffordshire *v*. New Zealand cricket match at Stoke (where he presented the

HRH Prince George formally opens the City Aerodrome on 1 July 1931.

touring team with Doulton figures) and attended the Hanley Park fête. Tall, handsome, and with an irresistible charm, he was acclaimed wherever he went by crowds of cheering admirers – girls in their summer dresses, pottery workers in white smocks, and children fluttering handkerchiefs. At the conclusion of a memorable trip, the Prince eventually returned to Meir and flew back to London.

On 13 September, the whole nation cheered as Flight Lieutenant John Boothman in Mitchell's seaplane S.6B won the Schneider Trophy for the third time in a row, which ensured that it would remain in Britain for ever. 'Heartiest congratulations on the part you have taken to achieve such a wonderful record' read the telegram sent to Mitchell by Stoke's Lord Mayor on behalf of the city. The average speed of the S.6B had been just over 340 mph, but the same afternoon Flight Lieutenant George Stainforth set a new world air speed record by achieving an average of 379 mph. Two weeks later, on 29 September, Stainforth again smashed the record with a speed of 407 mph, making the seaplane the fastest aircraft in the world. Despite such achievements, Mitchell remained relatively unknown; one journalist called him 'a silent mystery man'. At the year's end, however, he was notified that he was to be awarded the CBE in the New Year's Honours List – the only official recognition he would ever receive.

*

In the General Election of October 1931, Sir Oswald Mosley of the New Party stood for Stoke South and finished bottom of the poll, although Harold Hales won Hanley for the National Conservatives. Bennett's fictional 'card' became the Lord Mayor of 'Bursley'; the real one entered the House of Commons.

The Schneider Trophy.

At Meir the air taxi service was fully operational, and a telephone had been installed at the aerodrome so that a businessman had merely to ring up (telephone number 122 Blythe Bridge) and book a plane 'to anywhere'. At long last the new flying school was also taking off, and during the weekend of 10 and 11 October Captain E. B. Bartlett, the instructor in charge of the two-seater Avion biplane, had been kept at full stretch. 'It has been wonderful weather for flying this weekend,' he said. 'At times we could not cope with those wishing to go up.'

Further expansion was already on the cards. Mr R. Fullerton, the Chief Ground Engineer, announced that two more air taxis had been promised by National Flying Services, and he expected that they too would be put to good use, so great was the local interest in flying. This enthusiasm, he felt, stemmed from the fact that the aerodrome was so suitable. 'With one exception,' he said, 'it is the largest British aerodrome I have been on.' He was also optimistic with regard to the future of the aero club: 'A number of the members are already experienced flyers, and encouraged by their lead the others are taking to the sport like ducks to water. I anticipate that by the beginning of next season the club will be firmly established and will rank as one of the largest in the country.' Behind the optimism, however, was the stark fact that the aero club had barely a third of the 150 members it needed to make it a viable proposition. There were still some difficult days ahead.

On 15 November, the aerodrome had the rare privilege of playing host to its second royal visitor within a few months. The Prince of Wales (who became King Edward VIII in 1936) should have arrived in the area the day before, intending to stay overnight at Himley Hall in Dudley and then motor to his engagement, but he had been indisposed and it was feared that he would be unable to come. However, this seemed to be one engagement that he was determined to keep. At the last minute he decided to fly from Windsor to Meir, en route to open the Rosemary Ednam Memorial Hospital for Cripples at Hartshill. That Sunday the weather was very cold, and heavy local mist raised doubts as to whether the Prince would be able to land. A flare was lit before the hangar as a guide, and a considerable number of people gathered in the flying field enclosure and on the main road leading into the city as word spread of the imminent arrival of the most popular and charismatic member of the royal family.

At 3.30 p.m. the Prince's Puss Moth G-ABRR – 'a neat little red, white, and blue plane' – was seen heading straight for the hangar. It circled and then landed perfectly on almost the identical spot on which the Prince's brother had touched down in July and within a few yards of Viscount Ednam, who was waiting to greet him. Clad against the elements in a long, heavy coat over a dark lounge suit, the Prince emerged with his favourite pet terrier Jack who had flown with him. He quickly exchanged his close-fitting flying helmet for a bowler and declared that flying conditions had been 'bad – but not too bad'.

The Prince of Wales is greeted
by Viscount Ednam on his
arrival at Meir on
15 November 1931.

Already behind schedule, he then sped away for his engagement to resounding
cheers from the crowd.

At Hartshill, the Prince paid tribute to the woman who might have been his
wife and future Queen. 'You all know,' he said, 'the wonderful work Rosemary
Ednam did all the years she lived in these parts. It was she who inaugurated
the idea of this hospital and started the fund. [...] I now open this hospital, full
of great thoughts and sacred remembrances.'

Meanwhile, his pilot, Captain Fielden, having safely delivered his charge,
nearly came to grief himself. He had taken off to fly to Wolverhampton, but
on the way ran into a bank of fog and decided to return to Meir. At Fulford,
near Blythe Bridge, he again met with very poor visibility and had to make a
forced landing. Happily, neither he nor the plane sustained any real damage.

7

Sir Alan Cobham's Flying Circus

From 1932 to 1935, Sir Alan Cobham created what is probably the most celebrated flying show of all – his National Aviation Day Crusade with its slogan 'Make the Skyways Britain's Highways'. For three years in succession he visited Meir, the first occasion being on Thursday, 9 June 1932, when at about 11.10 a.m. 'a shimmering silver speck appeared in the blue sky. The machine wheeled and dipped, touched ground, and skimmed to a standstill – a graceful three-engined air liner with a seating capacity for ten passengers.' The *Youth of Britain II* had landed.

Like Captain Barnard before him, Sir Alan paid tribute to the aerodrome, describing it as 'a fine open space, wonderfully situated, [...] a great contrast to the make-shift grounds at which I have had to land at some towns during my tour'. Shortly afterwards, the city's first lady Lord Mayor, Miss Florence Farmer, and a number of council members arrived to welcome their distinguished guest on behalf of the city and then accompany him on a special sightseeing tour over the Potteries. Unusually, one of them, Alderman George Barber, the cinema owner, had by now become an experienced amateur airman who had flown extensively over the Continent and had recently returned from an aerial tour of Palestine and Egypt. Although over seventy, he had also been taking flying lessons for about three months from his friend Captain Mayer. For most of the party, however, it was their first ever flight, and Alderman E. Hughes, then in his eightieth year, described the new experience as 'grand'.

Sir Alan was then entertained to a luncheon at the North Stafford Hotel by the Chamber of Commerce. Proposing the health of their guest, the president (Colonel W. J. Kent) said that in the realm of aeronautical science Sir Alan had achieved a wonderful record and had played a great part in the establishment of municipal aerodromes, which were springing up all over the country. Sir Alan, who was accorded an enthusiastic reception on rising to respond, said that he had always believed in flying, and that since the war the progress of aviation had been phenomenal.

He went on to declare that the progress of the future would make present commercial speeds of aviation look foolish. In a visionary speech, he said that in a few years it would be possible to reach any part of the world in a matter of days – in fact it would take only hours to reach America by air. However, he continued: 'The aeroplane will not be able to prove its great

Left: The Lord Mayor (Miss Florence Farmer) welcomes Sir Alan Cobham to Meir on 9 June 1932. *Right*: Sir Alan chats to Ronald Copeland MP and Mrs R. Beresford.

utility in this country until every town has a landing ground, so that it will be possible to fly in a straight line from anywhere to anywhere. To ask aircraft to develop without landing grounds is like asking ships to go on the seas without harbours, and trains to run without stations.'

He congratulated the people of Stoke for going ahead with the aerodrome and urged them to hold on to it. Again in visionary mode, he continued: 'There is no reason why you should not have, in the future, aeroplanes arriving at Stoke in their thousands – just the same as you have motor-cars passing through the city today. [...] I can think of the time when suddenly, some Saturday afternoon, the sky will go dark and people will remark, "There goes the Stoke Light Aero Club".' He concluded on a note of optimism that sadly a few years hence would prove unfounded: 'Flying means speed of communication. Through it people will be able to get to know each other better, and when they do, I don't think they will squabble so much.'

The display at the aerodrome that afternoon was the most spectacular event seen in the Potteries since Buffalo Bill's Wild West show twenty-eight years before. It opened with a grand parade of the twelve aircraft taking part. As each of them in turn flew past the public enclosure, Sir Alan explained through a loudspeaker the role it would play in the coming show. A demonstration of formation flying followed, with all the aircraft formed on either side of Sir Alan's plane as they cruised over Meir in a neatly aligned wedge-shaped echelon. A Tiger Moth that had been specially built for the advanced training of Service pilots then amazed the large crowd with a spectacular exhibition of aerobatics, followed by a demonstration of 'crazy flying' and the sight of a Comper Swift dancing in the air to the rhythm of music broadcast from the Kolster-Brandes radio coach.

Also on the programme were delayed-drop parachute descents, auto-towed gliding (Lowe-Wylde was back with Sir Alan), upside-down flying and

Sir Alan Cobham's flying circus.

'big game hunting', when the pilot swooped low and with a revolver shot down a series of numbered balloons in sequence. The highlight, though, was undoubtedly the air race round pylons between the fastest machines at the aerodrome, the race being flown over three circuits of a triangular course. As a tribute to a local and national hero, it was listed thereafter in the programme as a 'miniature Schneider Trophy Race'.

At a council meeting at the end of the month, it was announced that a licence for the use of the aerodrome had been received from the Air Ministry and that the lease had also been taken up by National Flying Services. As usual, Mr Rogers was unimpressed, especially when the Town Clerk admitted that the city coffers had derived no benefit from the recent air pageant. He stated bluntly that it was time they considered the whole future of the airfield and asked: 'Is it not a fact that this aerodrome is a liability to the city?' It was a question that would hang in the air for many years to come.

On 1 July the *Graf Zeppelin* reached London on its 250th passenger flight. The following day, as it cruised around the country, sightings of the great German airship were made at Woore, Clayton and Loggerheads. Meanwhile, in Germany, Adolf Hitler became the first politician to use air travel in an election campaign.

*

This was proving a hectic year for Captain Mayer, one of the founder members and first chairman of the North Staffordshire Aero Club, who was often involved in air displays in the district and elsewhere. A native of Brindley Ford, he was truly one of the district's aviation pioneers, for his flying experience went back to pre-war days, when, aged sixteen, he had joined the Hall School of Flying at Hendon, one of the earliest flying schools, where he became an instructor in a remarkably short time. During the Great War, he had been granted a commission in the Royal Naval Air Service when he was only eighteen, and had gone on to command seaplane bases at Malta and Crete. Like most of the early pioneers he seemed indestructible, and had once drifted in the Aegean Sea for five days in a crippled seaplane before being rescued. He was later awarded a DFC for meritorious services and was still attached to the Air Force as a reserve officer.

On the 8 and 9 July he was among the competitors of that year's King's Cup Air Race, acting as navigator in a Sports Avian piloted by Captain G. H. Keat of London. A week later on 16 July, he was acting as clerk of the course at an air pageant at Meir organised by John Pepper, president of the aero club. Despite the unpleasantly dull flying conditions, thirteen visiting planes had arrived by the middle of the afternoon from all over the country. The centre of attention was undoubtedly the Lockheed Vega in which Commander Glen Kidston had made his recent record-breaking flight to the Cape, flown in from Hanworth Aerodrome by Lieutenant Owen Cathcart Jones.

On 27 August, Captain Mayer took part in the British Hospitals' Air Pageant at Coal Aston Aerodrome in aid of the Sheffield Royal Hospital – and ended up as a patient there. While 'bombing' a motor car, his plane inexplicably nose-dived into the ground and he was seriously injured, suffering multiple fractures. Dr Glass, chairman of the aero club, visited him the same day and

Captain John Mayer.

said: 'He is a man of wonderful vitality and cheery disposition. There is every hope of recovery.' He seemed to be making progress, but septicaemia set in shortly after the accident and his right leg had to be amputated two weeks later. He died on 6 October, aged thirty-four, a grievous loss to aviation in the area. At his funeral at Biddulph parish church, two of the many floral tributes reflected his passion from an early age – a floral propeller from his employers and an aeroplane modelled in laurel and yellow and white chrysanthemums from the aero club.

*

For Stoke City, the 1932-33 football season was proving momentous. From the outset, promotion prospects for the team were regarded as excellent, and their squad was further strengthened by the signing (at £5 a week) of an exciting seventeen-year-old from Hanley named Stanley Matthews, who had recently made his debut for the club.

On Saturday, 15 October 1932, the home fixture with Plymouth Argyle was highly significant, not only because the Potters were striving to retain the leadership of the Second Division against one of their closest rivals, but also because it marked an experiment that (it was said) might 'revolutionise football clubs' travel in the future'.

As usual, the Plymouth team had travelled by train to Stoke the day before and on the morning of the match were enjoying a tour of the Wedgwood works at Etruria. While they were there, Captain Barnard took off from Roborough Aerodrome in Plymouth with a party of nine of Argyle's directors and officials on board his famous *Spider* and flew them to Meir Aerodrome. Their aim was to test for the first time the feasibility of air travel for football teams.

The plane left at 10.10 a.m. and made a perfect landing at Meir at 12.45 p.m., having covered the 200 miles against head winds in just over 2½ hours. Despite a little buffeting on the way, the passengers described it as an 'exceedingly pleasant journey', and no one felt any adverse effects. They intended to fly back the following day, accompanied by one of the players, but for the moment they left for a quick lunch in Hanley before watching Stoke win 2-0 on their way to becoming Second Division Champions.

The cost of the return trip (which was being defrayed by the club's president) was £75, and no definite decision as to future air travel was being made until the League Management Committee had discussed the matter. However, Mr Robert Jack, the team manager (who had made the journey by train), ruled out for the time being any regular flying by his players because of the cost involved. He appeared dubious that it would ever catch on.

*

Not everyone was as enamoured of municipal aerodromes as Captain Barnard or Sir Alan Cobham. Despite days of intense activity, there were also prolonged periods when little seemed to be happening at the City Aerodrome – a fact noted by correspondents to the *Sentinel*. One wrote that a cynic might be tempted to describe 'this development of municipal activity as the result of an attack of megalomania' and told how 'a large and prolific flock of sheep are at present in possession' of the airfield.

As previously seen, some members of the Corporation were equally hostile. Throughout the 1930s, as the cost of clearing and preparing the Meir site began to mount, the City Council developed a 'love-hate' relationship with the airport that sometimes descended into farce. One such occasion took place on 2 February 1933 – three days after Hitler became Chancellor of Germany – when the Council discussed the costs associated with the airfield. Mr Rogers stated that he had opposed the aerodrome project (or the 'municipal luxury' as he called it) from the outset, and thought that his attitude had been justified by the publication of the accounts. According to these, the airport had so far cost £29,180, while for the past year the income had been £234 16s 6d and the expenditure £2,632 10s 10d.

When reminded by the Lord Mayor that a lease was in existence and the Council could do nothing, Mr Rogers lamented that fact and moved that a sub-committee be appointed to look into the matter. Mr J. A. Dale seconded the motion, declaring that the land should, if possible, be returned to the Corporation. The names of Mr Rogers and Mr Dale were then proposed for the committee of inquiry and carried to general laughter. Both the nominees instantly took umbrage at the 'insulting and light-hearted way' in which the matter had been treated and refused to serve. After this spat, the subject was allowed to drop – for the time being.

Over the weekend of 3 and 4 June, the British Hospitals' Air Pageant reached Meir on its tour of over 200 venues. This time the North Staffordshire Royal Infirmary, the Burslem Haywood, and Tunstall Memorial Hospital were to benefit from a percentage of the takings from the show, which lasted from early afternoon to dusk on both days. It offered an embarrassment of riches: sixteen aircraft, twenty events, and a host of top-flight stars, led by Charles Scott, a popular and celebrated aviator who had won the King's Cup in 1925 and whose record-breaking flights to Australia had made headline news. The *Sentinel* had hailed his 1931 triumph as 'a magnificent personal achievement and a new demonstration of the supremacy of British aircraft'.

A notable feature of this pageant was the number of women participating – the first to join the staff of an air circus in the UK. The record of the Hon. Mrs Victor Bruce (Mary Petrie) spoke for itself. Famous both in the motor-racing sphere and in the air, she was the first Englishwoman to fly solo around the world. Miss Pauline Gower had gained second place in the All Women's Air Race, while her mechanic, Miss Dorothy Spicer (who also held a pilot's licence) was the only practising woman ground engineer in the country. Together they had set up the first all-female air taxi service and travelled frequently to the Continent. One of the most eagerly awaited events was the racing between the men and women pilots, with commentary through a loudspeaker by Colonel J. C. Fitzmaurice, a member of the crew of the aeroplane *Bremen*, which had made the first flight across the Atlantic from East to West in 1928.

The various machines on show included the Gipsy Moth in which Charles Scott had flown to Australia, a 200 mph Fairey Fox, de Havilland and Handley-Page air liners, and several Avros, Fox Moths, and Spartans. There was also a fierce Chinese Dragon, a weird and brightly coloured monster of the air, designed and painted by the famous comic artist Heath Robinson especially for the pageant. This enormous winged reptile – in reality a BAC Drone aeroplane – was skilfully flown by the well-known glider pilot J. C. Longmore to the delight of the many children present.

The summer flying season was now in full swing, and on Thursday, 27 July 1933, Sir Alan Cobham and his barnstormers made a return visit, his advance publicity promising that 'this great display is twice as large and exciting as [his] display at Meir last year.' Another vast crowd turned up, including many children who watched from the roadside, unable to pay for entry into the inner sanctum beyond the six-foot canvas screens.

The programme started with a formation flight and flypast of all the aircraft involved, led by Sir Alan in his Handley-Page airliner. Aerobatics then dominated the programme, with a thrilling display by the Moth, followed by synchronised aerobatics by three aircraft in formation. A remarkable demonstration of inverted flying was given by Turner Hughes in a Fighting Scout, while Harry Ward plunged into space from around 1,000 feet and hurtled dizzily downwards for two or three endless seconds until his parachute unfolded 'like a giant lifebuoy of the air' and he landed safely on the airfield. Also on display were baby glider-planes fitted with motor-cycle engines and the latest types of autogiro. A new vehicle designed to facilitate rapid fuelling of aircraft was also seen in action for the first time in Stoke-on-Trent.

The programme was interspersed with humorous items (such as 'aerial pig-sticking' and 'how not to fly an aeroplane'), speed and height judging competitions, and the ever popular 'miniature Schneider Trophy Race'. A minor disappointment was the cancellation of the trapeze acrobatics and wing-walking owing to a very strong wind, but this was made up for by the generous provision of joyriding for members of the public, who were carried not only on 'ordinary flights' but also in many display events, such as the fly-past and the parachute descent. There was even a long queue of people eager to accompany the aerobatic pilots! At the end of the proceedings, Sir Alan addressed the spectators and gave a brief talk on 'Aviation Today'.

As the crowds happily dispersed, clutching their souvenir programmes and signed picture postcards of the pilots, the ground crew was already dismantling

Sir Alan Cobham returns to Meir
in July 1933.

and packing away the canvas screens, the tents, the toilets, and the crowd
barriers. Before long the road convoy would be well on its way to the next
destination, leaving behind scarcely a trace of their presence except for the
smell of crushed grass and the residual tang of oil and aero engines.

Two days before Sir Alan's visit to the Potteries, Reginald Mitchell had been
back for the funeral service of his father at Shelton parish church before interment
at Hartshill cemetery. He was himself taken ill later that summer and, with bowel
cancer diagnosed, underwent a major operation that August. The grim news was
that if the cancer returned, there was nothing that could be done for him. After
a short convalescence, he decided that it was high time he learned to fly himself
and took lessons in a Gipsy Moth, gaining his pilot's licence the following year.
Thereafter he flew himself all over the country and made several trips to Rolls-
Royce at Derby, though whether he ever touched down at Meir is a matter of
speculation. By then, fitted with a colostomy bag and often in pain, he was devoting
all of his remaining energy to the design of a new 'killer' fighter for the RAF.

8

Winners and Losers

During the First World War, Bert Challinor, one of the masters of the Oakhill School, Stoke, had been a colleague of several of the visiting airmen and he lost no time in getting some of them into the school. On 8 November 1933, Captain King, accompanied by Mr L. Bicknell of British Aero Films, spoke to senior scholars on aerial photography. At the end of the talk, a draw was held to select one of the students to take a photograph of the school – from the cockpit of an aeroplane!

The winner was John Rathbone, of Grosvenor Avenue, Oakhill, who was subsequently taken up in a Puss Moth from Meir Aerodrome for a 25-minute joyride. 'I did not feel the least bit nervous,' he said on landing,

I greatly enjoyed the flight, but was surprised at the lack of sensation. As I was going over the city I recognised such landmarks as Longton Park, the main road through the city, the canal at Sideway, Stoke, and of course my own school. I also saw my mother waving to me from our backyard as I passed over. When I got over the school, on the instruction of Mr Bicknell, I took the photograph.

The trip had obviously made an impression on the youngster. John now wanted to join the RAF.

In December, National Flying Services suddenly went into receivership. The Corporation's decision to lease the aerodrome to them for an astonishing 25-year period had been controversial from the start, and over the years had been criticised by both the aero club and the *Sentinel*. Now there was an opportunity to recover the lease and develop the aerodrome to its full potential – if only the Council would seize it. In the New Year, the *Sentinel* addressed the issue in a forthright article entitled 'What of the City Aerodrome?' It told how the aerodrome had already cost a staggering £32,000 and had become 'a byword of local politicians quoting examples of municipal extravagance'. Yet the site had considerable advantages: it was extensive; it was in the centre of England on the track of north and south air lines; and it was capable of being turned into one of the best provincial aerodromes. It was also seriously underused.

'What are we going to do about it,' asked the writer, '– leave it to become a derelict waste or make it a point of importance in air transport?'

The newspaper urged the Council to acquire the lease and operate the aerodrome itself, as other cities had done so successfully. In addition, it advocated that links should be forged with companies that were developing air services to ensure that the city was not overlooked: 'If some comparatively nearby town should secure air traffic when it is likely to be available in the not too distant future, Stoke-on-Trent would be left with little more than an aerodrome and regrets.' Such promptings had the desired effect. At their next meeting, the Council resolved to acquire the lease for £150 (which included the transfer of the hangar) and to investigate the possibility of air lines using the aerodrome. For once the decision had been 'almost unanimous'.

On 2 March 1934, Lord Londonderry, the Air Minister, announced long overdue plans to strengthen the Air Force. In the coming year, four additional squadrons were to be formed, bringing the RAF up to a total strength of eighty-one regular squadrons – a measure immediately attacked as inadequate. The news scarcely caused a ripple in the Potteries, where people's minds were fixed on the 6th round FA Cup clash against Manchester City at Maine Road the following day. That Saturday, a record exodus of fans began early and went on throughout the morning, with eighteen special trains carrying 17,000 people, and thousands more travelling by bus, car, and cycle. Over 25,000 Stoke City fans converged on the ground, two of them, Mr J. Hawthorne and Mr S. H. Beech (both members of the aero club), having made the short hop from Meir to Barton Aerodrome from where they took a taxi to the ground – one of the first instances of football fans flying to see a game. In a close match the Potters lost by what was described as a 'freak goal'.

Three weeks later, on the 25 March, William Joyce, the area administrative officer of Mosley's new party, the British Union of Fascists, addressed a large political meeting at Longton Town Hall. He was at his most seductive. 'The fascist movement in Britain is one of constructive patriotism,' he declared. 'In thought, word, and deed we are absolutely loyal to His Majesty the King.' Joyce was well known in the area; a few years later he had a much wider audience after he fled to Germany and, nicknamed Lord Haw-Haw, broadcast Nazi propaganda to the UK throughout the war.

Another visitor to the area was Joachim von Ribbentrop, head of a large wine company that owned vineyards in the Rhineland. He came at least four times, ostensibly to visit a friend who lived locally, a German by birth, but also to make contact with other German residents, many of whom were completely unknown to him, but whose names he had and letters of introduction to them. Someone who met him at the Castle Hotel in Newcastle, where he used to stay, later gave this thumb-nail sketch of a man who was soon to be a major player on the world stage:

He could be a very charming fellow, with quite an innocent air about him, but I would not call him a likeable man. He was sometimes serious and rather supercilious, but he could also be affable. It is amusing to me to read his speeches when he talks of the Nazis' concern for the working people, for he seemed to me to be the complete snob, and to have a faint contempt for anyone who would not be of use to his own personal ambitions.

In August 1936, he was appointed German ambassador to Great Britain and two years later became notorious as Hitler's Foreign Minister.

*

After an uncertain start, the North Staffordshire Aero Club was becoming more firmly established and now had about 70 members, both flying and non-flying. Since Christmas, it had opened its own rooms at the aerodrome and was confident enough of its continued existence to request permission from the City Council to build a proper clubhouse there. It also began to develop an active social side and on Friday, 23 March, held its first annual dinner at the Crown Hotel, Stone. Having pride of place in the dining room was a model of an aeroplane that had been specially made for the event by John Davison of Porthill, while the ballroom had been decorated to good effect in the club's colours – blue, black, and silver. Guest of honour was Captain R. R. Bentley, who had flown to Meir from London that day for the occasion. Other guests came from near and far and danced the night away to the music of Al Berlin and his Boys from Trentham.

Two months later, on Thursday, 7 June 1934, Sir Alan Cobham's air show was back for its third and final visit to Meir (though without Sir Alan, who was engaged on tests for the Air Ministry in preparation for a long non-stop flight that would necessitate refuelling in the air). Two displays were scheduled for 2.30 p.m. and 6.15 p.m., but just before the first show was about to start a mighty thunderstorm broke and rain lashed the airfield. Belatedly, when the weather cleared, the programme began and did not disappoint the doughty spectators.

An expensive fleet of twelve new aircraft had been assembled. The 'Three Aces' (Flight Lieutenant Geoffrey Tyson, Captain Cecil Bebb and Mr J. Mackay) were flying Avro Cadets, the most advanced type of sporting light aeroplane, in which they gave a sensational display of simultaneous aerobatics before racing each other over three laps of the aerodrome. Flight Lieutenant Tyson then performed in a high-speed Siddeley-Lincock fighter, in which he looped the loop through a hoop erected on the aerodrome, flew inverted at a height of only 50 feet, and picked up a handkerchief from the ground with a hook on his wing tip! The pilot was able to describe each manoeuvre for the spectators, as his voice was being relayed from the broadcast coach by loudspeakers. Although his machine was reaching speeds of 250 mph, he 'sounded no more concerned than if he had been seated in an armchair instead of a racing plane diving towards the aerodrome'.

Other items included 'Say it with Flour' (fun and games with flour bombs), the pilot's 'Silly Symphony' (trick flying), and the 'Paper Chase' (when the pilot dropped a paper streamer and repeatedly flew through it as it fell, trying to cut it to pieces). Joan Meakin, renowned as 'the Glider Girl', then put on a polished performance of her own. Her craft was towed to a height of 1,500 feet behind an aeroplane before she released the cable. As her Rhonbussard glided down to the aerodrome, she showed that aerobatics were just as possible in a glider and repeatedly looped the loop.

Afterwards Ivor Price demonstrated the 'pull-off' method of parachuting used for training by the RAF, which was being demonstrated to the public for the first time. Standing on a platform on the wing of an airliner, he pulled the release cord of his parachute when only a few hundred feet above the ground. Passengers in the plane were able to watch the whole process of the parachute's unfolding itself and opening, and see Price snatched from his platform and in due course deposited safely on the ground. Captain Phillips joined in by giving an astonishing display of aerobatics and 'crazy' flying in his Siddeley-Avro Trainer, and then took up local residents to share the experience. Two air liners – the Handley Page 1,000-hp Clive (which carried twenty-two passengers) and the Airspeed 3-engined Ferry (which carried ten) – were also on show and available for short trips. All who took up the offer were given a certificate signed by the pilot to say that they had flown with him and had 'supported British aviation'.

The City Council deserved such a certificate, for by its September meeting it was brimful with energy and new ideas regarding the aerodrome. An invitation had been extended for a squadron of the RAF to visit the airfield on 8 November; a meeting had been held with several airlines with a view to including Stoke-on-Trent as a stopping place; and the aeronautical consultants Airwork Ltd had been asked for advice on the proper development of the site. In addition, medical and crash equipment was to be brought up to the standard prescribed by the Air Ministry, public libraries were to be requested to obtain copies of the weekly periodical entitled *The Aeroplane,* and the aero club was to be approached with the object of promoting a gala day at Meir. Not all the sceptics had been silenced, but most council members seemed to agree with Alderman Sir Fred Haywood when he said: 'If Stoke-on-Trent wishes to be in the limelight in regard to the future of aerial transport, we must make arrangements now, or forgo for all time.'

In the limelight on the international stage, the 'greatest air race in history' was about to get underway. At daybreak on Saturday, 20 October 1934, 60,000 spectators watched as twenty of the world's finest aircraft left Mildenhall in Suffolk on the 12,000-mile dash to Melbourne, Australia. Taking part were several pilots who had already been to Meir (Neville Stack, Charles Scott) and several who would soon appear there (Amy Johnson, Tom Campbell Black). Favourites to win were Amy and her husband of two years Jim Mollison, a celebrated long-distance flyer in his own right. Their black and gold Comet *Black Magic* was the first to take off, the other contenders following at 45-second intervals. Only twelve of them would reach Melbourne. Some were forced to withdraw; two New Zealanders were killed when their Fairey Fox crashed in Italy; Amy and Jim's attempt ended at Allahabad in a blazing row after which they returned to England separately. (They were divorced in 1938.)

The winners were Charles Scott and Tom Campbell Black, whose Comet *Grosvenor House* covered the distance in a phenomenal 71 hours. The two men had shattered all former records and scooped the gold trophy and an enormous prize of £10,000. They were hailed as the most famous airmen in the world – a world that had suddenly shrunk as a result of their remarkable exploit.

*

That July marked the first complete month during which the North Staffordshire Aero Club operated its own aircraft, and flying hours totalled forty-six. The club had recently taken delivery of a new two-seater Miles Hawk monoplane trainer, G-ACNX, capable of a speed of 115 mph, which Stanley Hawley soon took for a spin to Limoges, returning via Ostend.

Meanwhile, Mr Leslie Irving and Mr R. J. Wenger had passed the tests necessary to qualify for their basic 'A' licences, under the tutelage of Flying Officer R. G. Weighill, the honorary instructor. (Mr Irving, a Director of the Paragon China Company at Longton, had made his first solo flight after only 6 hours' instruction – a record for the club.) In September, Mr W. I. Woodward, an ex-RFC and RAF pilot who held a 'B' commercial licence, was appointed the resident Pilot Instructor, and a few weeks later the club took delivery of a six-seater air liner – a new Fokker Universal monoplane. Always keen to promote the aerodrome, the club made both planes available to the general public for instruction, joyrides or taxi work, at 6d a mile. It had also introduced a Day Members' scheme, under which a party from the British Reinforced Concrete Engineering Company of Stafford had recently enjoyed short air experience flights at the aerodrome.

This steady progress was reflected in the large and enthusiastic gathering at the club's second Annual Ball, held at the Crown Hotel, Stone, on 16 November 1934, when parties from Birmingham, Stafford, and Chirk joined members to dance to the music of the Grosvenor Hotel Band from Chester.

Addressing the revellers after supper, Dr Glass, the club's president, lost no time in extolling its virtues. 'Flying nowadays is not a pastime for hare-brained lunatics,' he declared. 'It is a serious commercial proposition.' He went on to say that the club could offer much cheaper flying than any airline and offer instruction 'at as low a figure as any club in England'. The charges were 37s 6d an hour for dual instruction and 27s 6d for solo instruction, and he hoped that many more local people would avail themselves of the opportunity of learning to fly. 'We have one of the most modern and up-to-date machines,' he said, 'and we are hoping in the near future to have one even more modern, which would be capable of a speed of 235 mph. The club has experienced many dark and difficult days, but we are now on the crest of a wave and I think that we shall make excellent progress in the future.'

The joint honorary secretaries reinforced the message. Mr Hawley said that until recently the club had had 'rather a thin time', but it was now progressing favourably and they were trying to make it a really friendly affair. Mr Parkinson added that the Air Ministry had recognised them as a club suitable for subsidy – the only such club in Staffordshire at that time – and the new machine they intended to get was a Miles Hawk Major, similar to that in which Squadron Leader McGregor had finished fifth in the recent air race to Australia. The whole evening was a conspicuous success and no doubt quickened interest in aviation in general and in the North Staffordshire Aero Club in particular.

During April of the following year, the club flew 104 hours from Meir Aerodrome, and Stanley Hawley's wish to make it a 'really friendly affair' was fulfilled – at least as far as some members were concerned. That Easter, Mr and Mrs Badger took one of the club's machines for a flying honeymoon, while Stanley Hawley married fellow member Miss Phyllis Beresford at St Philomena's church, Caverswall. The bridegroom was one of the few pilots in North Staffordshire to hold his 'B' Certificate. His bride, not to be outdone, had made her first solo flight at Meir just days before her marriage.

9

Heads in the Sand

On 12 April 1935, it appeared that one of the Council's initiatives was about to bear fruit. In a well-publicised visit, officials of United Airways – an airline that operated over many parts of the British Isles – flew from London to Meir to discuss the inclusion of Stoke-on-Trent as a calling point with the Lord Mayor (Alderman A. C. Harvey) and the chairman of the Aerodrome Committee. The visitors, who arrived in an eight-seater plane, included Mr W. L. Thurgood, Managing Director of United Airways, and Mr Rhodes Marshall, chairman of the Aerodrome Committee of Blackpool Corporation. At the invitation of Mr Thurgood, a party took a trip over the city, this being the Lord Mayor's first experience of flying. He was immediately converted. 'I have enjoyed every minute of it,' he said, on landing.

A direct regular air service from the Potteries to London and Blackpool seemed not only probable but imminent, with the inauguration of the scheme provisionally set for the end of that month. Mr Thurgood was so impressed by the aerodrome that he held out the hope that Stoke-on-Trent would have its own separate service operating between these two points. 'It is an excellent aerodrome from the point of view of approach and area,' he said, and declared his intention of putting eight de Havilland Rapides on the new service.

As the visitors were preparing to leave for Blackpool, the Lord Mayor handed a message to Mr Marshall to be delivered to his opposite number there. It read: 'On the completion of my first air trip, I send to you the greetings of the City of Stoke-on-Trent, with my best wishes for the success of the new line. It is unnecessary for me to say how much we, in Stoke-on-Trent, appreciate the benefits of Blackpool, and I hope that during the summer, our towns will be linked by air.' Everything seemed set fair for the advancement of the City Aerodrome. Then the Council shot itself in the foot.

The RAF visit, originally scheduled for 8 November of the previous year, had been postponed at the Council's request because the poor weather and dark evenings would not have allowed people sufficient time to get there after work. It had been rearranged for the following spring, to form part of the celebrations for Empire Day. This annual event, held around 24 May (the birthday of the late Queen Victoria), was designed to commemorate the achievements of the British Empire, and provided an opportunity for RAF squadrons to travel throughout the country and put on a show in aid of their Benevolent Fund. Various aircraft were used – the Hart, Fury, Hampden, Lysander – and drew vast crowds, giving people the rare chance to see aircraft close-up on the ground and for children to clamber into the cockpits before experiencing a joyride. Sometimes a barrel of beer would be dropped by parachute or a bi-plane would flour-bomb a First World War tank.

The chairman of the Aerodrome Committee, Alderman Charles Austin Brook, had high hopes that this first visit by the RAF would be an outstanding event in the city. He was delighted to learn that No. 101 Squadron, stationed in Bristol, would be coming, for it enjoyed the reputation of being one of the fastest in the Service. A large marquee was to be erected on the aerodrome where all the RAF personnel would be invited to luncheon as guests of the Corporation prior to the display. Spectators were promised 'the opportunity to see some of the most interesting machines of the Force – the giant bombing craft'. In addition, the Air Ministry had sanctioned the bringing of 'bombs, machine guns, cameras, photographs, parachutes, and navigation equipment'. Thrills and spills were to be provided by the North Staffordshire Aero Club, which would stage a demonstration of aerobatic flying and offer special flights at reduced rates. On this occasion no charge was to be made for admission in order to attract as many people as possible to the airfield.

The event was scheduled for 25 May, but immediately after the first publicity things started to go wrong. At a council meeting held on 2 May, a heated debate on the visit reopened old wounds and split the council down the middle. It began when Mr F. T. Guest moved an amendment that 'the detailed arrangements for the visit be disapproved'. He asked if it was necessary that, to advertise the aerodrome, they should use 'the most fearful of all man's machines for his own destruction'. 'I cannot understand,' he went on, 'why so many of us seem to have been caught up in this wave of military-mindedness which is sweeping the world, and it seems to me that unless some of us who believe firmly in peace are prepared to make a stand, war and the destruction of civilisation will be inevitable.' He said that he felt he was speaking for the majority of the citizens of the city, but was interrupted by cries of 'No. Nothing like it.'

Mrs J. Barker then seconded the amendment, showing an obvious distaste for the RAF's 'bombs and machine guns'. Others opposed. Alderman Lloyd said the aerodrome had cost them 'many thousands of pounds' and they should do all they could to promote it. Alderman Sampson Walker, although no flying enthusiast, chipped in on behalf of the RAF: 'I am not air-minded. If I can help it, you will never catch me in an aeroplane. But if you wish to encourage air-mindedness, you must prefer to see the finest flyers in the world rather than the second or third best.' Mr Rogers could not have agreed less, declaring that he had opposed the aerodrome – 'which was a white elephant' – from the start. Civil aviation was all right, he said, but he thought the aerodrome site would be put to a far better purpose if it were handed over for housing.

Mr A. E. Hewitt, however, would have none of it. 'I have never heard so much bosh talked as I have in the last half-hour,' he declared. He contended that the people of Stoke-on-Trent should be allowed to see the instruments of war – which were ready to protect them and their wives and children. His attempt to sway the meeting was, though, in vain. When put to the vote, the amendment was carried by 49 votes to 41. The visit was cancelled.

Reaction to the decision was prompt and predominantly hostile. The Secretary General of the Air League of the British Empire, Air-Commodore J. A. Chamier, wrote to the Town Clerk, regretting the decision and the missed opportunity of strengthening the position of the aero club. 'A Britisher' was one of several correspondents who wrote to the *Sentinel* expressing astonishment and dismay that the visit had been cancelled in the interest of peace. 'On the contrary', he went on, 'I would remind the councillors who voted for the amendment that it is an irrefutable fact that the deplorable weakness of the air defences of this country at the present time constitute the greatest possible menace to the peace of Europe.' Lamenting the lack of air-mindedness among the community at large, he concluded: 'I would point out that this country is no longer an island surrounded by water, but is an island surrounded and covered by air, and that the Navy is no longer the first line of defence of these islands, but has, of necessity, been superseded by the air arm.'

In comment column and editorial, the *Sentinel* was scathing. 'Did [the Corporation] really think the RAF Squadron was coming to Stoke equipped with toy balloons?' it asked. It went on to deplore the ban and ridicule the stance taken by some members of the Council:

> As to the military aspect of aviation, it is obvious to everyone. There is not the slightest advantage in hiding our heads in the sand, ostrich fashion, and imagining that if we do not look at aeroplanes, they will no longer exist as machines of war. Let us face the facts that aeroplanes are the first line of offence and defence, and that, at a mere signal, they can operate long before an army can get on the move or a fleet can reach its sea stations. We shall not remove the potentially swift menace which the development of aviation has created by refusing to have a squadron of the RAF in our midst and by declining to admire the skill and courage of the finest airmen in the world, evinced in an Empire Day demonstration.

It is not known if the decision also affected the plans of United Airways; at any rate they did not proceed.

At least there was nothing controversial about the 'flying visit' of the Prime Minister of Australia, the Rt Hon. J. A. Lyons, who flew from Hendon to Meir on Saturday, 18 May, accompanied by his wife, who was making her very first flight. The purpose of the trip was to declare open the bazaar organised by members of St Gregory's church in aid of their New School Fund. The location was Longton Town Hall, which had been converted for the occasion into a representation of a medieval English village, with market stalls and village greens. Mr Lyons was also invited to the customary luncheon at Stoke Town Hall, where he was presented with a tea service in recognition of the honour done to the area by his visit.

A few days afterwards, as if to rub salt into the wounds, the *Sentinel* reported on the activities that had taken place at many other aerodromes on Empire Day, declaring that Stoke-on-Trent, 'which put itself in the forefront in providing an aerodrome has put itself *off* the map for the present'. The aero club, equally critical of 'the cavalier attitude of the council', had closed for the day and its members had taken themselves off to Tollerton Aerodrome in Nottingham to take part in events there.

Later that May, a report by the Aerodrome Committee was presented to the Council on the possible consequences of their decision, particularly with reference to the probable future development of the aerodrome, to the future relationship between the Council and the Air Ministry, and to the encouragement of new industries in the area. Clearly exasperated, Alderman Brook said that he had 'begged and prayed to the RAF to give this display' and felt that the cancellation had been an insult both to the RAF and to the Aerodrome Committee. He appealed to the council members to make up their minds whether they wanted an aerodrome or not, and starkly presented the alternatives – to keep Meir as a civil aerodrome or have it taken from them and run as a military aerodrome. 'There are certain things on the carpet at the moment,' he said, 'which to my mind mean the making or breaking of the City Aerodrome.'

Events were rapidly overtaking the reservations of certain council members, as Alderman Brook seemed to be implying. On 22 May, plans for a large expansion of the RAF were announced simultaneously in both Houses of Parliament. In effect, the home strength of the RAF was to be virtually trebled, which meant that some civil aerodromes would have to be utilised. Although Meir was not yet on the list, there was every possibility that it might eventually be used.

10

An Airport at Last

In May 1935, twenty-five years had elapsed since King George V had acceded to the throne, and many events were held throughout the nation and beyond to commemorate his Silver Jubilee. One of the aero club's contributions was the offer of a flying scholarship to the value of £25, open to anyone between the ages of eighteen and thirty, which would allow the recipient to enjoy free flying instruction up to the point of obtaining a pilot's 'A' licence. Entrants had to attend for a trial flying lesson of 30 minutes' duration, during which Flying Officer Weighill would assess their aptness and proficiency according to a fixed programme, a copy of which was to be sent to each candidate in advance. The winner would be the one with the highest score.

Intense interest was aroused, both in Staffordshire and in neighbouring counties, and during May eighty entrants underwent practical flying tests at Meir. The eventual winner was Mr D. C. Smith, of Nantwich, with a score of 74 per cent, closely followed by Mr J. S. Gaunt, of Birchall, Leek, with 71 per cent. Other worthy contenders were Mr R. Guest, of Shrewsbury, Mr J. E. Boulton, of Stafford, Miss Dorothy Clive, of Willoughbridge, and Mr G. D. Brown, of Nantwich. As the runner-up had reached such a high standard, the aero club decided to award a second prize consisting of the right to receive instruction for the licence at half the usual cost.

Another commemorative event staged at the City Aerodrome was the Jubilee Air Display, led by Lieutenant Cathcart Jones, who, with Ken Waller, had finished fourth in the great air race to Australia. On Monday, 24 June, six pilots put on a daring show of trick flying and aerobatics, and other stunts included a parachute race. The outstanding feature, though, was the very low cost of the flights –3s 6d for joyrides, 15s for a 100-mile cruise or an hour's flying. It was not surprising that in the torrid June heat so many people found the most refreshing place to be was up in the air.

The following month members of the aero club put on an aerial display of their own at the Caverswall Castle fête on the afternoon of Saturday, 13 July. The club also celebrated the award of the pilot's 'A' licence to Miss Clive, who had recently achieved fifth place in the scholarship competition. After only

Dorothy Clive and Flying Officer
R. G. Weighill.

6½ hours of dual instruction with Flying Officer Weighill, she had flown solo, thus becoming the first woman in Staffordshire to qualify for her licence.

The same month brought one of the great occasions of the Jubilee Year – George V's review of his fleet from the Royal Yacht *Victoria and Albert*. In the blue-grey waters of Spithead, the King saw 160 battleships and 40,000 officers and men – ten miles of armed sea might. A quarter of a million people thronged the water front from Lee-on-Solent to Southsea to marvel at the magnificent spectacle. John Millar, a member of the aero club who lived at Leek, had flown over to the Isle of Wight for the event in the club's Miles Hawk, picking up a passenger on the way. On their return journey on 17 July, the plane got into difficulties. An eye-witness heard 'loud popping noises' and saw the aeroplane 'circling round as though the pilot was trying to land. It just missed a tree.' The plane came down at Staines, Middlesex, and overturned in a cornfield. The pilot was thrown clear, but his passenger was trapped in his seat until some workmen arrived and lifted the plane. This was the first mishap to any of the club's machines, but fortunately the pilot, passenger, and plane all survived to fly another day. Other accidents would prove more serious.

The City Council, trying to recover from the debacle of the RAF visit, was again seeking to promote the use of the aerodrome and had granted an option to Airwork Ltd to establish a flying school there at an annual fee of £300. Meanwhile, in the House of Commons, Harold Hales had asked the Minister for Air to consider Stoke-on-Trent as a possible site for the establishment of air service factories. These, he said, would have the advantage of being close to Meir Airport, 'one of the finest aerodromes in the country'.

The Council had also spent several months in negotiations with feeder airlines, including Hillman, Spartan, and Railway Air Services, and had appealed to would-be travellers from the aerodrome to get in touch with the Town Clerk so that information on numbers and destinations could be obtained. Success was finally achieved that autumn. The *Sentinel* proudly proclaimed 'Stoke Becomes Airport' when, on 12 August 1935, Railway Air Services called at Meir for the first time as part of their Glasgow – Belfast – Croydon service. 'Today is a very important day in the history of Stoke-on-Trent Aerodrome,' the *Sentinel* announced, 'as it marks the commencement

AIR SERVICES
TO & FROM STOKE-ON-TRENT

Commencing on Monday next, 12th August, arrangements have been made for the London, Belfast, Glasgow Air Service to call at the City Aerodrome, Stoke-on-Trent, on request, for passengers proceeding to London in the one direction, or beyond Manchester and Liverpool in the other, and vice versa. This will provide a link-up at Croydon with the air services to and from the Continent and at Manchester with Railway Air Services "Manx Airway" Section to and from the Isle of Man.

The air liner will, when it descends at Meir, proceeding in a Northerly direction, be due at 4.20 p.m. and leave in the shortest time possible thereafter. In the Southerly direction the due arrival will be 11.50 a.m. and the departure similarly immediately thereafter.

Notice will require to be given in advance by intending passengers as under:—

(a) In the case of passengers joining at Meir — to the Station-master at Stoke Station, not later than 24 hours previously; and

(b) In the case of passengers alighting at Meir at the time of reserving seats for the journey to Meir.

The fares will be:—

STOKE and	Single		Return
London	47/6	......	81/-
Blackpool	25/-	......	41/-
Isle of Man	47/6	......	81/-
Belfast	67/6	......	121/-
Glasgow	77/6	......	131/-

E. B. SHARPLEY, Town Clerk.

Town Hall, Stoke-on-Trent.

The new air services are announced.

of a direct communication by air to the large cities of this country and to all parts of the world.'

Inauspiciously, owing to weather conditions, the de Havilland Mercury had started late and reached Meir at 12.25 p.m. instead of the scheduled time of 11.50 a.m. Miss Florence Farmer and the Deputy Town Clerk, Mr Harry Taylor, were the first passengers on the inaugural flight and travelled from Meir to Croydon. A few weeks later, the local and international swimming celebrity Norman Wainwright was pictured as he too took advantage of this new and swifter method of transport to fly to Belfast. More adventurously, Alderman George Barber set off with Russia as his destination, but owing to a mishap to the plane at Birmingham and a series of missed connections, he had to turn back. (The following year he tried again, this time successfully.) In September, Crilly Airways wrote to the Council intimating that they were prepared to call at Meir on request in connection with their Leicester to Liverpool service, and this too was publicly advertised. British Airways also expressed an interest, although it finally decided to concentrate on developing its continental routes.

In spite of the optimism being expressed, the services offered were at first limited and minor; indeed, by today's standards they would be regarded as quaint if not downright primitive. Meir was a grass airfield with a hangar;

Regular air services at Meir are inaugurated when Miss Florence Farmer and Mr Harry Taylor board a plane for London on 12 August 1935.

one de Havilland Mercury or Jupiter – which could seat only ten passengers – called each way daily (except Sunday) 'on request'. Travellers had to give at least twenty-four hours' notice of their intentions to the station master at Stoke. As far as Health and Safety was concerned, one of the staff kept fire-fighting equipment in his own car for use in any emergency. Later that year, though, when the Watch Committee bought a new fire engine, the Council asked it to give the Aerodrome Committee first option on the old one.

*

On Friday, 13 September, Sir Alan Cobham returned for his final visit to the area – not to Meir, but to Bradwell Lane, Porthill. He brought with him a range of aircraft, from the Flying Flea and autogiro to the great Astra airliner, which seated twenty-two passengers. Accompanying him was Miss Joan Meakin, who performed in her new Wolf glider.

Other attractions included looping in formation (three aircraft joined by ribbons from wing to wing); aerobatics by Mr Rowley, who flew inverted only 30 feet from the ground; a 'Children's Hour' from 5.30 to 6.30 p.m. when children were escorted round the aircraft park with numerous novelties arranged for their entertainment; and 'Flying's Most Difficult Feat', when Mr Rowley picked up with his wing-tip a flag held in a man's hand! Various aircraft were available for joyrides, and the final attraction was the customary parachute descent. Some of the novelty, however, was disappearing from such shows, and with dwindling attendances and several fatal accidents to both performers and members of the public, Sir Alan sensed that the age of the flying circus was nearing its end. Later that year, he sold his show to Charles Scott in order to concentrate on other commercial interests.

On Sunday, 3 November, a few weeks after the Italian invasion of Abyssinia, Miss Sylvia Pankhurst, a prominent member of the suffragette movement, addressed a crowded meeting at the Methodist Central Hall in Longton. Speaking of the international situation, she said that the League of Nations was the only hope of avoiding another war and warned that if Mussolini were allowed to proceed, there would be others ready to follow his example. Three days later the prototype of a new aircraft from Hawker made its debut flight. Designed by Sidney Camm, it was the first British fighter to exceed 300 mph. It was to be called the Hurricane. Until then the Air Ministry had shown little interest in the plane; now it had a change of heart and ordered 600.

At the end of the month Flight Lieutenant Tommy Rose returned to Meir, his plane bearing a legend that marked his latest achievement: 'King's Cup Winner 1935'. He was guest of honour on the evening of Friday, 29 November, at the aero club's annual ball at the North Stafford Hotel in Stoke, when 120 members and their guests attended what turned out to be a sparkling occasion.

A fortnight afterwards, in mid-December, the aero club had its first real emergency to contend with when Miss Clive was piloting the club's Miles Hawk G-ACTN. Suddenly she was caught in a snowstorm – as bad, according to one of those present, as a sandstorm. Mr J. McGuinness, the chief pilot, was in the air at the same time and managed to land in a field close by. Miss Clive attempted to land at the aerodrome, but then decided it was too dangerous as her goggles were blurred with snow. She tried to rise above the storm so that she could wait until it abated, but struck a large tree with such force that parts of the plane were scattered over a wide area. Miss Clive was thrown clear and escaped with severe cuts and shock. Not so lucky was her passenger (and cousin), twenty-one-year-old Roger Clive, who was trapped in the wreckage. Mr McGuinness was first on the scene and with other members of the club managed to get him out. Miss Clive was allowed home after treatment, but her cousin was taken to Longton Cottage Hospital where he later died from his injuries.

*

Early in the New Year, the nation was plunged into mourning with the death of King George V on 20 January 1936. As heir apparent, the Prince of Wales had sometimes been criticised for his passion for flying; on 21 January, as King Edward VIII, he demonstrated his intention of being a thoroughly modern monarch by flying from Sandringham to London – the first time a sovereign of this country had made use of an aircraft. His coronation was set for 12 May of the following year, an event that would proceed without him.

On 5 March, Reginald Mitchell was at Eastleigh Airport, Southampton, to watch the prototype of his new fighter take to the air for the first time. He celebrated quietly by returning to Stoke-on-Trent and taking his two brothers out to dinner, when they reminisced about flying model planes in the garden of their childhood home at Normacot. It was to be one of his last visits; within months his illness would recur.

The aero club was back at the North Stafford Hotel on 6 March to hold a complimentary dinner for its new president, Mr C. R. Anson. Committee members past and present were out in force, and distinguished guests included Lord Sempill, Group Captain Charles Darley, and the Lord Mayor, Alderman J. A. Dale. The principal speaker was Group Captain Darley, Commander of the Tern Hill Aerodrome, who had served with the Royal Flying Corps during the First World War and been shot down by the German fighter ace Max Immelmann in 1915. In 1922 he had been awarded the Albert Medal (subsequently replaced by the George Cross) for trying to save his brother from a blazing aircraft, and in 1931 he was made a CBE.

After submitting a toast to 'the North Staffordshire Aero Club and the president', he told how the club now had sixty flying members and forty

Guests at the North Staffordshire Aero Club dinner on 6 March 1936 include (left to right) Colonel H. Clive, the Lord Mayor and Lady Mayoress, Alderman C. Austin Brook, Mr C. R. Anson, Mrs Anson, Lord Sempill, Miss Harrison, OBE, Dr Glass, and Miss Dorothy Clive.

non-flying members, but appealed for general support since no club could be sustained on such numbers. In a prescient speech, he continued:

> The value of civilian flying clubs is enormous, for they are both a municipal and a national asset. If there does come a time when there is war, such a war will start in the air, and there is no knowing how quickly it will develop. The Air Force will have very heavy casualties in a very short time, so they must have big reserves behind them of apparatus and trained pilots, and that is why the flying clubs are such a national asset.

He recalled the 'colossal disorganisation' caused to this country by limited bombing in the last war and the advances made since then in the speed, range, and bomb load of modern planes. Once he had been pleased to have a fleet of aircraft with a speed of 65 mph; now there were bombers capable of 200 mph which could carry a ton of bombs, and every town in the country was within their range. 'It is a question of self-preservation to support clubs such as this,' he concluded.

> It is our duty to see that those reserves are there. The enthusiasts of Stoke-on-Trent are a national asset – they are as much enthusiasts as flying men were twenty-three years ago, when I started flying. So I wish to emphasise the importance of everyone backing up the club from every point of view, and I wish the club always Good Landings.

The president then responded and said that if civilian clubs were to flourish, the government would have to provide them with new control stations and satisfactory weather forecasts. He also hoped that the City Council would provide the lighting equipment that was needed at the aerodrome: 'In the Bible it says that a city on a hill cannot be hidden – but an aerodrome on a hill 600 feet up can very easily be obscured by cloud or fog, and it is not always easy to find it. At dusk it is not always easy to find Stoke Aerodrome.' The Lord Mayor, responding to a toast to 'the Corporation of Stoke-on-Trent', said that the progress made at the aerodrome since the Corporation had taken it over showed the sincerity of the city in its desire to stimulate civil flying. With reference to the plea for effective lighting, he said the Corporation would act as soon as its finances allowed.

In truth, the Council budget was already being stretched to provide basic amenities such as waiting rooms, lavatories, wireless sets, grass cutting, weather reports, signs, and an electricity supply in connection with the passenger services, while the income from the aerodrome was still negligible. Apart from the aero club's rent of £50 per annum, 10 per cent of the gross gate receipts from air shows was now going to the Corporation, with a minimum of £10 and a maximum of £25. Landing fees in respect of commercial aircraft were 9d per passenger embarking or disembarking and 1s per aircraft landing or taking off. A new company, Midland Aircraft Repairs Ltd, had set up its HQ at the aerodrome in 1936 for the purpose of overhauling aeroplanes for the certificate of airworthiness and aircraft repairs generally. Its rent was £20 per annum. A fee of 7s 6d a week was also being charged for each of two Flying Fleas that were being housed at the aerodrome. Important as it was, the lighting would have to wait.

Next day, 7 March, Lord Sempill travelled to Meir to open the new clubhouse and was delighted to see the improvements made at the aerodrome since his last visit. The clubhouse itself, which had cost in the region of £1,000, was spacious and well-equipped, containing a dining-room, lounge, bar, kitchens, and accommodation for administrative offices. During a brief ceremony, it was now the turn of Lord Sempill to stress the importance of such clubs: 'I hope the people of Stoke-on-Trent will take the point of view of people in other parts of the Empire when they realise that flying clubs are a national necessity and not merely a focal point where those purely interested in such matters can meet together to discuss flying matters.' Leslie Irving then presented the aero club badge to their guest, who had become an honorary member.

It had been hoped that planes from a number of flying clubs would visit for the ceremony, and three Hawker Hart bombers from Tern Hill were expected during the afternoon. Owing to the rain and poor visibility, however, events were somewhat curtailed, and a planned flying excursion to Leeds for the principal guests had to be abandoned. On the same day German troops reoccupied the Rhineland.

11

The Birdman of Meir

By now the *Sentinel* had got wind of Mitchell's latest aircraft and on 27 March mentioned it for the first time: 'Observers in and around Southampton have been noting the remarkable high-speed performance of an aeroplane which has made occasional flights.' The plane was still shrouded in secrecy, but it was known that it was an all-metal construction, had a Rolls-Royce Merlin engine and could fly at 5 miles a minute – or more. Mitchell told his sixteen-year-old son that he was 'reasonably happy' with his creation, though Gordon felt it could do with a good coat of paint. Later, at the insistence of Sir Robert McLean, Chairman of Supermarine, it was called 'the Spitfire'. Mitchell thought it 'a bloody silly name'.

Not so fast was the 'Flying Flea', designed by the French engineer Henri Mignet, which was part of the aeronautical craze of the 1930s. It could be built at home from a manual for less than £100, and a number of these diminutive craft took to the air at Meir (and elsewhere), often with calamitous results. One such had been built by Harold Burns of Congleton with the help of his father, and they decided to take it for a spin at the aerodrome on the evening of 5 April. It crashed, not far from the main Uttoxeter Road, striking the ground with such force that an eye-witness described it as 'a mangled wreck'. He was astonished to see the pilot emerge from the wreckage relatively unscathed. Mr Burns smiled ruefully at him and passed it off as 'part of the flying game'.

Another Flying Flea in the public eye during the first week of May 1936 was the one on display in Tom Byatt's Longton showrooms. It belonged to Charles Scott and was in action at the aerodrome on 7 May when his air display came to town. Also performing in the show were Idwal Jones, the 'Welsh wizard of the air', and Winifred Crossley, a stunt pilot who would one day become the first woman to fly a Hurricane. Apart from the (by now) traditional items, the major attraction was the reappearance of Charles Scott himself, still basking in the fame of his triumphant flight to Australia in 1934. His aim was to make the people of Britain 'air-minded' and demonstrate that it was possible to fly at little more cost than to go by road or rail.

One of his pilots, Captain Stonhill, had visited Oakhill Council School that morning, to answer pupils' questions and sign autographs, while Mr A. Harris,

Scott's Flying Flea is depicted in a local advertisement.

the show's well-known parachutist, had demonstrated 'packing' the parachute he was to use in the show. A special treat awaited one hundred senior children that evening when they were to visit the City Aerodrome and be addressed by Charles Scott himself.

The *City Times* had also splashed out and given 100 free admission tickets to children who entered its Shirley Temple painting competition. In addition, twelve adults were awarded free 15-minute flights in a Ferry Airspeed Air Liner. One of them was Luke McDonald, a blind masseur of Waterloo Road, Burslem, who believed that he was the first blind man in the Potteries to take a trip in a plane. On landing, he stated that the swaying of the machine had made him think that he was on a steamer on the river at Chester rather than in the air. He was also surprised that there was no jolting at all as they touched down. 'I should think that the experience to a sighted person would be rather pleasant,' he mused. It certainly was for another winner, Mrs Minnie Ellis, of Norton-le-Moors, who sent an enthusiastic letter of thanks to the newspaper. 'One has to have a flight to know that there is nothing whatever to be afraid of,' she wrote.

A fortnight later, on 23 May, RAF aircraft were seen at Meir for the first time when the aerodrome at last participated in the Empire Day celebrations and a flight from No. 10 Flying Training School (FTS) at Tern Hill visited from 4 to 5 p.m. The planes were under the command of Flight Lieutenant Harvey, who was flying a Gloster Gauntlet – 'one of the latest and most formidable types of fighter machines in existence' – and they gave demonstrations of formation and high-speed flying. During the afternoon an exhibition of aerobatics was also given by Flight Lieutenant Maxwell, who had flown a Sparrow Hawk from Reading. Other aircraft on view were a Hawker Hart bomber and an Avro, but for the several hundred people who turned up the event may have seemed something of a postscript to the main display taking place at Tern Hill. This was perhaps reinforced by the fact that members of the aero club were offering return trips to the RAF station at Market Drayton throughout the day in the Miles Falcon they had recently bought.

In June, the American millionaire Whitney Straight, an ex-Grand Prix motor racing driver and future fighter pilot, offered to take a twenty-one-year lease on the City Aerodrome. As the Director of the Straight Corporation, which operated airfields throughout Britain, he proposed to form two local private companies: Stoke-on-Trent Airport Ltd, to operate the municipal aerodrome, and Stoke-on-Trent Aero Club, to operate the club and a flying school that he would open. For this he was willing to pay a rental of £750 per annum plus £250 per annum as a minimum percentage of his turnover. The Council seemed extremely interested in the proposal and interviewed Mr Straight to discuss it with him at length.

However, Mr R. F. E. Parkinson, auditor and financial secretary of the aero club, made a rigorous analysis of the offer and concluded that 'the Corporation [would] be much more likely to save money in the long run by retaining full control of their own aerodrome'. This was published in the *Sentinel*, which had already declared that 'it would be the gravest mistake to grant another lease'. After some initial indecision, the Council did not consider the proposal further. On making enquiries, it had learned that the Air Ministry looked favourably on the possibility of establishing a flying school in North Staffordshire, and Cannock Chase had been proposed as a possible site. The Council was determined that it should be at Meir, and a deputation was dispatched to the Ministry to support its application.

Equally determined to succeed was Harry Ward, a parachutist who had previously performed at the City Aerodrome with Sir Alan Cobham's Circus. Now he was to make his debut at Meir as 'Britain's First Birdman', the star attraction of Campbell Black's air display. Aged thirty-three and an experienced ex-RAF parachutist, Mr Ward wore a special suit that gave him a wing span of nine feet. On the eve of his performance, he outlined what he hoped to achieve: 'When I launch myself into space, I shall set off a smoke bomb so that the crowd can see where I am. I shall make a series of swoops and, if possible, a couple of turns. I cannot really say where I shall land. So much depends upon the wind.'

Harry Ward demonstrates his 'wings' at Meir shortly before his debut.

On Saturday, 15 August, several thousand spectators turned up to watch despite the very cloudy conditions. The plan was for a DH-Dragon to take him up to 10,000 feet, which would give him plenty of height to sort out any problems on the way down. There had been no opportunity for a test drop. Fellow parachutists Ivor Price and John Tranum were already dead. This time Ward himself faced disaster.

The plane took off and as it rose everything beneath them quickly became opaque. For some time they proceeded to circle, searching in vain for a break in the clouds, until the pilot lost his bearings and had to descend to locate the aerodrome. When they finally emerged into clear air at 4,000 feet, they found themselves over the moors of the Peak District!

By the time they returned to Meir, the crowd had been waiting expectantly for an hour or more, and so Ward felt obliged to jump and from a much lower height than he would have wished. He edged to the door of the Dragon, stood momentarily on the wing step, and then plunged headlong into thin air. Everything went wrong. When he tried to swoop he immediately started to spin and could not control his wings at all. He was flipped onto his back, still spinning helplessly and falling ever more sharply. Suddenly he was flung face downwards again to see the aerodrome hurtling towards him. In the nick of time he jerked the release cord of his parachute and went crashing down in an inglorious heap on the edge of the field. The crowd thought he'd been killed and were amazed to see him slowly get to his feet. Undismayed, he said that he would try again another day.

If the Birdman's first outing proved something of a damp squib, the firework display at the new headquarters of the aero club on 5 November was more impressive by far – though it too did not go quite according to plan. Before the traditional Guy Fawkes' celebration that was to take place on the landing ground, a vast quantity of fireworks was being sorted on the billiards table in the new clubhouse. Suddenly one exploded, showering sparks over all the rest. Within seconds there was pandemonium. Catherine-wheels, jumping jacks, Roman candles, and blue devils were set alight, and the room erupted, with cascades of fiery stars, ear-shattering explosions, and the whoosh of blazing rockets. Some fireworks that resembled a plane in flight circled the room, soaring upwards, and then swooping down, trailing black smoke.

At the first explosion those present had made a frantic dash for the door, the last one being helped on his way by a rocket that shot across the room and struck him in the back. The din in the confined space was horrendous, as was the heat. When they dared return, one of the members smashed a window with a brick to let out the smoke. Then a few ventured inside with fire extinguishers and soda-water siphons to tackle any flames. The club steward, who had been unable to get out, was found cowering behind the bar, unharmed but temporarily deafened. By the time an officer of the Hanley Fire Brigade arrived to carry out a safety check, the situation was well under control.

Part of the ceiling was burnt out, together with the linoleum, the billiard-table cloth, and the curtains. Rocket shafts were embedded in the asbestos panelling; in some places the walls were bristling with them like an archery target. Stanley Hawley said: 'It was an absolute inferno while it lasted and everybody dived for cover. There was an amazing amount of damage in a short space of time.' Other members arrived later with additional supplies of fireworks, and a celebration of sorts took place on the airfield. According to those present at the time, however, it was not a patch on the impromptu pyrotechnic display that had occurred earlier indoors.

12

Turning-Points

In December, Meir acquired a new cinema and the country a new king. The Broadway, built on farm land adjoining the crossroads and within a stone's throw of the aerodrome, provided a much-needed amenity to the area and within a few years would offer a refuge for many a lonely airman. It was described by experts as being 'one of the finest examples of cinema architecture in the country', and boasted a seating capacity of 1,100 (with some double seats, immediately called 'necking' seats) and a café where hot meals would be served before or after the performance.

The new king became monarch suddenly and dramatically. With pottery firms working flat out to produce up to eight million souvenir items for the coronation of Edward VIII, the sensational news of his intention to marry the American divorcee Mrs Wallace Simpson provoked the abdication crisis and his permanent exile. Prince George, undoubtedly the most talented member of the royal family, was at first considered as his replacement, but perhaps his earlier playboy lifestyle disqualified him. The mantle fell on his shy, stammering brother Albert, who had visited the area in 1924 as Duke of York; his next visit would be as King George VI, the title he took on his accession. By the time he was crowned on 12 May 1937, his more glamorous brothers were almost forgotten in a week-long extravaganza of rejoicing throughout the kingdom – as if everyone sensed that this would be the last great national celebration for many dark years to come.

Public and private buildings through the length and breadth of the six towns were decorated on a truly elaborate scale and brilliantly illuminated by night. Activities were as varied as they were numerous, and there were days of parades, concerts, banquets, parties, tree-plantings, festivals, fêtes, and bonfires. Galas were organised for the children in the city's parks; the Lord Mayor gave a Coronation Luncheon in the Jubilee Hall; a grand Coronation Ball was held at Trentham Gardens.

On Coronation Day itself a massive parade of Territorials, Police, and ex-Servicemen marched to Hanley Park, where a 21-gun Royal Salute was fired. At Stoke parish church a Coronation Service was held, with a broadcast of the ceremony taking place in Westminster Abbey. Jazz bands in multicoloured costumes (in which red, white, and blue predominated) then meandered through the main streets of the city before assembling in Hanley Park for a massed performance, with dancing taking place around the bandstand. A spectacular firework and searchlight display brought a memorable day to a close.

The aerodrome played its part by hosting a Coronation Air Pageant on 15 May before a large crowd. The intrepid Birdman was back, but this time bad weather clipped his wings and he was unable to get off the ground. The Empire Day Air Display followed on 29th. As usual, the aero club did its best, putting on a series of free flights and competitions, while members of the Territorial Army gave demonstrations with searchlights and other equipment, but again it seemed more of a sideshow to the major event at Tern Hill. The RAF presence consisted solely of a flight of three Gloster Gladiators from No. 3 Squadron, based at Kenley, which arrived late in the afternoon. Perhaps the abrupt cancellation of 1935 still rankled.

The aero club, however, continued to flourish and was always eager to forge links with like-minded individuals or organisations. One of its flying members, Mr E. D. Pimble, became the honorary secretary of a new Aeronautical Society in Stoke-on-Trent, and it seemed only natural that he should negotiate special flying concessions for its members with the club. Only a few days later he had a lucky escape when he took Mary Peach for a flip at Meir. The plane overran the airfield on landing, crashed into a fence and turned over. Neither was injured, however, although the propeller was smashed.

Another member of the aero club, Ken Bishop, had just left his post at the Leek and Moorlands Building Society to join the Hanley Economic in Stoke-on-Trent, becoming one of the youngest Building Society Secretaries in the country. He obviously encouraged others to be air-minded, for a young employee, John Waite, was rewarded for his good work with a flying lesson at the aerodrome, paid for by Ken. Within a few years, both would be serving in a conflict that only one of them would survive.

The 'Golden Age' of flying was drawing to a close. That April, the Basque town of Guernica had been savagely bombed by the Luftwaffe, a precursor of the horrors to come. In May, while mooring at New Jersey, the German airship *Hindenburg* had exploded in flames, killing 36 people. In June, Mitchell had died, at the shockingly young age of 42. As his ashes were being interred at South Stoneham, near to Eastleigh Airport, three RAF planes flew low over the cemetery in a final salute to the man soon to be called 'the first of The Few'.

*

With the war clouds gathering that would eventually curtail all civilian flying, a notable accolade was awarded to the aerodrome when it was announced that the organisers of the King's Cup Air Race had accepted the aero club's invitation to use Meir as a 'turning-point'. The race, the climax of the British Air Calendar, was a prominent social occasion that attracted royalty, government ministers, and the 'top brass' of the armed services, as well as many overseas visitors. It was a unique event in which private, commercial, and service pilots were able to compete against one another for the prestigious prize. The cup had been given by the late King to encourage the development of civil aviation, and there was nothing a pilot coveted more than to win this 'blue riband of the air'.

There were some important 'firsts' for this particular race. For the first time part of the course would be over water; for the first time the race would be televised; and for the first time every one of the thirty-one entries was a monoplane. 'A few years ago,' recalled the *Sentinel*, 'a monoplane was an object of wild curiosity – even among flying men.' Indeed, every squadron in Fighter Command was still flying open-cockpit biplanes – not so dissimilar from those flown by their predecessors in the Royal Flying Corps in 1918.

As usual some famous flying men were competing, including Captain Geoffrey de Havilland and four previous winners of the cup. Flight Lieutenant Tommy Rose was to pilot a Miles Hawk, Mr Charles Gardner (the eventual winner) a Percival Mew Gull, Mr H. R. A. Edwards a Wicko and Captain W. L. Hope (three times a winner) a Comper Swift. Only one lady was taking part, Miss Lily Dillon from Ireland, who was to accompany Captain Neville Stack in her Vega Gull. A mystery plane, the experimental de Havilland TK4, added spice to the event. It had been entered by Lord Wakefield and was to be flown by Mr R. J. Waight, but the only definite thing known about it was that it could average 130 mph – since this year any plane not up to that speed had been automatically excluded. It was being whispered that the TK4 had a maximum speed of 245 mph.

On this occasion the race was to take the form of a circuit of Britain over two demanding days, Friday and Saturday, 10 and 11 September 1937. The first day was over 786 miles, from Hatfield to Dublin via York, Aberdeen, and Glasgow. The second day of 656 miles was from Dublin to Hatfield via Newtownards, Portpatrick, Carlisle, St Bee's Head, Blackpool, Stoke-on-Trent, Leicester, and Cardiff. Once more race fever gripped the nation with

The prestigious air race comes to the Potteries.

its heady brew of glamour, speed, and danger. The first day brought gale-force winds and tragedy. When Wing Commander E. G. Hilton in his Falcon Major G-AENG was turning over the control point at Scarborough Castle Hill, he was flung right through the cabin roof and decapitated by the propeller. His passenger, Wing Commander P. Sherren, crashed to his death in the plane.

On the afternoon of the second day, a vast crowd turned up at Meir to see the race as it passed through on its way to Leicester, Cardiff, and the finishing line at Hatfield. The aero club had pulled out all the stops to ensure that the day ran smoothly for the flyers and spectators. Three of its members – Stanley Hawley, Leslie Irving, and Captain Wilf Green – had been appointed official observers for the race and made their report as each plane passed. The club had also arranged an enclosure on the airfield for the benefit of members of the public. There they could obtain the best possible view of the aeroplanes as they flew over Meir at a height of not more than 500 feet between two points marked out on the ground 150 feet apart. A loudspeaker had also been set up, and a commentator was on hand to explain the position of the remaining seventeen aircraft after the previous day's eliminating flight.

The first planes appeared at 3.10 p.m. with the almost simultaneous arrival of Lewin and Harvey, both flying Miles Whitney Straight machines. Shortly afterwards the crowd was thrilled when the 'hush-hush' TK4 and a de Havilland Comet (which had been flown on the record-breaking flight to Australia by Charles Scott and Campbell Black) appeared within a few seconds of each other. The Comet was approaching the aerodrome at approximately 180 mph, but the TK4 streaked past it before reaching the turning-point and then 'zoomed away into the distance, travelling at phenomenal speed'.

At about 4 p.m., one of the competitors was forced out of the race at Meir. This was doubtless a major disappointment, but the pilot would soon go on to achieve considerable fame and success, as would the plane itself. Alex Henshaw had already been awarded the Siddeley Trophy in the King's Cup Race of 1933 – the youngest pilot ever to receive it. He had also taken part in the Birmingham Contact Races of 1935 and 1936, on the first occasion flying an Arrow Active, on the second a Leopard Moth, in which he had won. On both occasions Meir was part of the course, with entrants having to land, get out of the machine, and sign the marshal's book. He had now acquired one of the fastest planes in the country – a Percival Mew Gull – and was determined to scoop the Cup itself. His failure in 1937 was but a hiccup towards that ambition, as he later recalled in a letter to the author:

I landed at Meir with my Mew Gull G-AEXF owing to engine misfire due to special fuel that had been prepared for the race. I only remember landing on a small grass airfield with – I think – a Bellman-type hangar.

The following year XF won the King's Cup Race at the fastest speed ever recorded and in 1939 broke every record in all classes to Cape Town

Alex Henshaw.

and back. This Mew Gull is now the only aircraft ever to hold World Long
Distance Records unbroken for 67 years.

The air routes that Alex Henshaw and others were now flying were being
studied in their geography lessons by pupils at the Moorland Road Girls'
School in Burslem, and on 12 November twenty-five of them were taken to the
City Aerodrome for some novel practical instruction. Two lucky girls chosen
by ballot – Glenis Barker and Gertie Lymer – were then taken up for their first
ever flight, courtesy of the aero club.

The year ended on a high note. The City Council was told that the Air
Ministry, having inspected the aerodrome, proposed to establish a 'Type B'
Volunteer Reserve Flying School there at a rent of £850 per annum on a
twelve years' lease. Control of the ground would be retained by the Council
and there would be no interference with the arrangements for civil aviation. It
seemed like manna from heaven. The Council adopted the proposal 'without
comment'. The RAF was coming to Meir.

13

Undertones of War

The need to expand the aerodrome had been obvious for some time and had already been discussed by the Council. At its meeting on 27 January 1938, it confirmed the purchase of 93 acres adjoining the aerodrome at a total cost of £11,000. The site was thereby increased to 275 acres, making it one of the largest provincial aerodromes in the country. The way was now clear for the Air Ministry to begin building two hangars (each 180 by 90 feet) with mess-room and other accommodation. The Ministry was in a hurry. It wanted its reserves to be flying by the summer.

A week later the 'bombshell' that rocked the Potteries had nothing to do with international events – indeed, momentarily, it drove them from the headlines. Stanley Matthews had asked to be placed on the transfer list. Within days, letters, news reports, and editorials in the local press made the same point: Matthews must not be allowed to go. Pottery manufacturers were soon complaining that the matter was affecting production, and five leading industrialists called a public meeting to try to resolve the issue. On 14 February, the King's Hall in Stoke was packed to capacity an hour before the start, with another thousand supporters having to stand outside and listen via a loudspeaker. Two days later the club's directors turned down the request. Matthews was staying. Although Stoke-on-Trent had recently been named the 'third most sober town in England', there was much celebration.

Respite was brief. In March, Hitler incorporated Austria into the Nazi Reich, the *hors d'oeuvre* on his menu of acquisition. Newspapers made grim reading with accounts of mimic attacks, blackouts, and the provision of air-raid shelters. In this context Empire Air Day on Saturday, 28 May, took on an extra significance. At Meir it was finally to have been a major event in its own right. As the Hendon pageant was not being held that year, provincial centres were looking forward to an abundance of service machines in their displays, and Meir had been specially favoured on account of the development of its training school.

Thirty aircraft were promised from four squadrons, and a bumper afternoon was in prospect, with 5½ hours' flying. Then bad weather intervened. Only sixteen planes were able to make the journey, twelve of them Gauntlets from No. 46 Squadron, and actual flying lasted for only half of the scheduled time.

Nevertheless, more than 3,000 people turned up and witnessed an extraordinary exhibition of formation flying, aerobatics, and aerial combat, in which three fighters were scrambled to intercept and force down three 'enemy' bombers. A loudspeaker kept spectators in the picture by giving a running commentary of what was happening in the air. An Anson, an Oxford trainer, and a Hawker Fury were on the ground and available for close inspection, and inside the hangars there were parachutes, flag targets, a complete armament bay, and a demonstration of machine-gun operations from a fighter. Representatives of Stoke-on-Trent's Air Raid Precautions Unit (ARP) under Mr R. G. Totty had a stall with various types of respirators and gas clothing, while eleven members of a contingent of the 41st Anti-Aircraft Battalion under the command of Major H. M. Powell also gave a display. Proceeds from the event totalled £236, a sum that was gratefully received by the RAF Benevolent Fund.

Nothing now was too much trouble for the RAF personnel, who had been accorded a civic welcome and entertained to lunch before the display. Proposing a toast to their guests, the Deputy Lord Mayor, Alderman J. A. Dale, said that they could not receive a warmer welcome in any part of England than in North Staffordshire. He continued by referring to the training school to be established at Meir, with a permanent fleet of twenty-five machines, and concluded: 'I think it shows we are air-minded and we hope to train some splendid young men there.' Wing Commander Crawford responded by expressing his appreciation of the co-operation of the Aerodrome Committee and the aero club. Not only were they helping charity by these provincial displays, he went on, but they were also assisting in recruiting. He congratulated the Aerodrome Committee on having realised the value of an airport and said that the location was 'ideal'.

The former Air Minister and current president of the Aerodrome Owners' Association, the Marquess of Londonderry, also paid tribute to the city's 'remarkable aerodrome' after he touched down at Meir on 22 June on his way to lay the foundation stone of a new sanatorium at Hanchurch. He praised the City Council's progressive policy and said: 'The need for aerodromes increases every day, and I am sure there is no superior site for one anywhere in the country to yours in Stoke-on-Trent – and I can assure you that I speak with some little knowledge on this very difficult subject. I was glad to see the progress that is being made with the School, and I am sure that in the future this will be a centre of communication.'

Suddenly the Council's former doubts and misgivings were being swept aside in a new mood of optimism that bordered on self-congratulation. Councillor G. Battison, the present chairman of the Aerodrome Committee, reflected it when speaking of these latest developments:

I am extremely pleased with the way the aerodrome is coming into its own. The action of the Corporation in taking over the land will prove, ultimately,

Aircraft take part in the Empire Day display on 28 May 1938.

Visitors inspect an Anson.

to have been one of the best steps ever taken in the district. Already we are assured of a good income, while in addition the value of the land has increased three-fold since the time we first took it over. As we become more air-minded, the aerodrome will become of more and more importance. I look forward to the day when people will go along to Meir to catch an LMS plane just as now they go along to a railway station.

Sadly his expectations were not to be fulfilled, for although the airfield would shortly achieve significant importance, it was in an entirely different way from the one he foresaw. By now the whole country was gearing up for war. On Sunday, 19 June, there had been a practice blackout over the whole of South Staffordshire, followed on the 21st by the first trial of the air-raid warning system in Stoke-on-Trent. On the 23rd the Air Minister, Sir Kingsley Wood, launched the greatest RAF recruiting campaign Britain had ever known by appealing for more than 31,000 men.

This was an opportune moment for the North Staffordshire Aero Club to make an appeal of its own, which it did on 29 June, asking for support from local businessmen. The club had a proud record: until then it had survived by virtue of the enthusiasm of its committee and members, and now flew three machines – two Hawk Majors and a slower version used for initial instruction. In the last three years, up to eighty pilots had undergone the full course at Meir and qualified for civil flying. In addition, the two faster machines had recently been working with anti-aircraft forces in the area and at Derby and Nottingham. The club now wished to widen the scope of its activities; in particular it wanted another Hawk in order to produce more trained pilots. It did not have long to wait.

On 15 July 1938, the Air Minister placed the largest ever aircraft order with a single firm when he signed a contract with Lord Nuffield for 1,000 Spitfires to be produced at his new factory in Birmingham. Sir Kingsley followed this up on 25th with a scheme to create a vast new reserve of RAF personnel by the formation of the Civil Air Guard. This scheme, open to men and women aged from eighteen to fifty, slashed the expense of learning to fly by subsidising light aeroplane clubs. Once it had cost about £40 to qualify for an 'A' licence; now it would be approximately £3. In exchange for this governmental largesse, recruits undertook to offer their services in a national emergency for RAF duties, or in any other area concerned with aviation. For the first time flying was no longer the preserve of the affluent, and the *Sentinel* foresaw the stampede that would follow: 'The chance of learning to fly for less than may be spent on a motor-cycle will captivate adventurous youth.' The newspaper was right: enquiries (from both sexes) swamped the aero club – making an additional aircraft not merely a hoped-for ambition but an urgent necessity.

Meanwhile the Air Ministry had awarded a contract to Messrs Reid and Sigrist Aviation to run the RAF centre at Meir. It was officially opened on

1 August 1938 as No. 28 Elementary and Reserve Flying Training School, the first military flying unit to be established in Staffordshire prior to the Second World War. In charge was Flight Lieutenant Tindall, with Flying Officer A. C. Richardson and Sergeant Pilot E. T. Heelds as his instructors. The rest of the staff, though, were mostly civilian, as were the pupils, who received free tuition in one of a number of the jobs of an airman for signing up to the Volunteer Reserve (VR). This was another way that people could afford to fly, and the courses proved extremely popular right up to the outbreak of war, the Avro Anson, Hawker Hart, and Miles Magister becoming common sights over Meir.

The centre quickly had 36 pilots under training, but within months was aiming at a strength of 106 pilots and 112 observers and wireless operators. Pilots were given the rank of Sergeant, other pupils that of Leading Aircraftman. Payment was one shilling an hour during the time trainees were attending the aerodrome or instructional centre, with compensation for travelling expenses. In addition they had to undergo fifteen days' annual training during which payment varied according to rank, from 8s to 10s 6d a day. For special occasions, all trainees wore a uniform that differed little from the regulation RAF dress. At other times, 'a blazer and tie of smart design' were to be worn.

Their temporary headquarters were at 43a Church Street, Stoke, until they were able to occupy the Trentham Institute, a large black and white timber building that stood on the Stone Road. Trainees would attend two nights a week for lectures on administration, airmanship, navigation, theory of flight, gunnery, bombing, wireless telegraphy, signals, photography, and reconnaissance. A tall tower at the rear of the Institute was also used to teach the basics of parachute jumping. Weekend flying at Meir was the highlight for budding pilots, the average flight lasting about half-an-hour. After twenty such flights, a pupil was expected to fly solo. The observers and wireless operators received four months' ground instruction before being allowed to fly in the second stage of their training.

By September 1938, the international crisis was so grave that Neville Chamberlain, the Prime Minister, was making his first journeys by air (at the age of sixty-nine) to confer with 'Herr Hitler'. As he did so, trenches were being dug in the city's parks and gas masks distributed at 156 stations across Stoke-on-Trent. After three visits in a fortnight – perhaps the earliest example of what is now termed shuttle diplomacy – Chamberlain returned from Munich saying he believed it would be 'peace for our time'. The world breathed a sigh of relief and he was given a hero's welcome. For the moment, however, Hitler had won. On 3 October, German troops occupied the Sudetenland.

*

The aero club had declared itself full after enrolling 300 of the multitude of applicants for the Civil Air Guard. These attended a packed meeting at the

Above: Flying Officer A. C. Richardson, Flying Officer L. S. Tindall, Sergeant Pilot E. T. Heelds, and a pupil walk towards the planes.

Left: The pupil is given instruction on directions before take off.

Above: Three Miles Magisters leave Meir Aerodrome.

Below: A formation of Hawker Harts fly over Meir.

SPEND YOUR SPARE TIME IN THE ROYAL AIR FORCE **VOLUNTEER RESERVE**

It's service you'll like!

VOLUNTEERS NOW WANTED FOR TRAINING AS

WIRELESS OPERATOR- —AIR GUNNERS
(Age 18 to 32)

Free Training—Expense Allowances— Annual Gratuities.

Full particulars from :—
The Commandant R.A.F.V.R., Stone Road, Trentham, Staffordshire

The RAFVR is established at the Trentham Institute.

Crown & Anchor Hotel, Longton, on 21 October, when Leslie Irving outlined the scheme for them. He said that the training of the Guard had been left to local aero clubs all over the country, with the clubs working under the direction of a Board of Commissioners headed by the Marquess of Londonderry.

The club at Meir hoped to take trainees in groups of five to the standard of the 'A' licence in about seventeen hours. Depending on ability, four to eight hours would be spent on dual instruction, followed by three hours' solo work. Various tests then awaited them, including landing without the use of the engine and landing within a prescribed area. The final hurdle was an oral examination on major points of 'air sense' – akin to a test on the 'rules of the road'. Instructional talks on ground work would also be arranged, which trainees were urged to attend. To encourage people to fly off-peak, the government had made the charge for mid-week flying half what it would be at weekends – 2s 6d per hour on light machines and 5s on heavier planes.

Also present at the meeting were club officials Captain Wilf Green and Hugh Sharpley, the former an ace of the First World War, the latter soon to be one of 'The Few'. Captain Green (the brother of the late Lieutenant Thomas

Seaman Green) was an inspiring (if not awe-inspiring) figure for the would-be flyers in the audience. Serving with No. 32 Squadron, he had accounted for seven German planes and been shot down himself three times. He had also been mentioned in French dispatches, awarded a DFC, and been decorated in the field by General Pétain with the Croix de Guerre and Légion d'Honneur.

Those sitting in front of him were all ears as he told them that the Guards would be of great value to the country in time of emergency and warned that their training should therefore be taken very seriously. 'Flying,' he said, 'was rather more than taking a machine off the ground and flying around the aerodrome.' He stressed the importance of understanding the machine and the value of the instructional talks referred to by Mr Irving. He concluded the evening by declaring that they were fortunate in having one of the finest instructors in the country: 'I have never met another who has as much patience with a pupil as has Mr McGuinness. A trainee can feel he is absolutely safe if Mr McGuinness says so.' In the bar afterwards, young men got to know one another and talked of the exciting prospects ahead.

Although Meir now busied itself with instruction and training, there was still time for less serious interludes, and the coming of another VIP was eagerly awaited. A telegram from Reykjavik had been received giving details of Father Christmas's arrival at the aerodrome and inviting boys and girls to meet him there. The traditional figure duly arrived on Saturday, 5 November, to be welcomed by Guy Fawkes. Afterwards he processed in a gaily decorated

Captain Wilf Green.

coach through Longton and Fenton to Lamb Street, Hanley, where he was greeted by his retinue at Lewis' before climbing the Golden Ladder to the first floor to open the Toy Fair. He proceeded to the Snow-White Grotto with its 'six wonderful mechanical scenes, a wishing well, and Sneezy, Dopey, and their confederates', and then began to receive the many children who were already queuing to see him.

Another pleasant episode for all concerned was a return visit by pupils from the Moorland Road Girls' School to gain first-hand experience of aerial developments. The visit, on 24 November, was another example of the continuing efforts being made by the aero club to encourage flying and air-mindedness among local people, and Messrs Battison and Hawley were on hand to welcome their sixty guests.

Five lucky girls seized the chance of making their first air trip when they were taken up individually by Mr McGuinness. On their flight over the Potteries, they were surprised to discover that although bright sunshine flashed on the wings of the aeroplane, the smoke clouds hanging over the city permitted them only a hazy view and they could hardly recognise familiar landmarks. Meanwhile, the other pupils were shown the layout of an aerodrome and the practice adopted for take-off and landing. They were also taken into the hangars of the RAF Training School and allowed to experience the thrill of sitting in the pilot's seat and imagine for a few seconds that they were Jean Batten or Amy Johnson.

*

Stanley Matthews' daughter was the first baby to be born in the New Year at the Limes Maternity Home, Hartshill, arriving on 1 January 1939 at 7.30 a.m. On 11th, Anna Neagle braved heavy snowfalls to visit the Odeon Theatre, Hanley, in connection with the launch of the film *Sixty Glorious Years*, in which she was starring as Queen Victoria. Elsewhere Barcelona fell to Franco's forces. At the end of the month, the RAF made an urgent appeal to employers to release reserve and volunteer pilots for 6 months' intensive training.

In February, the progress of Meir's Civil Air Guard was reviewed at a well-attended meeting at Hanley Town Hall. The chairman, Captain Green, said that 300 members had joined and 390 hours' flying had been achieved since September – an excellent performance considering that they had only one instructor. Six members had already qualified for their 'A' licences and nine others had made their first solo flight. About thirty more were currently receiving instruction. To speed up the work, another instructor had been appointed who would start within a few days. In addition, a new clubhouse, donated by Mrs E. Hawley, was being erected, and on its completion many more members would be able to start ground training. A dance was to be held to raise funds to equip and furnish the new building.

Despite this optimism, the aerodrome was about to suffer a double blow. The 'on request' passenger services, begun in 1935, had by then increased to two flights daily, but these were discontinued in 1939, despite protests by the City Council. Meir was no longer a port of call.

Misfortune also struck the aero club. During the storms early in March 1939, Mr Percy Wilson Fell, who had been appointed as second instructor only three weeks before, had a remarkable escape as he was attempting to land at Barton Airport, Manchester, in a 70-mile-an-hour gale. As he was trying to regain height after a failed first attempt, a strong gust of wind made one of the wings catch the surface of a ploughed field. The wing was torn off, the plane overturned and immediately smashed into the ground. An eye-witness said the machine had been 'tossed like a leaf in the wind' before it crashed. Mr Fell, despite suffering a fractured leg, managed to get out of the wreckage and was then dragged to safety. The club's Miles Hawk Major lay in pieces in a ditch.

In the same month Hitler took over the rest of Czechoslovakia, and 'war' was declared locally at 11.45 p.m. on the 20th when a trial blackout was made over a large part of North Staffordshire and South Cheshire. By that time city air-raid wardens were at their allotted posts, all street lighting was extinguished, and from midnight until 2 a.m. RAF bombers were expected

IMPORTANT NOTICE

AIR RAID PRECAUTIONS

'BLACK-OUT'

NIGHT OF MARCH 20th/21st, 1939

In connection with the Home Defence Exercise to be held this month, it is intended to "black-out" a large part of the country for a short period during one night of the Exercise, and the Home Office has asked this District to co-operate by securing that no lights are visible from the air between mid-night and 2 a.m. on the night of March 20th/21st, 1939.

The darkening of areas exposed to air attack may be expected to be an essential feature of the defence of this country in time of war, and useful information on the best means of effecting this may be derived from the present Exercise.

Householders and all other occupiers of premises are accordingly asked to assist by ensuring that lights in their premises are extinguished, or screened by dark curtains or blinds, between mid-night and 2 o'clock on the night of March 20th/21st. It is particularly desirable that external lights and other lights directly visible from the sky should be extinguished or screened.

As lighting in streets will be restricted, vehicles should, so far as possible, keep off the roads during the two hours' darkened period.

It is emphasised that there is no intention, in connection with the "black-out," of cutting off lighting or power supplies at the mains.

Notification is given of the ARP exercise to test the effectiveness of the area's blackout.

to cruise over the whole of the area, with observers taking photographs and collecting material for written reports. Worries had been expressed concerning the night glare of pottery ovens and the Shelton Bar steelworks.

In the event, two of the three bombers from Yorkshire had to turn back because of gales and low cloud, and the one that reached the district caught only the merest glimpses of the area. The people of the Midlands were perhaps reassured that the English weather combined with their own industrial haze could thwart the dreaded German bomber. A few days later in the House of Commons, Neville Chamberlain guaranteed Great Britain's help to Poland if she were attacked. A marker had at last been put down. *Thus far and no führer*, as a wit had chalked on a wall in Stone. The Poles thought that the crisis was over and invited the Stoke City team to tour the country. Some weeks later, however, after passports had been prepared and all arrangements made, a telegram reached the Victoria Ground advising cancellation 'owing to increased international tension'.

In Berlin on 20 April, Hitler's 50th birthday 'was marked by pomp and glory befitting an Emperor'. For five hours, 45,000 men of the German Armed Forces goose-stepped, marched or rode in tanks through the Tiergarten, with Hitler taking the salute. Stoke-on-Trent meanwhile staged a monster parade of its own. It was the climax of a National Service Week, during which nightly recruiting rallies had been held in the open-air simultaneously in all six towns. On Sunday, 30 April, the week's events culminated in a gigantic parade in Hanley Park, watched by 10,000 people. Regular and Territorial units, with guns, searchlights, and other equipment, together with several thousand men and women of Stoke's citizen army of National Service, marched past the Earl of Harrowby, who stood with the Lord Mayor on the terrace in front of the park's pavilion. It was 'one of the most impressive spectacles ever seen in the district'.

That April also saw the approval of a scheme for the affiliation of RAF squadrons to the chief cities and towns of the country so that ordinary citizens could become familiar with RAF personnel and their machines. The unit affiliated to Stoke-on-Trent was No. 46 Fighter Squadron from Digby, Lincolnshire, whose Gauntlets had performed at Meir the previous year. Their second appearance was to be little short of sensational on what was to be the last ever Empire Day Air Display at the City Aerodrome on Saturday, 20 May.

Tern Hill had secured the services of Amy Johnson, who was to take part in a gliding demonstration, but Meir had treats of its own in store. A civic welcome was again extended to all the airmen from No. 611 Squadron, who were to give the display, and they were then entertained to a lavish luncheon at the aerodrome. Visitors, meanwhile, were able to see the static display close up, which consisted of the latest machines that the Service had at their disposal. Among them were Hawker Demons, a Handley Page Hampden, a Fairey Battle, a Blenheim, a Whitley, and an Avro Tutor. The city's ARP Department had their usual display of equipment, including gas masks old and new, protective clothing, and a decontamination plant.

The main proceedings began with a demonstration of formation flying by five Hawker Hinds that 'flew at high speeds, forming and reforming in various patterns with wonderful precision and finishing with a marvellous dive'. Individual aerobatics then thrilled the crowd, the pilots performing a series of 'hair-raising loops, dives, rolls, and turns'. Mimic warfare was provided by a series of attacks by fighters on 'enemy' bombers and a low-flying attack on a convoy. The display ended as usual with a flypast of the various types of aircraft that had been taking part.

Stealing the show, though, were three new frontline fighters from No. 46 Squadron whose sudden appearance in mid-afternoon stunned the huge crowd with their speed. The Hawker Hurricane had arrived.

*

After Munich, enrolment had quickened at the VR Training School. Among its early recruits were the sons of Mrs R. A. Yates of the local Waggon and Horses Hotel. Richard, the elder, had been the first apprentice at the City Aerodrome. After serving his three years, he had then been employed by Reid and Sigrist before he and his brother Thomas (who was also a member of the mechanical staff) joined the Reserve. Both were to serve as flight mechanics at RAF airfields throughout the war.

Vic Reynolds, of Hartshill, trained initially at the Trentham Institute as a wireless operator/air gunner, as did John Waite, the young clerk from the Hanley Building Society. Both went on to serve with distinction with Coastal Command. John Ashton, from Newcastle, Don Edwards, from Fenton, and Cedric Moores, from Miles Green, all learned to fly at Meir and eventually became fighter pilots. Of the three, only Ashton survived.

'Volunteers' also came from the aero club and included Oswald ('Tim') Massey and his future brother-in-law Hugh Sharpley. The former was engaged in his father's ironmonger's business, W. Massey and Sons, at Newcastle. During the war, he would go on to serve as a Flight Lieutenant with Coastal Command and be mentioned in dispatches for his distinguished service. Hugh Sharpley, the younger son of the Town Clerk of Stoke-on-Trent, was the complete all-rounder: an accomplished marksman, a fine horseman who had won several steeplechases, a prominent member of the North Staffordshire Polo Club, and vice-captain of Swynnerton Cricket Club. After leaving Rydal School in Colwyn Bay, he had gone into the engineering section of the Stoke-on-Trent Sewage Works Department and was then appointed engineering assistant in the Staffordshire Potteries Water Board. He had taken up flying in 1935 when he joined the aero club and was soon one of its star performers. It

Far left: Oswald Massey.

Left: Hugh Sharpley.

seemed almost inevitable that he should become a fighter pilot and take part in the most celebrated air battle in history.

Other 'weekenders' came from further afield. Vernon Page, originally from Gloucester, had taken up a student apprenticeship with the English Electric Company in Stafford; Bill Astell lived at Spire Hollins in Derbyshire, but joined the Meir Reserve while working for one of his father's textile mills at Tean; Dennis Armitage and Eric Bann, both from Macclesfield, were employed as engineers by Norton and Biddulph Collieries and Fairey Engineering respectively. One of the youngest volunteers was Eric Lock from Bayston Hill, near Shrewsbury. Ever since he had been taken for a joyride by Sir Alan Cobham he had wanted to join the RAF, but after leaving school he had had to help on his father's farm. As soon as he was old enough, however, he seized his chance and joined the Reserve at Meir. He cut a rather unprepossessing figure – in his Sidcot flying suit he stood just 5 feet 6 inches in height and was soon nicknamed 'Sawn Off'. One of his instructors was to describe him as 'the world's worst pupil in any kind of aircraft'.

The dangers inherent in their part-time training were brought home to them on Sunday, 28 May 1939. Clare Norman Parish from Adlington, near Manchester, was already a pilot at the training school and was about to take his final examination as an instructor. That Sunday, while on a training flight from Meir, his plane crashed into a wooded hillside near Wincle at the head of the Dane Valley. A group of boy scouts from Leek, who were camping nearby, managed to extricate the pilot from the wreckage, but he died soon afterwards. He was twenty-one.

His death must have made some of the others wonder what lay in store for them as war seemed to grow daily more imminent. They could scarcely have imagined, however, that one would distinguish himself in the Battle of France; that another would become the first North Staffordshire airman to receive the

George Medal; that a third would take part in the most famous bombing raid of the Second World War; and that five would join the immortal ranks of 'The Few', among them a flyer who, in his brief meteoric career, would become one of the highest-scoring pilots in the Battle of Britain, a top gun, an ace of aces.

*

Later that May, the 1939 London–Isle of Man air race had an absence of continental competitors because of the international situation. One Me 108 had been entered, only to be withdrawn when permission from Field Marshal Hermann Goering was not forthcoming. The race was won by Flying Officer Geoffrey de Havilland in the TK2 with Alex Henshaw a close second in his Mew Gull. A casualty among the nineteen starters had been Francis Dawson-Paul, who had to put down his Chilton at Meir with a seized valve. This was unfortunate as his plane was reputed to be 'unusually fast' – though it was as nothing compared to the Spitfires he would be flying within a year as a Royal Navy pilot alongside 'The Few'.

On 1 July, the Air Minister himself flew into Meir shortly before 4 p.m., accompanied by the famous First World War ace Squadron Leader Ira Jones. Although Sir Kingsley's visit was described as 'informal', the reception party included the Lord Mayor, the Deputy Town Clerk, Mr Andrew MacLaren (MP for Burslem), Squadron Leader G. H. Reid, DFC (Managing Director of Reid & Sigrist), Wing Commander P. Y. Birch (Town Centre Commandant of No. 28 Flying Training School), Mr L. F. Tindall (Chief Flying Instructor), Flight Lieutenant Gyll-Murray (RAF Examining Officer), and Mr J. R. Brittain (Chief Ground Engineer).

Sir Kingsley watched 'a normal Saturday afternoon's activity' at the School before making a 40-minute tour of the hangars, workshops, offices, first-aid rooms, kitchen, mess-room, pupils' room, and an instruction room. In the engineer's office, he saw the teleprinter that had been supplied by the Air Ministry so that a direct land line was now available with the Ministry control room and meteorological office at Barton, Manchester. He also inspected the Link trainer – the forerunner of today's flight simulator. He then left by air for the next stop on his whirlwind tour, the RAF station at Shawbury, near Shrewsbury. A few days later in the House of Commons, he announced further expansion at Meir with the establishment of a Repair Depot and the prospect of up to 2,500 jobs on offer. The Air Ministry also approached the City Council to ask if it would camouflage the aerodrome.

Less than a week after Sir Kingsley's visit, a second Minister of State arrived when Mr Geoffrey Lloyd, Secretary for Mines, flew into Meir from Windsor, where he had been in attendance on the King and Queen at the Royal Show. He wanted to get first-hand information on the mining industry in the area, and on 6 July he visited Sneyd Colliery, going underground to see the working conditions for himself. He then went on to open a school for pit lads at Knutton before flying back to London.

On Sunday, 6 August, 'aircraft practice' took place over Trentham and the surrounding districts. Despite advance notice of the exercise, this led to a flurry of letters to the *Sentinel*, beginning with one from a resident of Abbey Hulton who complained about planes 'skimming the house-tops', to the discomfort and distress of local inhabitants. Cecil Plant, of Harpfields, an officer in the Volunteer Reserve, pointed out that the pilots were probably men like him who had given up their holiday to train. 'Surely he does not mind the noise,' he went on, 'when he weighs it against the thought that these planes are his guarantee of not hearing the motors of a foreign power, who would not stop at just noise.'

Other residents fretted about accidents, and their apprehension seemed justified when, on the evening of 8 August, an aeroplane struck and broke a high-tension line and cut off electrical supplies to the Caverswall area for a time. This plane belonged to the aero club, and Peter Massey was instructing his pupil, Mr Seekings, on forced landings when they had to make a real one in a field at Cookshill. Neither was injured, however, and after a short delay they managed to take off again and return to the aerodrome.

A welcome distraction was provided by the arrival of Pat Collins' Fair at Regent Road for the Hanley and Stoke Wakes Week. It offered 'super dodgems de luxe, motor bicycle speedway, famous waltzers, the Moon Rocket, and a circus', but the undoubted sensation proved to be the appearance of the 'World's Tallest Man' – Vaino Myllyrinne from Finland, who stood eight feet four inches tall and was said to be still growing!

In spite of the indifferent weather, the Potters' annual exodus to Blackpool and the North Wales' seaside resorts was also well underway, with 136,000 people leaving the district in two days. But this year all the talk was of war.

14

A Few of 'The Few'

On Friday, 1 September, Germany invaded Poland. Britain and France immediately ordered full mobilisation, and an evacuation of three million children began – 'the greatest exodus in history' – with 12,000 of them destined for North Staffordshire. A complete blackout was imposed in the Potteries and Newcastle-under-Lyme that evening, and schools publicised the fact that they would not be re-opening as planned the following week. At 11.15 a.m. on Sunday, 3 September, Neville Chamberlain formally declared war on Germany.

Early casualties were Sergeant P. B. Sproston of Caverswall and Sergeant W. H. Stevens of Newcastle, who had met and become friends at the Meir training school. As a result of the closeness of their surnames, they were posted to the same squadron and shared the same sleeping quarters. Both were promoted to sergeant on the same day and had their first taste of action on the same day, flying alongside each other. At the end of the month, both were reported missing when they were shot down into the sea on the same day.

Another casualty was Flying Officer A. C. MacLachlan who had done much of his civilian flying from Meir Aerodrome before joining the RAF. While on a reconnaissance flight over the Siegfried Line, and with his observer-gunner engaged in taking photographs, their plane was riddled by a German fighter and seen to crash in flames. At first it was feared that they had been killed, but MacLachlan was later posted as a prisoner of war.

The Air Ministry now requisitioned the aerodrome – which became known as 'RAF Meir' – and No. 28 Flying Training School was soon disbanded. All civilian flying was banned, and the club's aircraft were stored at Hanley High School where a former pupil saw them: 'Some very interesting stuff including a rather pretty little Hillson Praga, but the whole lot disappeared during the war and I suspect they were taken out and burned by the official vandals.'

By November, twenty-three members of the North Staffordshire Aero Club were serving with the armed forces, and others followed them some months later. Fourteen had enlisted in the RAF, while Stanley Hawley became a Flight Sub-Lieutenant with the Fleet Air Arm. Within a year, four of them would be lost. Sergeant Pilot Wilfred Walker, of Oakamoor, serving with Bomber Command, died of wounds in July 1940. Sergeant Pilot Peter Garvey, of Talke, also with Bomber

> ## POLICE NOTICE
> # AIR RAID WARNINGS
> ## FACTORY and WORKS SIRENS and HOOTERS
>
> **Notice is hereby given that from now onwards sirens and hooters must not on any account be used except for sounding air raid signals**
>
> *Warnings of impending AIR RAIDS will be given by A FLUCTUATING OR "WARBLING" SIGNAL OF VARYING PITCH or A SUCCESSION OF INTERMITTENT BLASTS SOUNDED BY HOOTERS AND SIRENS. The "RAIDERS PASSED" signal will be a CONTINUOUS SIGNAL AT A STEADY PITCH.*
>
> FRANK L. BUNN, Chief Constable.
>
> 1st SEPTEMBER, 1939.

The air-raid warning system is explained on the eve of the war.

Command, was reported 'missing' that August. In the same month Pilot Officer Ken Bishop, of Leek, was killed during a training flight. Sergeant Pilot Hugh Sharpley, of Hanchurch, died in November serving with Fighter Command.

Another of the club's flyers, Thomas Aston Heath, was an Old Boy of Newcastle High School and the nephew of Captain Wilf Green. He began his service career as a Pilot Officer, but eventually rose to the rank of Acting Wing Commander with No. 169 Squadron. He was awarded an Air Force Cross and Bar, then a DFC, and was finally mentioned in dispatches. He also received a congratulatory letter from Air Chief Marshal Sir Arthur Harris.

Eight other members of the flying club had joined the Army, among them Major A. R. Harley-Jones, who had been the works manager of Bilton's (1912) Ltd, earthenware and tile manufacturers. As well as being a member of the aero club, he was also in the Territorials and had been called up almost immediately. He went on to serve with the Royal Artillery and was taken prisoner at Tobruk in 1942. During his captivity in North Africa and Italy, he made three escape attempts, but was recaptured and sent to Germany where he was finally liberated by American forces at the end of the war.

The remaining club members, now grounded, tried to maintain some of their activities and in December 1939 they held the first of a series of dances at the Grand Hotel, Hanley. The aim was to create a fund so that cigarettes and other comforts could be sent to airmen serving overseas, and 300 guests turned up to support the endeavour. They were royally entertained. The ballroom had been exquisitely decorated by Mr A. Cooke, of Burslem, and music throughout the evening was provided by Jay Hollins and his Grand Hotel Orchestra. A welcome surprise was the cabaret put on by Lord John Sanger's Circus, the 'boxing to music' act being the undoubted hit of the night. Several of the prizes that were awarded were handed back to be sold for the fund, and Captain Green conducted a spontaneous auction, which raised a further £5 15s. Overall it was confidently expected that the occasion would bring in more than £30.

On 12 February 1940, the first RAF personnel arrived at Meir and preparations were made to convert the airport into a war-time RAF station. New buildings were to include two Bellman hangars, lecture rooms, hospital, guard huts, NAAFI canteen, and a rifle range. The latter would prove a magnet to local children, who would delight in collecting the shells of spent bullets before retiring to their 'hay igloos' in the fields alongside the aerodrome.

In March, No. 1 Flying Practice Unit (FPU) was established at Meir and began its task of honing the skills of 120 Acting Pilot Officers and 120 Sergeant Pilots who had completed advanced courses. Within months some of them would be at the forefront of the Battle of Britain. They included men like Maurice Mounsdon, who had joined the RAF on a short service commission before the war; Henry Goodwin, who had held a commission in the Auxiliary Air Force since 1933; and John Laurence Bickerdike, from New Zealand, one of a contingent of Commonwealth pilots who had come to assist the Mother Country. Among them were two future aces, the New Zealander Bill Hodgson and the Canadian Keith Ogilvie.

Some, like Geoffrey Page, were barely out of their teens. He had learned to fly as a member of the University of London Air Squadron and had just completed his training at Cranwell. After the RAF College, Meir – which he described as 'set amid the sordid slag heaps of the Potteries' – must have been something of a shock, and Page was no doubt glad that his stay was brief. As there was no on-site accommodation, three large houses had been taken over for the officers, while the NCOs were billeted at Longton Town Hall. In the ballroom, clothes lockers were used as space dividers, but there was little privacy, washing facilities were minimal, and the food was 'terrible' – overcooked cabbage, mushy potatoes, and meat whose origins remained a mystery. Later Meir Drill Hall was used to relieve the pressure on the NCOs, and residents living near the airfield were encouraged to entertain RAF personnel, many of whom were readily invited to Sunday tea; some of them were glad to take up residence with local families.

The people of the Potteries were by now used to welcoming newcomers, and many had taken in as lodgers the thousand bank clerks who arrived when Barlaston Hall temporarily became the headquarters of the Bank of England, with the ballroom and restaurant of Trentham Gardens serving as the London Clearing Banks. Soldiers of the French Foreign Legion and Polish army were also soon encamped in the adjacent Trentham Park. (One of them was Stoke-born James Williamson, who had joined the Foreign Legion shortly before the war in order 'to see the world'!) Refugees from Czechoslovakia and elsewhere had been arriving for several years and had recently been joined by the influx of evacuees from London – 'evaporated children', as one woman was heard describing them. Later Longton High School, just over the road from the airfield, was commandeered by the War Office, and a section of the Military College of Science specialising in Field Artillery moved in.

Apart from familiarisation flying, No.1 FPU was involved in military exercises in the area, including a mock attack on Alton Towers on 14 May. A few days earlier Winston Churchill had become Prime Minister, and the real conflict in the West began with the German *Blitzkrieg* on France and the Low Countries. Suddenly one of Meir's earlier trainees, John Ashton, then based in France as a Pilot Officer with No. 85 Squadron, was thrust into action for the first time. On 10 May, the first day of the onslaught, he destroyed two He 111s and on the 13th claimed two other 'kills' in some of the fiercest fighting of the war. On 15 May, his own Hurricane was shot up over Belgium, forcing him to crash-land, but he escaped unhurt and returned to the battle a day later.

At the end of the month, striving to protect the British Expeditionary Force's desperate withdrawal, he was shot down in flames and, somewhat the worse for wear, had to become a 'footslogger' himself, joining a straggle of soldiers on their way to Dunkirk. There, dug in on the beaches and under fire, he may have been cheered to hear the voice of another Potteries' man, Able Seaman Fred Nixon, who was in charge of his ship's boat during the evacuation. On reaching the shore he would roar out repeatedly 'Any more for Stoke?' Ashton eventually embarked and reached England after a nightmare journey lasting twelve hours. He then went on a brief leave to the family home in Newcastle to find that he had been reported 'missing in action', much to the astonishment of his parents who believed that he had a desk job.

John Ashton.

*

With the country now facing the threat of invasion, No. 1 FPU (the only one of its kind to be formed) was disbanded on 16 June 1940 and its pilots sent to operational stations. One of them, the New Zealander Clive Saxelby, would go on to take part in the first 1,000 bomber raid on Cologne and later celebrated his twenty-first birthday in a German prison camp.

As soon as the unit left, its Hawker Hinds and Hectors were replaced by dozens of Miles Magisters of No. 5 Elementary Flying Training School (EFTS), which had been posted there from Hanworth in Middlesex. Civilian pilots serving as members of the Air Transport Auxiliary helped fly in the Magisters, one of them being Amy Johnson, whose flight on the 15 June 1940 was duly recorded in her log book, seemingly her only visit to Meir. A few days later Newcastle and Hanley were bombed.

No. 5 EFTS was soon upgraded to a Class A Unit, and the shortage of pilots was now so acute that within days the 'Maggies' were up and flying, and on fine days made 1,200 landings. Frank Goff was one of the new arrivals:

We moved to Meir because London barrage balloons made it too dicey for training flights. I was an NCO and we were billeted in Longton Town Hall. I well remember an elderly couple who ran a fish and chip shop quite near. When we arrived in the evening, we were ushered through to a room with plates and cutlery on the table. We found the local people very friendly.

One incident comes to mind. One day on solo flying, I climbed to 5,000 feet and tried a slow roll before I'd been instructed on this manoeuvre. Having got upside down the nose dropped so I pulled the stick back and dived straight down to about 500 feet over an industrial estate being built quite near before levelling out! That evening I was having a beer in a local, and there were some Irish labourers who had been working on the site describing how some idiot pilot had nearly crashed on them!

Inevitably there were accidents. The first occurred on 2 July 1940 when a Magister hit high-tension cables and spun out of control, crashing at Beechcliff, near Trentham. The instructor, Pilot Officer Reginald Sankey, of Tunbridge Wells, and his pupil, Sergeant Dennis Green, of Leamington, were both killed instantly. On 6 July, the Reverend 'Bobby' Bell, the parish priest of Holy Trinity church, Meir, officiated at their funerals – the first of a number of such ceremonies he would be called upon to perform. The two airmen were then interred in Longton cemetery.

Despite such setbacks, pilots were turned out at an impressive rate throughout the summer with 134 sent on for more advanced training. Two such were twenty-one-year-old Trevor Oldfield and nineteen-year-old Ken Rees, both of whom arrived at Meir cherishing hopes of becoming fighter pilots. Trevor Oldfield had originally joined the Auxiliary Air Force in 1938 as an air gunner, but with the outbreak of war he was selected for training as a pilot. Ken Rees had enlisted in 1939, but had been left kicking his heels in Cambridge until his brother-in-law pulled a few strings to get him a posting to Meir. Both were itching to begin flying.

Rees' account of the first stage in his *ab initio* training was typical of the experience awaiting hundreds of young airmen at training schools throughout the country. Soon after his arrival, togged up 'in a flight jacket, helmet, and goggles out of Biggles', he was ready for his maiden trip with Flight Lieutenant Purdy, whom he regarded as 'superior to God'. His first reaction to their aircraft was a mixture of love, fear and bewilderment:

> It was a Miles Magister, with a fixed undercarriage, an open cockpit (hence the WWI helmet and goggles; even in August you would freeze) and a tiny propeller tacked onto its front like the nose of a dachshund. I didn't see how that flimsy piece of machinery could possibly get me and Purdy off the ground. [...]
>
> I watched Purdy climb into the front cockpit while a cheerful airman strapped me into my parachute. 'That, matey,' the airman held up the ripcord, 'is the handle you pull when the wing drops off.' He grinned, watched while I gingerly squeezed myself into the rear cockpit, and then began strapping me in, parachute and all, with the Sutton harness which stopped you falling out of the open cockpit to the earth below.
>
> 'How can I use my parachute in this?' How could I move at all?
>
> He grinned again, the bastard. He'd done it all before, many times. 'Oh, there's a pin in the front that will release the harness.'
>
> 'When the wing drops off.'

Ken Rees.

He nodded, still grinning, and jumped down.

I sat there, all strapped in, and watched over Purdy's shoulder as he prepared for take-off. I was surprised to see how long it took him. It had never occurred to me that one had to do more than simply start the engine and go, just as they did in the films. [...] One of the airmen held his thumb up. Purdy said, 'Switches on. Contact.' The engine burst into snarling, rumbling life [...] and we bounced and clunked our way into take-off position. I watched him do more checks, then, turning into the wind, he opened up. Instantly we gathered speed; I felt myself being pressed hard back into the seat with the sudden acceleration, then the tail lifted and we were airborne.

After ten hours of basic exercises ('for stalling, spinning, climbing, gliding, turns, etc, etc'), he flew solo, and his fifty hours' elementary training were rounded off by another instructor, the cheerful, red-moustachioed Desmond Lancelot Plunkett, who introduced aerobatics as a matter of course, no matter what exercise they were supposed to be doing. Their paths would cross again some years later in one of the most infamous episodes of the Second World War.

Trevor Oldfield gained his wings at Meir that August, and a conversion course to fly the Spitfire followed. In the same month, despite a recommendation for fighters, Ken Rees was posted to No. 11 FTS in Shropshire to train as a bomber pilot. He was devastated.

*

With the Battle of Britain now entering its most dangerous phase, the shortage of pilots grew acute. The indomitable Lady Bailey, who had inaugurated Meir Aerodrome ten years earlier, was spoiling for the fray and pestered Churchill – in vain – to let her become a fighter pilot. She was then fifty.

However, more of the men who had passed through Meir had already been committed to the fight. Sergeant Pilot Eric Bann had had a turbulent few days at the end of May with No. 253 Squadron and, like John Ashton, had had to make his way home from Dunkirk, as he told his parents in a letter a few days later:

Well, Mother and Father, I'm back with the BEF, London, Saturday night, one of the lucky ones. What a scene on Euston station – never seen anything like it. Crowds gave we boys a wonderful welcome. [...] All the boys were arriving [...] still wet after swimming to the rescue boats. Mothers, fathers, wives, sweethearts were all waiting there. Some poor devils just stood looking dazed when they realised that their man had paid the price, their faces almost haunted.

He was subsequently posted to the newly formed No. 238 Squadron and thereafter was in the thick of the action, getting reacquainted with the Channel in July when he was shot down into it – 'Gosh, it was cold so early in the morning! Well, I broke all swimming records and was eventually picked up by a boat and landed at Portsmouth.' In the same month he shot down an Me 110, and an He 111 in August. By then the constant combat stress was taking its toll, as his brother Maurice recalled: 'Eric was given seven days' sick leave (nerves), immediately reduced to four days, and on the second day to 48 hours. My mother wanted him to report sick, but he refused. His hands were shaking, and his eyes were blinking.'

Early in September, Eric and five other squadron members took on twenty-five German fighters. 'Four of them each made things just too bad,' he wrote to his parents. 'Well, I ducked and fought like a madman – I am sure at those moments one is not normal. I looked up once and the air was full of machines and lead all milling round for that final burst. Well, here I am, not touched, thank God, and have one fighter to my credit. We chased every one away and got the warmest praise from all.'

On 15 September – the climax of the Battle of Britain – he was again at the cutting edge of the action: 'Old 238 gave them hell. We got twelve Huns in one scrap – just went in as one man and held our fire until very close range, then blew them right out of their cockpits.' Later that month he was recommended for a commission, but on the 28th his Hurricane was 'bounced' by a German fighter while on patrol over the Isle of Wight. Eye-witnesses saw Eric's aircraft on fire and heading towards Portsmouth at speed. Seconds later he decided to bale out. His parachute failed to open and he plunged to his death on Brading Marshes.

*

Dennis Armitage never forgot 'those lovely Hawker Harts we had at Meir', but in 1940 he had graduated to flying Spitfires with No. 266 Squadron.

Eric Bann and his wife May.

Unlike Eric Bann, he saw little action initially and 'settled down to a long, lazy summer at Wittering, interrupted only by a rather abortive visit to Dunkirk'. In August, however, the squadron was posted south to the cauldron of Tangmere, Manston, and Hornchurch, and 'from then on our life took on the more or less conventional Battle of Britain pattern. We took off, and after a time we came down, reloaded, and took off again. We lost our CO after only a few days.' The Commanding Officer, Squadron Leader Rodney Wilkinson, had been machine-gunned after baling out.

In a memoir, Armitage vividly recalled the arena of the skies over the Home Counties with 'vapour trails of a scrap already in progress looking like a giant skein of white wool that a kitten has been playing with'. At first enemy formations appeared as 'just a long, thin, horizontal dark cloud on the horizon, and then as we approached it became a mass of little black dots'. Their attack brought chaos:

For a minute or two there would be aeroplanes everywhere, Spitfires and Hurricanes and Me 109s above and below, to the right and left, all with throttles hard forward and sticks hard back, twisting and turning in a mad whirlpool. The carefully thought-out formation attacks which we had practised so long and assiduously were gone with the wind the moment the enemy fighters appeared. Soon you would find yourself going round and round in a tight circle with two or three Me 109s, and because the Spitfires had a slightly better turning circle you would gradually get the better of them, but just as you were getting your sights on they would flick onto their backs and dive away, and because they were quicker in the dive and there might be some more up in the sun waiting to dive on you, you did not follow. And then you would look around for the rest of the party and for miles in every direction there would not be a single aircraft in sight.

Dennis Armitage.

The twenty-three pilots of the squadron who went south were quickly reduced to nine, and within the space of a few days Armitage was promoted from Junior Flight Commander to Acting Squadron Leader. He too did not escape unscathed, as he later recalled:

> There had been the usual shemozzle which had eventually sorted itself out into one or two Spitfires and three or four Me 109s buzzing round in tight circles, and I had just had the pleasure of seeing the three I had been closeted with diving down towards the sea with one of them smoking nicely. Another 'possible', perhaps even a 'probable', but not a 'confirmed' because I was not silly enough to follow him down in case there was another waiting for me up in the sun – and there was. I have no idea how he slipped under my tail, but suddenly I heard a loud explosion, something hit me on my left leg, and there was a terrifying noise of rushing air. I whipped into a vertical turn, looking fearfully up towards the blazing sun and then, as confidence returned, I spotted what was probably the cause of the trouble diving away, already some 5,000 feet below. I realised the noise was simply due to the Perspex hood having been blown out by the explosion and, that apart, my machine seemed quite manageable. But my left leg was numb from the calf down. I put my hand down gingerly to feel if my foot was still there and, reassured on this point, I headed for home.

Although hobbling around on a stick, he continued to fly – 'fortunately there is no place other than bed where full use of the legs is so unimportant as in an aeroplane' – until the squadron was ordered to return north to reform. It was less than a month since it had set out from Wittering and by then was reduced to five pilots. When the squadron eventually rejoined the Battle, it formed part of the Duxford 'Big Wing' led by Douglas Bader, who had also found that legs were not so important in an aeroplane.

*

Geoffrey Page and Maurice Mounsdon had both been posted to No. 56 Squadron and were involved in the air battles from early June to August. In twelve days Page claimed three 'kills', but on 12 August his Hurricane was hit by fire from a Dornier and set ablaze. Suddenly his cockpit was an inferno:

> Fear became blind terror, then agonised horror as the bare skin of my hands gripping the throttle and control column shrivelled up like burnt parchment under the intensity of the blast furnace temperature. Screaming at the top of my voice, I threw my head back to keep it away from the searing flames.

Somehow he managed to bale out over the Channel, but as he was descending 'the odour of my burnt flesh was so loathsome that I wanted to vomit'. When he hit the water it took a supreme effort with his injured hands to get free from the octopus-like grip of the parachute that was dragging him under. He was eventually picked up by an old tramp steamer and taken to the RAF's hospital at Halton. There, just before he lost consciousness, he caught sight of himself in the reflector mirrors of an over-hanging light and saw 'the hideous mass of swollen burnt flesh that had once been a face'.

From 25 July to 26 August, Maurice Mounsdon destroyed four enemy aircraft and damaged two others. However, on 31 August his Hurricane was shot down over Colchester and he was severely wounded, spending the next nine months in hospitals, some of the time at the Queen Victoria at East Grinstead for plastic surgery. Fortunately he survived, unlike Henry Goodwin who had joined No. 609 Squadron. On 14 August he vanished after his Spitfire was shot down off Bournemouth. Ten days later the body of the twenty-five-year-old was washed ashore on the Isle of Wight.

*

The Kiwi pilots John Bickerdike and Bill Hodgson had gone on to serve with No. 85 Squadron and also took part in the torrid air battles of that Spitfire summer. On 12 July 1940, Bickerdike shot down a German bomber while protecting a convoy, but ten days later he was killed in a flying accident near Debden. Hodgson's baptism of fire came on the 18 August when the squadron was scrambled to intercept around 200 Messerschmitts and Dorniers. He shot two down and damaged another. Then, out of ammunition, he was chased home by thirty Me 110s. In the following two weeks he shot down or damaged twelve enemy aircraft, earning the nickname 'Ace Hodgson'.

Bill Hodgson.

On 31 August, the squadron engaged thirty Dornier 215s, escorted by about 100 enemy fighters. Hodgson made a head-on attack on one of the Dorniers, inflicting heavy damage on it, and then shot down an Me 109. In the turmoil his own Hurricane was hit and set on fire, but as he was over a densely populated area and near to oil tanks at Thames Haven, he resisted the urge to bale out and instead took the riskier option of crash-landing in a field in Essex. He emerged unhurt and was then royally entertained by officers of the 2nd Glasgow Highlanders who got him 'tanked'. 'Boy, they treated me well,' he recorded in his flying log.

On 1 September alone, seven fellow pilots were killed or wounded, and the exhausted squadron was then withdrawn to the north, where in October he was awarded a DFC. The following year he hitched a lift in one of the first Douglas-Havoc night-fighters to reach the unit. It is thought that a nose panel flew off, jamming the rudder and causing the plane to crash. The three men on board – all Battle of Britain veterans – were killed outright. When their funeral cortège left Debden Camp a few days later, the roads were lined with airmen, among them other members of 'The Few', including the squadron commander Peter Townsend.

Meanwhile the Canadian Keith Ogilvie had arrived at No. 609 Squadron as the replacement for Henry Goodwin, his fellow pilot at the Meir unit. Known as 'Skeets' or 'Oggy', he had formerly been the star kicker on the football field for Ottawa University. Now he was to shine in an altogether different sphere. On the 7 September, flying a Spitfire over West London, he shot down an Me 109 and claimed an Me 110 as a 'probable'. On 15 September – now celebrated

Keith Ogilvie (extreme left) and other pilots of 609 Squadron welcome representatives of the foreign press.

as Battle of Britain Day – he took part in one of the most notable episodes of the battle, during which Buckingham Palace came under attack from a Dornier 17. Ogilvie shot up the plane, which was then set on fire by the Czech Jan Kaucky of No. 310 Squadron before Cheshire-born Ray Holmes of No. 504 Squadron delivered the *coup de grâce* by ramming it – a truly international effort. The bomber crashed in the forecourt of Victoria station, while Holmes' Hurricane came down in Buckingham Palace Road. Ogilvie was credited with a third of the 'kill' and received the congratulations of Queen Wilhelmina of the Netherlands, in exile in London, who had witnessed the action. A DFC soon followed – and nearly four years in a prisoner-of-war camp.

*

Also in action that autumn was Trevor Oldfield, who had joined No. 92 Squadron at Biggin Hill. After some inconclusive skirmishing, the real action began for him on 27 September when the squadron was scrambled three times, each time engaging the enemy with losses on both sides. During the second scramble at midday, Oldfield was detailed to weave above the squadron, from which position he saw it split up and attack the enemy. His combat report gave this account of the engagement that followed:

> Owing to my being above the squadron, I was able to turn sharply to the left and attacked an Me 109 from quarter astern. I saw pieces fly off the enemy aircraft near to the wing roots after I had given him a 3-second burst. I had

Trevor Oldfield.

only time to see him half roll and dive away before I spun out. I could not see whether the aircraft crashed, but about two minutes later I saw someone making a parachute descent.

He subsequently claimed his first victory, but during the third scramble of the day he was himself shot down and killed, his Spitfire hurtling violently onto Hesketh Park in Dartford. Eyewitnesses believed that he had stayed with the plane to avoid houses in the area. A typed copy of his earlier combat report had to remain unsigned.

Hugh Sharpley had been operational with No. 234 Squadron from July 1940 and claimed several victories. In November, however, a fortnight after he had unexpectedly turned up at the family home at Hanchurch on a brief leave, his father received the dreaded telegram that reported him 'missing, believed killed'. It was later confirmed that his Spitfire had dived into the sea off the coast of Cornwall. He was thirty. His name is recorded on the Runnymede Memorial (for those with no known grave) and on the small war memorial that stands in the cemetery at Trentham.

In October 1940, Vernon Page was posted to No. 610 Squadron and came through the last weeks of the Battle of Britain unscathed.

*

During this fraught period, the most exciting thing to have happened to 'Sawn Off' – Eric Lock – was his marriage in July 1940 to Peggy Meyers, a former 'Miss Shrewsbury'. Apart from that, as a member of No. 41 Squadron, he had been languishing for the most part at Catterick, North Yorkshire, while the battle raged in the south. That all changed on 3 September when the squadron flew their Spitfires into RAF Hornchurch, close to the Thames estuary. Two days later they were unleashed into the action.

It was a day of frantic activity. In his first patrol over Maidstone, Lock joined a formation of Me 109s and shot two of them down. After landing, the squadron was scrambled almost immediately to confront a large bomber force with its covering fighters. In his combat report Lock recorded the ferocious dogfight that followed:

> I engaged an enemy Heinkel 111 which crashed into the river. [...] I climbed back to 8,000 feet and saw another Heinkel, which had left the main formation. I engaged same, and his starboard engine was set on fire. I closed in to about 75 yards and fired two long bursts and smoke came from the fuselage. [...] I then stopped firing and followed him down. I was then attacked by an Me 109, who fired at me from below and wounded me in the leg. As he banked away, he stall turned. I fired at him and he exploded in mid-air.

In one day the 'world's worst pupil' had claimed four 'kills' plus one probable – more than most fighter pilots would claim during the entire war.

His first DFC was awarded on 1 October, which cited the fact that he had destroyed 'nine enemy aircraft, eight of these within a period of one week'. Three weeks later he was awarded a Bar to his DFC, the citation now referring to the destruction of 'fifteen enemy aircraft within a period of nineteen days'. Despite his late start in the battle, he rapidly became one of its top-scoring pilots and was lionised in the press. However, on 17 November, after shooting down two more Me 109s, he was himself seriously wounded and forced to crash-land. He was to spend the following four months in hospital with cannon-shell wounds in his arms and legs. Part of this time was spent at the Queen Victoria Hospital where he shared a ward with Maurice Mounsdon.

While still in hospital, he became the youngest officer of the war to be awarded a Distinguished Service Order (DSO) – the citation now referring to 'at least twenty-two' enemy aircraft that he had destroyed. On 1 April 1941, just before his own twenty-second birthday, he had recovered sufficiently to attend an investiture at Buckingham Palace where, uniquely, he collected all three of his decorations at the same time. 'Will you be flying again soon?' asked the King. 'I think I will, sir,' he replied, and at the end of June he did return to active service as a Flight Lieutenant with No. 611 Squadron. On 3 August 1941, he failed to return from a sortie over France. His body was never recovered.

Eric Lock.

15

The Potteries Invaded

Accidents continued to happen on and around the Meir site, due to the bad weather, the industrial haze of the Potteries, and pilot error. One Magister buried itself in the roof of a house in Sandon Road; another spun into the airfield, killing both pilots; a Blenheim crashed on landing; a Tiger Moth came down at the Broadway. Ron Rushton remembered a Spitfire going in too low over George Avenue and clipping its undercarriage on a chimney or a power line, flipping the aircraft on its back. He later saw it from Meir Railway Bridge, upside down on the embankment. The pilot had been killed.

The frenetic activity of yesteryear was, however, already winding down. The Battle of Britain had been won, and it was announced that those who had given their lives were to be honoured at the war's end with a permanent memorial in Westminster Abbey.

As if to symbolise the victory, the wreckage of a Messerschmitt was put on show in Huntbach's car park, Hanley, in November 1940 – 'admission to view 6d, the proceeds going to the Lord Mayor's Charities'. The weather also intervened, with thick fog, torrential rain, and then snow severely curtailing flying activities until the following spring. Some trainees used the time to visit local pottery manufacturers and mines; other pilots willingly supported the 'Spitfire Funds' sponsored by towns and cities eager to buy one of Mitchell's planes for the nation. Stafford, Leek, and Stone raised the necessary £5,000 and named their aircraft *The Staffordian, The Spirit of Leek,* and *The Star of Stone* respectively. Newcastle meanwhile organised a mile of shillings to help pay for theirs.

That autumn Ted Eley staged the show *Sunday Night on Broadway* – at the Broadway Cinema – in aid of the city's fund. The two hours' entertainment featured his Red Carnations Concert Party, and Mr Eley compered the proceedings, during which a tea-set was sold by auction to RAF officers from the aerodrome. They immediately organised a competition with the tea-set as the prize. Afterwards, in a brief ceremony, Flying Officer W. G. Rayne and Flight Lieutenant E. L. Purdy presented the proceeds to the manager, thereby increasing the amount raised that day to £185.

The bombing of Shelton and Chesterton in December 1940 gave added impetus to donors large and small. At Shelton there were several fatalities, including children, but the Chesterton bombing was the most destructive raid on North Staffordshire during the war, in which sixteen people were killed and many injured. One elderly lady turned up with a bagful of coins for the city's fund and said, 'For years I have been saving them to divorce my husband, but that man Hitler is more wicked.'

The New Year began bleakly. On 5 January 1941, a pilot who had baled out was seen descending into the icy waters of the Thames estuary. Rescue attempts by boats in the area failed, but personal belongings picked up identified the pilot. It was Amy Johnson on another assignment for the Air Transport Auxiliary. 'Wonderful Amy' was gone, her body never found. She was thirty-seven, the first member of the ATA to be killed.

A morale-boosting visit took place on 10 March 1941 when the Inspector General of Flying Training, Sir William Mitchell, inspected the airfield accompanied by Air Commodore B. E. Baker. He then visited No. 239 Squadron of the recently formed Air Training Corps (ATC) at Longton High School in nearby Sandon Road. The scheme had been introduced by the Air Ministry the previous January in order to mobilise boys (and later girls) aged between sixteen and eighteen as an aid to recruitment. Stoke-on-Trent had been the first authority in the country to seek information regarding the new scheme and had inaugurated it locally in the same month as it was formed. Members of the committee running the scheme included Leslie Irving and Captain Wilf Green of the aero club and Wing Commander N. H. Woodhead, Commanding Officer of RAF Meir. Cadets were soon being offered privileged visits to the airfield, thereby forging a link that would last for many years to come.

On arrival, Sir William was welcomed by the Headmaster and Acting Commanding Officer, Mr M. V. Gregory, who introduced him to the various acting officers and instructors, several of whom had served with the RAF. Four flights were operating at the school, made up of 170 young men, and Sir William saw two flights in action – one engaged in physical training, the other in mathematics and Morse. He declared that he had been very impressed by what he had seen and by the keenness of the lads, who no doubt wished to emulate illustrious old boys like the Battle of Britain pilots George Bennions and Ralph Carnall, or the bomber pilots Bob Genno and Francis Finney, whose exploits were featured in the news throughout the war.

Another pilot who was making the news locally was Roy Beaston. Already an experienced fighter and bomber pilot, he was about to go to one of the dominions as a test pilot and instructor. On Sunday 18 May, he flew back to the Potteries in an American Lockheed Hudson and came in low over his home in Trentham Road – so low that residents came to their doors concerned that he was in trouble or lost. There was no need to worry. Sergeant Beaston was merely dropping a message for his father asking him to pick him up in the car at the airfield. Although the message landed in the next-door garden, his father was soon on his way. Meanwhile Sergeant Beaston had touched down in one of the largest planes yet seen at the aerodrome.

*

Despite so much military activity, an air of complacency was becoming evident in certain parts of the region. Although the Potteries had already come under air attack several times – in one raid seventy-four incendiary bombs had been dropped close to the airfield – residents of Meir had grown very slack in observing the blackout, according to Chief Inspector Edge at the Longton Police Courts when a number of them were fined for various infringements. A reminder that the threat of invasion had not disappeared was needed, and it was therefore timely that in the summer of 1941 – just days after the German offensive against the Soviet Union – North Staffordshire should be at the centre of one of the largest mock invasions ever held in the provinces.

It ran from 3 p.m. on Saturday, 12 July, to noon on the following day (though local inhabitants were assured that it would not interfere with sports fixtures or the opening of places of amusement on the Saturday!). Experience of blitzed areas at home and invasion strategies abroad had been drawn on to make sure that the operation was as comprehensive and realistic as possible. Phase One – an extensive civil defence exercise – began with heavy air raids, in which high explosive and incendiary bombs were assumed to have been dropped over a wide area of Stoke-on-Trent. Tunstall was the scene of the first attack when a garage was 'hit', resulting in petrol igniting, fractured water, gas, and electricity mains, a blocked road, and an overturned bus. Fourteen people had been 'wounded', with civilians making the most of their bit parts as casualties. The incident, typical of

A local store advertises its blackout material.

many about to be played out throughout the Potteries and Newcastle, immediately involved firemen, wardens, special police, rescue parties, ambulances, and first-aid units, not to mention emergency rest centres and mobile canteens.

Within hours the Potteries was said to be 'ablaze'. Streets were blocked or cordoned off because of 'unexploded bombs'; railway bridges were reported demolished, houses, schools, shops, and cinemas devastated with the occupants buried beneath. In Newcastle, the Town Hall 'collapsed' when a delayed-action bomb exploded. Two collieries had also been bombed, bringing into play their own fire-fighting and ARP services. Only a handful of planners knew how events would unfold and they were determined to put the defenders under the most extreme pressure. Static water supplies were suddenly put 'out of action', forcing fire-fighters to improvise. Telephone communications then went down, necessitating the dispatch of girl cyclists with urgent messages. In the early evening gas bombs were dropped – in reality tear gas – and there was some panicky fumbling as people tried to don their respirators in time. Some had forgotten them, and there were many streaming eyes in Hanley's Market Square. One young lady was seen wiping away tears under the government's poster *Hitler Will Send No Warning* that urged everyone to carry a gas-mask. By this time – another grimly realistic touch – long lists of casualties were appearing outside the town halls.

So overwhelming had been the 'attack' that the mutual aid scheme was activated whereby substantial reinforcements could be rushed in from elsewhere. But exacting as it was, the conventional air attack was merely the prelude to Phase Two – the invasion itself – that began with the landing of 'parachutists' during the night, and was aided by fifth-columnists and saboteurs who had infiltrated into the district some days before. The 'invaders', consisting of 700-800 men of the regular army, were a 'rough lot' whose cunning was matched by their ruthlessness. They commandeered cars and buses in an attempt to seize key points quickly, but were opposed at every turn by men of the Home Guard backed up by other regular units.

Martial law was proclaimed by Colonel W. Greene, the Military Commander, and no quarter was asked for or given. Fists and rifle butts were used freely in skirmishes in Longton, 'rare scraps' occurred in Glebe Street, Stoke, while Kidsgrove and Etruria had some nasty surprises in store for the enemy. Some civilians entered enthusiastically into the spirit of the occasion and turned amateur sleuths, sniffing out 'spies' and 'fifth columnists'; others complained of delays and being constantly harassed to produce identity cards. A few seemed to believe that the invasion really was happening. An old lady was at the booking office window at Stoke station when Captain Shenton fired a blank from his revolver as a signal to the defenders. She immediately fled, leaving ticket and money behind, and was last seen haring down Station Road. It was as well that she did not witness the 'pitched battle' that followed, which spread further afield and led to the occupation of Stoke Town Hall. By then the Lord Mayor, Town Clerk and all important papers and seals of office had been whisked away to a secret headquarters.

At the close of hostilities there was time for the participants to lick their wounds – or in the case of Captain Eric Carhart to have four stitches inserted in a gash above his eye that he sustained in a brisk engagement at Hanley police station. The overall verdict of the umpires who had been ever present was that victory had gone to the defenders. Others felt it had been too close to call.

Among German documents seized at the end of the war was one entitled *Stadtplan von Stoke-on-Trent* (1942). This map of the city showed not only every street, railway station, and factory, but farms, churches, disused pitshafts, and even allotments. It was one of the preparations for an invasion that never came.

*

Censorship prohibited any mention of the airfield and so it is unknown what part, if any, it played in the exercise – though it may well have dispatched a few low-flying aircraft to mimic the dive-bombers that were supposed to be active. With armed soldiers at the gates, machine-gun posts inside, and several hundred RAF personnel trained to reinforce the military guard if necessary, it was already fully prepared for any attack, real or simulated. Life at the base was in any case dangerous enough without any external threat – that July alone five airmen were killed and four others injured.

Among those pilots still undergoing their initial training was Edward Sniders, for whom 13 May 1941 was the red-letter day when he took to the air for the first time. 'For two months,' he recalled, 'we flew wonderful little Miles Magisters, monoplanes, with our heads in the air behind the windscreens and lots of aerobatics.' He went on to gain his wings and qualify as a bomber pilot. Two years later he was flying a Mosquito, the fastest British aircraft then in operation, in sorties over Cologne, Hamburg, and Munich as part of the famous No. 139 Squadron.

Another of Desmond Plunkett's protégés who trained at Meir in July of that year was Colin Cole Jerromes, from Rubery, near Bromsgrove. He too was posted to Bomber Command and served with several squadrons, including No. 218, flying Stirlings. On two separate occasions in 1942, he went on to complete bombing missions despite having one of his engines out of action. He was twice mentioned in dispatches and awarded a DFC for gallantry and devotion to duty. Later he was engaged in clandestine Lysander operations to occupied Europe, about which little is known even today.

In August 1941, a twenty-two-year-old American pilot from one of the Eagle Squadrons flew to Meir with a British colleague to visit six pits in the area. They timed their visits to coincide with the beginning or end of the shifts and went into the pithead baths or winding gear shops to speak to groups of miners. Their message was simple: 'We fighter pilots need more coal to build more fighter airplanes.' After their pep-talk, one of the miners started talking

Trainee pilots and instructors at No. 5 EFTS at Meir in 1941 include Colin Cole Jerromes (back row, second from left) and Desmond Plunkett (front row, fourth from left).

about coal-mining, and 'very soon', recalled the American, 'he was giving the pep-talk to me, not me to him.' As a result an invitation to spend a complete shift at the coal face was offered and readily accepted. 'I would sooner be in the air than down a mine,' said the American. 'But I will go down your deepest pit, stay with you men for a whole shift and tell the airmen – and, of course, America – how you work. We pilots realise how dependent we are on you colliers.'

He kept his word and on a return visit in October went down one of the Chatterley-Whitfield Collieries and then broadcast to America about his experience. 'Instead of going up on patrol today,' he said, 'I went underground – down a coal mine. Yeah, a real coal mine, 1,500 below sea level and not a bit of cloud cover in sight. It was one of the grandest experiences of my life to go down that mine and work alongside those guys, who are doing one of the toughest, most vital jobs in this war.' After vividly describing the hazards faced daily by the miners, the pilot ended: 'No eight-gun Hurricane, no battleships or tanks with fancy names in this industry. Just a lot of dirty coal-tubs and some sticks of explosive. No uniform or medals for these guys. Just a pair of dirty trousers and coal dust and sweat. No sir, give me a Hurricane any day. I'm not tough enough to be a miner.'

*

With the immediate crisis over, many pilots were now being sent abroad for instruction. Typical of them were John Watson Foster, from Belfast, and Christopher William House, from Brecon, South Wales, who were posted from Meir to Moose Jaw, Canada, where they both qualified as fighter pilots. In October 1941, No. 5 EFTS was downgraded from its Class A status to Class B, which meant fewer aircraft and fewer students. Desmond Plunkett managed to get himself transferred from instructing to active service, and was posted to RAF Lyneham for training as a bomber pilot. He did though fly back to Meir in a borrowed Avro Tutor in November for his wedding to Patricia Wildblood, a local girl, at Longton Methodist church. From the airfield he thumbed a lift with some factory workers who, hearing he was about to be married, plied him with Guinness. He just made the ceremony, well-lubricated, and afterwards the happy couple left for a brief honeymoon – by train. Six months later he was shot down over Holland and taken prisoner.

Shortly after the Japanese attack on Pearl Harbour, No. 5 EFTS finally reached the end of its useful life. It was closed on 23 December, its instructors posted elsewhere, and the RAF presence was much diminished. Some of Stoke's earlier Volunteer Reservists continued to lead remarkable lives, however. The wireless operator Vic Reynolds had first seen active service with No. 206 Squadron before being posted to the Gambia to help form the new No. 200 Squadron. In January 1942, instead of taking off on a routine operation, their Hudson ploughed into a Blenheim and several other aircraft. Reynolds forced open a door and got three Army officers swiftly out as the plane was engulfed in flames. A few months later he had an even closer shave when their Hudson was shot down by troops loyal to the Vichy regime, and, wounded by shrapnel in both legs, he was held captive for a time.

His contemporary John Waite had a remarkably similar experience with No. 120 Squadron. Early in the New Year, he was one of the crew of a Liberator that was preparing to take off. What happened next was graphically described in the official account of the action:

One night in February 1942, an aircraft loaded for an operational sortie crashed during the take-off. Sergeant Waite, a member of the crew, was thrown clear some 20 yards in front of the aircraft, which was on fire. He was told by another survivor to run from the scene as fast as he could, as the high explosives on board the aircraft were likely to detonate at any moment.

Sergeant Waite, although injured about the face, back, and leg, ignored this advice and, with complete disregard of danger, went to the blazing wreckage and extricated the observer, who was lying on the floor of the aircraft in the flames.

Having extricated the observer, Sergeant Waite carried him for about 100 yards, then got him through a barbed-wire fence and, finally, behind the shelter of a ditch just as the explosives blew up.

Vic Reynolds (seated, second left) is seen as a member of the University of London Air Squadron on 4 August 1944.

In circumstances of exceptional danger, this airman, although himself seriously wounded, displayed great bravery. Unfortunately, the observer whom he had so courageously rescued died some three days later.

In October 1942, at a ceremony at Buckingham Palace, Sergeant Waite was presented with the George Medal by the King, the first time any North Staffordshire airman had received the award.

Throughout 1942 there was little activity at the airfield at Meir, although No. 45 Gliding School was established there in August, one of the first gliding schools of the Air Training Corps. At the time the Air Ministry could offer scant support, and the first glider at the school was cobbled together from three damaged machines requisitioned from the Lancashire and Derbyshire Gliding Clubs. Two scrap barrage balloon winches were then made serviceable and adapted for towing purposes.

In its early years all training at the school was done solo in single-seater gliders, novices being taught to fly in a series of hops near the ground and allowed to fly only in a straight line across the aerodrome from a height of about 100 feet. Reg Bott, who had been born at Burslem, recalled his own experiences there as an eighteen-year-old cadet:

We used a Dagling glider, which was essentially an open keel with an overhead mainplane and bucket seat. In spite of its primitive appearance,

The wife of Sergeant John Waite admires the George Medal he has just received at an investiture at Buckingham Palace.

it had the essential controls for learning basic flight. It was towed between a pair of barrage balloon winches located on opposite sides of the airfield. After adequate practice doing low hops, we were eventually winched up to about 200 feet or so at which point we pulled the release and enjoyed flying the craft back to earth.

I remember one occasion when I was towed from a position near the entrance of the airfield towards the boundary on the town side of the field. I have an image of getting too close to the edge of the airfield with houses just beyond the fence, and my landing between the fence and a large concrete emergency water tank, quite safely but with more luck than judgement perhaps. It was definitely no sailplane but we were happy and as far as I know there were no accidents.

Despite these small beginnings, the school proved to be outstandingly successful under its Commanding Officer, Flight Lieutenant Bill Nadin, a First World War fighter pilot. Each year it passed out more cadets than any of the other 53 ATC gliding schools in the British Isles, and in its first 4½ years, 400 cadets and a dozen instructors made a total of 20,153 launches without mishap. By then the school possessed seven gliders ranging from a primary training machine to a sailplane suitable for soaring. It had also received a letter of commendation from the Air Council. Although RAF Meir was undergoing many changes, the school would remain at the airfield for the next twenty years, an unbroken link with its military past.

16

Wings for Victory

In April 1943, Stoke-on-Trent's 'Wings for Victory Week' was by far the city's biggest war savings effort to date. During the same campaign, other towns and cities had saved for a variety of aircraft – Stirling bombers featured in Stafford's advertisements – but for the people of the Potteries only one aircraft could be considered. Their target was a staggering £1,500,000 to provide 300 Spitfires, and the spectacular nature of the events that were organised merited comparison with those of the Josiah Wedgwood celebrations thirteen years before. An ambitious programme included 'Wings for Victory' dances at four Town Halls, RAF bands playing in local parks, and a concert at the Theatre Royal in Hanley given by RAF personnel with Kitty Masters, star of radio and stage, as guest artist. In the days leading up to the opening, Spitfires were displayed in all six towns of the city – at Fenton (Town Hall Square), Burslem (St John's Square), Tunstall (Market Square), Longton (Stafford Street car park) and Hanley (Market Square) – the largest number on view in any city in the country.

The sixth Spitfire was on the stage of the King's Hall, Stoke, the centre-piece of a superlative display by the RAF and Fleet Air Arm (for which admission was free, souvenir programme 6d). 'It is an exhibition of remarkable scope,' stated the *Sentinel*, 'certainly the most effective ever staged in this district, and probably one of the most fascinating that has ever been assembled in the country.' Students from the Burslem School of Art had decorated the hall in the RAF colours and had reproduced the RAF crest above the Spitfire on the stage. Painted on the front of the balcony, which was illuminated by red, white, and blue lamps, were the roundels of the Royal Air Force, and over the balcony a single-seater glider had been fixed. From the high ceiling a dummy airman could be seen 'parachuting' to safety, while just inside the main entrance was a dinghy of the type that had saved so many pilots from a watery grave, with an invitation to visitors to throw coins into it as contributions to the RAF Benevolent Fund. Here too was the special stall for the Reginald Mitchell Memorial Appeal that had recently been launched by the Lord Mayor. It was hoped to raise in the region of £100,000 in order to erect the Mitchell Memorial Youth Centre, a model of which was on display.

Left: Stoke's 'Wings for Victory Week' appropriately featured the Spitfire.

Below: A contemporary sketch gives an impression of the 'Wings for Victory' display at the King's Hall, Stoke.

A series of bays along the sides of the hall demonstrated how airmen were trained, how they carried out their duties on operational flights, and how a whole range of ground and air equipment supported them in their endeavours. Enclosed in the cockpit of a Link trainer, visitors could 'fly' like any novice pilot and share the sensations of climbing, spinning, and stalling – all without leaving the ground! They could then go on to see a complete panel of the wireless equipment of a typical modern bomber – and send messages to another part of the hall where the rear gun turret of such a bomber was installed. Other stands displayed the powerful engines of various planes, such as the 9-cylinder Pegasus engine used in Swordfish and Walrus aircraft and the famous Merlin, standard not only in the Spitfire but in almost every single-seater fighter in the RAF.

Other areas contained a working model of the Wellington's bomb beam and bomb panel; a plane-repairing display; and a full range of model aircraft built to scale of British, American, and German planes. Down the centre of the hall were ranged bombs of every description – from grenades and parachute mines to aerial torpedoes. The largest bomb of all – an operational 4,000 pounder – was conveniently situated next to the Savings Stamp stall so that visitors could buy stamps to stick on the bomb, knowing that it would shortly be on its way to Germany. As he travelled to the aerodrome to welcome the distinguished guest who was flying in to open the proceedings the next day, the Lord Mayor (Alderman C. Austin Brook) may have recalled the cancellation of the RAF visit that he had organised eight years before because of such fearsome weapons being brought to the city. Times had indeed changed.

His overnight guest was Air Marshal Sir Trafford Leigh-Mallory, who had commanded 12 Group during the Battle of Britain and was now head of Fighter Command. The following day, Saturday, 10 April, while a huge crowd was assembling for the ceremonial opening, he inspected a guard of honour of local members of the Air Training Corps, accompanied by Flight Lieutenant A. E. Hewitt, Commander of the Stoke-on-Trent Wing of the ATC. Then, in a speech declaring the exhibition open, Leigh-Mallory at once paid tribute to the designer of the Spitfire. He, if anyone, knew just how much was owed to the man and to the plane:

Mitchell was quite certain in his own mind that we had this war coming to us, and he was determined that England should have the finest fighter aircraft in the world. He set himself that task, and you know he fought against all difficulties of one kind and another and, by indomitable spirit, he overcame all of them. His was an example of selfless desire – he actually ruined his own health through it – and I feel that a city which has produced such a man as that will carry the thing through to the end and give us every assistance in its power, right to the very end of the war.

Air Marshal Sir Trafford Leigh Leigh-Mallory, Chief of Fighter Command, taking the salute during the **Stoke parade.**

A smart naval contingent who helped to swell the ranks of the fighting services in the procession.

Top: Air Marshal Sir Trafford Leigh-Mallory takes the salute during the great 'Wings for Victory' parade at Stoke. *Centre*: A naval contingent marches past. *Bottom*: Sir Trafford at the opening of the RAF exhibition.

(The idea perpetuated here that Mitchell had somehow worked himself to death on the Spitfire had been popularised by the film *The First of the Few*, which made no mention of cancer. It was a notion that Mitchell would have found risible, for he had been accustomed to hard work and extremely long days from a young age. It could just as well be argued that it was his determination to see the Spitfire project through that kept him going.)

Adding colour and pageantry to the official opening was the massive parade that followed. With Leigh-Mallory taking the salute at the Cenotaph just outside the hall, personnel from each of the armed services – including a contingent of US troops – marched from Hanley to Stoke, together with units from the Women's Royal Naval Service, the Women's Auxiliary Air Force, the Home Guard, the Civil Defence, the St John's Ambulance Brigade, the British Red Cross Society, the Women's Voluntary Service, the British Legion, the Old Contemptibles' Association, the ex-Naval and Marines' Association, and Sea, Army, and Air Force cadets. A Spitfire, turrets from RAF bombers, and anti-aircraft guns also formed part of the parade.

Representatives of the Fire Service (one of whose members had been killed after being sent to the aid of Coventry in November 1940) brought up the rear with their mobile units and trailer pumps. So long was the procession – it stretched for more than two miles with over 7,000 people and five bands involved – that as the leading ranks were passing the saluting base outside the King's Hall some detachments were still waiting to set off from Hanley. It was undoubtedly the greatest parade ever seen in the city. At the end of what had been a momentous day, the Lord Mayor accompanied Leigh-Mallory back to the airfield to see him off. 'I well remember him leaning out of the aircraft and waving goodbye as he left the aerodrome at Meir,' he later recalled. They were never to meet again. The following year a plane carrying the Air Marshal crashed in the French Alps. No one survived.

Over the weekend that followed 25,000 people visited the exhibition, and by the time it was formally reopened on Monday, 12 April, more than £500,000 had already been raised. The celebrated guest that day was none other than Jean Batten, New Zealand's world-famous pioneer aviator, a friend and rival of Amy Johnson's. Like Leigh-Mallory before her, she lost no time in expressing her admiration for the area's most renowned son:

> I consider it an honour to reopen the "Wings for Victory" exhibition in the city where Mr Reginald Mitchell spent his childhood. The people of Stoke-on-Trent need no further inspiration than that to spur them on to achieve and exceed their target. When the history of this war comes to be written, there will be a great chapter dedicated to the memory of Reginald Mitchell and his great work in helping to win the war. But for the heroism and devotion of the Air Force in the Battle of Britain we should have lost the freedom we love so much, the freedom without which life is meaningless.

Bill Astell.

A number of distinguished local pilots had also been invited to pay an official visit to the city during the week of the appeal. One of them, twenty-five-year-old Flight Lieutenant Leslie Rickinson, DFC, was another Old Longtonian often in the news. In a recent operation his plane had been badly mauled by a German fighter, the second pilot having a hand shot away in the attack, but Flight Lieutenant Rickinson still managed to bring the bomber home. Initially he had accepted the invitation, but at the last minute cancelled his visit, explaining that his duty had to take precedence. He continued to fly bombing missions with No. 101 Squadron and was killed shortly afterwards with most of his crew. He was buried in Amersfoort general cemetery in the Netherlands. In one of his last letters home he sent a donation for the 'Wings for Victory Week', which helped swell the amount raised to a triumphant £1,801,950 – the highest sum ever achieved by the city in any of its campaigns.

Just over a month later on 16 May, Operation Chastise, now better known as the Dam Busters' Raid, took place. No. 617 Squadron had practised for its attack over the Derwent Reservoir in Derbyshire, not far from Meir Aerodrome, and it is reported that some of its Lancasters visited the airfield at this time. Certainly one of its pilots, Flight Lieutenant Bill Astell, DFC, knew the aerodrome well, for he had carried out his initial training there as a member of the Volunteer Reserve in 1939. On the night of the raid, he was flying in Guy Gibson's formation to attack the Möhne Dam. However, on the way there his aircraft, flying at only 100 feet above ground, hit an electricity pylon and crashed in a ball of flame with the loss of all on board – one of eight planes that failed to return.

17

The Great Escape

By the time he was twenty-one, Ken Rees had flown fifty-six night missions over Germany, taken part in the siege of Malta, and been shot down over Norway. In November 1942, he arrived at Stalag Luft III, near the small town of Sagan in what is now western Poland. First impressions of the camp were bleak indeed: there were five miles of barbed-wire fencing, and every 100 yards stood a watch tower with a guard, a searchlight, and a machine gun. Dense black conifers surrounded the entire area and reinforced the overwhelming sense of isolation.

As he trudged through the gates, past the enormous Nazi flag flying from the flag-post, he was astounded to see the familiar face of Desmond Plunkett, his former instructor at Meir. Plunkett told him that he had joined No. 218 Squadron and his initial combat missions were the first of the 1,000 bomber raids on Cologne and Essen. On his third trip out, however, his Stirling had been set on fire over Holland and he had made his one and only parachute jump from an aircraft. Two other Meir 'graduates' were also there, the Canadian Spitfire ace Keith Ogilvie, shot down over France in 1941, and the New Zealander Clive Saxelby, who had recently baled out of his blazing bomber over Düsseldorf.

After surviving the Battle of Britain, Ogilvie had seen considerable further action by helping to provide a protective shield for bombers attacking targets in France. However, on 4 July 1941, on one of his final operations before he was rested, he came to grief. His own account tells of what happened:

Over North Foreland the bombers crawled in beneath us and wings of the fighters formed up ahead, behind, and on either side – an inspiring spectacle, and I never lost the thrill of being a part of the show. Far below we could see the white streaks as the air-sea rescue launches put out from Dover and Ramsgate. On crossing the Channel and progressing inland we were greeted by 'ack-ack', first at Dunkirk, then St. Omer. Away to the side tiny specks represented the wary Hun climbing so as to be above and behind us when we turned down-sun for home. We had already started when about fifteen 109s floated over us, breaking up into fours, then pairs. A pair came down to attack the bombers and I had turned in to attack them when there was one hell of a 'pow' and I was smacked into the dashboard, my port aileron floated away,

Keith Ogilvie (left) larks with fellow ace
'Teeny' Overton, DFC, shortly before he
was shot down.

and a great rip appeared up my wing. There was blood all over and I felt sick,
so I blew my hood off and turned the oxygen full on to keep awake. If I could
reach the Channel I'd bale out, because I could not land the kite as it was. But
I must have passed out because suddenly everything was quiet and through a
haze I could see my prop sticking straight up, and smoke coming from under
my cowling. I figured this is where I leave and let go of the stick. Sometime
later I came to in a field, surrounded by sympathetic Frenchies who tried to get
me up and away, but I could not make it. I had been hit twice in the arm, once
in the shoulder, and had lost too much blood. A little while later a sad-eyed
German informed me, 'For you the war is over' – and he was not kidding.

Ogilvie was in hospital for nine months and was then sent to Sagan. His
capture was obviously regarded as a coup by the Germans, as news of it
was broadcast by Lord Haw-Haw himself. It at least brought much relief to
Ogilvie's comrades, who thought that he had been killed.

Since leaving Meir, 'Big Sax' had led an apparently charmed life. A veteran
of more than 50 operational sorties, he had been awarded a DFC for 'his
coolness and skilful piloting under most hazardous conditions'. One occasion
specifically mentioned in his recommendation was the first thousand bomber
raid on Cologne, in which he too had taken part. In fact Saxelby's aircraft
was first over the target, and soon after he started for home a night fighter
pounced. Their situation instantly became precarious:

The second pilot was killed immediately and the rear gunner wounded. The
rear turret was shattered, the fuselage aft of the astro hatch set on fire, and the

hydraulics damaged, causing the undercarriage and bomb doors to fall down. In addition an oxygen tube in the second pilot's position caught fire, filling the system with choking fumes. F/Lt Saxelby with great skill managed to right his badly damaged aircraft at 6,000 feet. He was again attacked at this height, so decided to take his aircraft down to ground level and at 300 feet he finally managed to shake off the enemy fighter. He gave a magnificent example of courage and determination in bringing his badly damaged aircraft back to England. He made an excellent crash landing at Honington without further injury to his crew.

His luck finally ran out on the night of 7 September 1942 in an operation over Duisburg. As he approached the target, he was attacked by two fighters that killed the rear gunner and shot away the plane's elevators. The aircraft stalled and then went into a spin, with the surviving crew rushing to bale out. One of them escaped back to England, but the remainder were captured and became guests of the Third Reich. Saxelby was taken first to Dulag Luft, an interrogation centre at Frankfurt-am-Main where he celebrated his twenty-first birthday, and was then transferred to Sagan. Two months later Rees arrived, and in the New Year they were room-mates in the new North Compound.

Following in their flight path was another trainee from Meir, the Mosquito pilot Edward Sniders. On the night of 27 July 1943, on his way to Duisburg, his port engine failed but he continued on one engine to bomb the target. Almost immediately after he had turned for home, the port engine caught fire and he struggled to bale out, his parachute all but jamming in the hatch as the plane tilted into a dive.

As he floated down in complete darkness, he had no idea which country lay beneath him, but eventually discovered he was in Holland and made contact with the Dutch resistance. With its help, he crossed into Belgium and then into France, in the hope of being spirited away by Lysander. Unfortunately, the escape line had been penetrated by the Gestapo and he was arrested at a bistro where he was hiding. In August, he became an inmate of the Centre Compound at Stalag Luft III.

He did not intend to let the grass grow under his feet, especially since the famous 'wooden horse' episode shortly after his arrival showed that escape from the camp was possible. His own initial efforts were equally bold. As he was fluent in German, he first of all walked out dressed as a German carpenter; then he was engaged in several tunnelling ventures, one of which – from the latrines! – promised quick success. So much so that when he was invited to join a big escape from the North Compound, he declined, preferring his own smaller project. It was a decision that almost certainly saved his life.

What is now known as 'The Great Escape' went on without him. Ogilvie and Saxelby were engaged on the planning and organisational side; Rees was heavily involved in tunnelling; Plunkett (on whom Donald Pleasence's character was loosely based in the film) ran a section of fourteen men who produced hundreds of maps for the escapees, many of them tailor-made for the individual's escape route. On the night of the getaway – 24 March 1944 – he was the thirteenth man through the tunnel, as no one else wanted that number, and he had soon boarded a train at Sagan station with several other early escapees, including Roger Bushell, the charismatic mastermind of the breakout. Plunkett was then at large for two weeks, being one of the very last to be rounded up when he was only a day's travel from the Swiss border.

During the escape Rees was acting as a 'dispatcher', and among the escapees that he hauled through the tunnel were Ogilvie and Saxelby. By then, after numerous delays, fewer than half of those selected had made it to the surface. It was time to call a halt, and Saxelby brought an order for his room-mate. 'That's it. That's all,' he told Rees. 'You follow me out, all right?' Hearts racing with excitement, they had almost reached the exit shaft when a shot rang out. For an instant they froze. In the confusion on the surface, Ogilvie made a dash for the woods and disappeared, though he was free for only a day. In the tunnel Rees frantically started to scurry back like a mole, followed by Saxelby, whose six-foot frame threatened to bring a cave-in. When they finally emerged, Rees narrowly escaped being shot in the camp by an apoplectic guard. As he was marched off to the cooler, an automatic in the small of his back, he cursed his bad luck and envied the many friends who were even then enjoying the luxury of a brief moment of freedom. He had no inkling that he would never see most of them again.

Of the seventy-six PoWs who made it through the tunnel, only three evaded capture and returned to England. Of the remainder, fifty were subsequently murdered on Hitler's orders, an outrage denounced by the British government. Fortunately, both Ogilvie and Plunkett survived the massacre. After his recapture, Ogilvie was kept in a cell with three other escapees, all of whom were shot. Ogilvie, however, was returned to Stalag Luft III where he joined Rees in the cooler. Plunkett was kept in harrowing conditions in Gestapo prisons in Czechoslovakia, though he derived some comfort from the fact that the building used as the Gestapo Headquarters in Prague had urinals made in Stoke-on-Trent, his wife's home town. He was eventually taken to Stalag Luft I where he first learned of the massacre and, as a consequence, suffered a breakdown and almost committed suicide.

Just as his own tunnel was nearing completion, Sniders and all the other British officers were transferred from the Centre Compound to another camp 6 kilometres away. It was there that the Senior British Officer had them assembled and told of the massacre of their fellow pilots, who had been shot while 'attempting to escape'. (In reality, they had been taken to remote areas singly or in pairs and shot in the back of the head.) The impact of the news was stunning, as Sniders recorded: 'To us it was vast thunder, unimagined, huge as the Day of Wrath.' All theatricals and sports were suspended, and all escape attempts forbidden until further notice. In the meantime, the Germans were sent to Coventry.

The *Sentinel* reports the aftermath of The Great Escape.

On 13 April, all the PoWs paraded for a memorial service for their lost comrades. A defiant requiem was sung by the camp choir, followed by the poignant solemnity of the Last Post.

*

On 10 April, as if by way of reprisal, the Allies launched one of their greatest ever raids over Occupied Territory. The targets were five focal points in the railway systems of France and Belgium, and 900 planes pounded them with a record 3,600 tons of bombs in preparation for the invasion of Europe.

One of the pilots, twenty-seven-year-old George Anthony Davison, had been born and educated at Newcastle-under-Lyme. Before the war he worked as a director in his father's pottery company at Burslem and had begun flying with the North Staffordshire Aero Club. After marrying Miss Betty Leach from Meir, he took up residence there in Weston Road, not far from the aerodrome. As soon as war was declared, he enlisted as an aircraftman and was commissioned in 1941. Now, a Flight Lieutenant with No. 576 Squadron, he flew his Lancaster in the attack on Aulnoyne, a rail junction on the Franco-Belgium border. The following day he gave a brief account of the action for readers of the *Sentinel*:

> There was little opposition on the outward trip. On arrival at Aulnoyne there was some flak. Our rear gunner saw good fires in the target area.
>
> Fighter activity began soon after we left and was intense all the way to the French coast.
>
> Ground defences were also more lively and there was plenty of flak and also a big searchlight belt just before we got to the Channel.

The German response had in fact been ferocious. Twenty-two planes were reported lost.

A few weeks later, on 6 June 1944, came the D-Day landings, and by 9 June convoys of wounded commandos from the Normandy beaches were arriving at the North Staffordshire Royal Infirmary and other local hospitals. Engaged in these momentous events was Pilot Officer John Rathbone, who eleven years earlier had flown from Meir to take an aerial photograph of his school at Oakhill. He had since achieved his long-standing ambition to join the RAF and was flying operations in support of the landings. On 15 June, he was killed in action over northern France and buried in Valenciennes communal cemetery, another corner of a foreign field.

*

From 13 June onwards, German reprisals came in the sinister form of 'pilotless aeroplanes' or 'robot planes' as they were called (later known as the V1 and V2). Such actions led the comedy duo Elsie and Doris Waters to comment that 'Hitler is getting wild; he is throwing his toys out of his pram.'

That autumn, the daring but ill-fated Battle of Arnhem was raging, and the surviving paras had to attempt a 'great escape' of their own. On 20 September, Lance-Sergeant Jack Baskeyfield, of Burslem, serving with the First Airborne Division of the South Staffordshire Regiment, was killed when he single-handedly took on several German Tiger tanks. For his 'gallantry beyond praise', he was posthumously awarded the Victoria Cross – the only North Staffordshire recipient of the war.

Helping to provide air cover for the Red Devils was Geoffrey Page, back in action with a vengeance after recovering from the horrific burns he had sustained in the Battle of Britain. After D-Day he had been flying from captured airfields in France, and his tally of 'kills' had risen to fifteen – one for every operation he had had to endure. However, that September, after attacking ground positions close to the Arnhem bridgehead, he was hit by anti-aircraft fire and forced to crash-land, fracturing his back. For him, too, the war was over.

18

The Shadow Factory

Early in the conflict, the Ministry of Aircraft Production had earmarked the Meir site because the last of its aircraft 'shadow factories' was being built a short distance away at Blythe Bridge. This was eventually occupied by the Rootes Group and the control, maintenance, and camouflage of the airfield was vested in Rootes Securities Ltd in November 1942. A few months later the company took over the whole of the airport buildings from the RAF.

Aircraft production had begun in 1941, with five Blenheims a week. This number gradually increased to between fifty and sixty planes a week before production switched to Beaufighters in 1943. These aircraft were towed from the factory along Grindley Lane and into the airfield's flight sheds, ready for test flying by Major E. G. Shults before ferry pilots delivered them to RAF stations. A year later the workforce started to modify the Mustangs that were flown in and to assemble the Harvards that arrived in packing cases from America. During that year alone, 1,025 aircraft were built, assembled or modified at Meir. To accommodate the heavier and faster planes, a 1,000 yard concrete runway was constructed and in service by May 1942, which was extended to 1,400 yards in June 1944. By then the last Blenheim, EH517, had been completed and flown away on 6 June 1943; the last Beaufighter, KW416, was flown out in April 1944.

With production continuing on a three-shift system for 24 hours each weekday, staff welfare was also a priority, and various medical and social facilities were developed. The factory had its own surgery and fire-service; it ran two football teams and a hockey team; it organised dances, film shows, and other events; and it set up a social and athletic club in the building previously used as the North Staffordshire Aero Club's headquarters and more recently as the RAF mess. With slight alterations, the premises then comprised a squash court, billiards rooms, and a lounge with a licensed bar. Netball was also popular among the ladies during their lunch breaks.

In the main factory, a platform had been erected at the west end of the canteen, to which a proscenium was added, together with footlights and adjoining dressing rooms, to form a stage for ENSA productions, which could be broadcast to other parts of the factory. (ENSA – Entertainments National Service

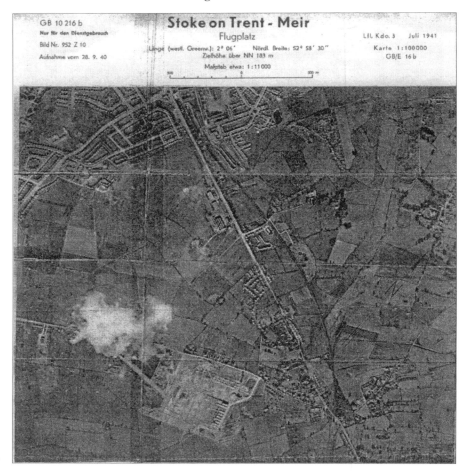

GB 10 216 b

Nur für den Dienstgebrauch

Bild Nr. 952 Z 10

Aufnahme vom 28. 9. 40

Stoke on Trent - Meir

Flugplatz

Länge (westl. Greenw.): 2° 06'   Nördl. Breite: 52° 58' 30"
Zielhöhe über NN 183 m

Maßstab etwa: 1:11000

Lfl. Kdo. 3   Juli 1941

Karte 1:100000
GB/E 16 b

The Rootes factory can be seen under construction in the bottom centre of this Luftwaffe reconnaissance photograph of September 1940.

Association – provided entertainment for troops and factories throughout the war. The acronym was popularly translated as 'Every Night Something Awful'.) The dining area also provided a suitable venue for special occasions such as the big drive by the factory's National War Savings Group during the 'Wings for Victory' Week in February 1943 (when over £10,000 was subscribed) or the 'Health Week' that was promoted for all staff in October 1944. During the latter event the canteen was decorated with flags, bunting, and hanging baskets of flowers, while a 'Health Week' banner was hoisted on the flagstaff at the main entrance. Various films were shown (including one discreetly entitled *Subject for Discussion*, which dealt with venereal disease) and the week ended with a Brains' Trust with a panel of doctors and Sir Ralph Wedgwood as Question Master.

The factory's own Home Guard unit was formed in February 1942, under the command of Major Shults. This eventually increased in number to 450, split into six platoons. Its sole function was to protect the airfield and factory from occupation or sabotage by enemy parachutists, and a number of its men were available day and night, with a picquet also being maintained in a barracks room at the aerodrome at week-ends and when the factory was shut down. After a period of retraining, it was later converted to an anti-aircraft unit. Also on hand, as a security officer, was Sergeant Ernest Egerton, who in 1917 had single-handedly carried out an attack on enemy dug-outs at Passchendaele Ridge. For his 'gallantry beyond praise', he had been awarded the Victoria Cross.

Many of the female employees had started their working lives in local potbanks in the 1930s, earning – at fourteen – a wage of 3s a week. Their recruitment by Rootes meant that they had to learn a variety of totally different skills to fit them for work in any department of the factory. Some of them had probably never seen a plane before, now they were constructing them. Hilda Ridge, who had previously worked at Dennis's Pottery in Fenton, was engaged in spraying camouflage on Blenheim bombers and Mustangs. Another recalled how she had left a Longton potbank and became a skilled riveter, working on the Blenheim's bomb doors and the pilot's walkway. Once she was standing on the wing when she slipped and started to fall. Her wedding ring caught on part of the plane and left her suspended, with the men she was working with rushing to help her. 'My wedding ring was bent,' she said, 'but it saved my life.' When the first plane that she and the others had been working on was finished, they were all allowed to go to the airfield to watch it take to the skies for its maiden flight. Some locals were even taken up – Roy Harris recalled how as a boy of fourteen he flew in Blenheim K7161 from Meir.

Eric Clutton, a sixteen-year-old who worked at the flight sheds on the airfield during the latter part of the war, remembered the sheer variety of aircraft that landed at Meir from time to time – the P47 Thunderbolt, the then top secret Typhoon, the Fairey Barracuda, the Curtis Helldiver, the Martin Marauder – not to mention the gigantic Coastal Command Liberators that were somehow squeezed in. Air Marshal Trafford Leigh-Mallory seemed to have a penchant for German planes, for he arrived on one occasion in an Me 108, on another in a Fieseler Storch.

As someone who had been bitten by the 'flying bug' from an early age, Eric was in his element and was even able to 'run up and taxi a few Mustangs, even if it was not quite legal'. One such occasion almost led to disaster:

I never trust aircraft parking brakes due to a couple of incidents at Meir. I was directly involved in one when I was running the engine of a P51D Mustang. I had my head in the office with the canopy closed tight to keep out the cold wind and the rest of the universe when I felt the aircraft lurch forward. I ought to mention that we had probably a hundred or so Mustangs all parked in neat rows with just sufficient room between the rows to taxi the aircraft, so my panic reaction was to stand on the toe-brakes and slam

Two views from March 1942 of the No. 10 Factory at Blythe Bridge.
(1) The dope shop.

(2) The rear-fuselage department.

the throttle shut! The tail came up and I swear I looked down the nose at the grass until the tail fell back with a crash and everything went quiet. I crept out and went around to the nose and my propeller was only a foot behind the Mustang in the next row! A near miss caused by failure of the parking brake (or me not setting it right!).

Only a week later four or five ferry pilots came in to collect several Mustangs and off they went, weaving down the track, heading for the runway, each trying to see past that long Mustang nose. The pilot in the lead stopped, as did all the others – except the poor guy at the rear who must have been unsighted and caught at the wrong part of his weave, and with a sickening CRUNCH he ran into the aircraft ahead of him! His own Mustang was not too badly damaged, but the one he ran into was in a much worse way. The whole rear fuselage was twisted and wrinkled like a very coarse thread. The horizontal tail was now at an angle of about thirty degrees to the ground and the fabric-covered rudder had vanished! This was a real object lesson for me – a case of 'there but for the grace of God!'

A second such incident involving a Beaufighter – 'a magnificent and mighty machine somewhat resembling an aerial pitbull' – could have been much worse:

A small wooden hut at the side of the parking apron was used by various ground crew members to thaw out in the winter. It was also the home of a thriving card school, and one day a Beaufighter was undergoing engine testing on the other side of the parking apron, its two mighty 1400-hp Hercules radial engines really putting out lots of noise. One of the card players looked up in some annoyance and is reported to have said, 'If he revs that bugger much more he will be in here!' At that point the Beau overcame its brakes and headed straight for the hut, the engine tester apparently not immediately noticing the movement on the smooth concrete. The scene inside that small hut must have been like an early Keystone Kops movie – first one to the door was George, who happened to be of ample girth – too ample to fit through the door in his panic, making the other card players climb under and over him. Fortunately they all got out before the aircraft, still with its engines going full blast, hit the hut and the propellers reduced it to tiny fragments! [...] I kept finding bits of pin-up pictures all over the airfield for months afterwards.

It was not only planes that set the teenager's pulses racing. The women's section of the ATA had been set up on the outbreak of war under the command of Pauline Gower (who had performed at Meir with the British Hospitals' Air Pageant in 1933). Their nickname 'Always Terrified Airwomen' did no justice at all to these remarkable pilots, many of whom were better flyers than their male counterparts. By this stage of the war they were allowed to fly almost any class of aircraft, and so hazardous was their work that nearly one in ten of them died. Such women were still something of a novelty, however, and always created a stir whenever they descended from the skies.

Eric well remembered the day a Mustang came in, circling around the airfield to use excess fuel as only one gear leg had come down.

> The pilot was a very good-looking blonde who wound the canopy back (for a quick escape) and removed her helmet so this mass of golden hair was flying back! She did a great job, but unfortunately our little diesel roller was out there flattening the metal mat runway extension and she hit it with the one extended leg. The diesel driver was skittled several yards and suffered a broken leg. The Mustang stopped abruptly and stood on its nose. The blonde had a bruise on her gorgeous forehead.

Local ferry pilots included John Fisher, of Newcastle-under-Lyme, Harold Burns, of Congleton, and Rita Baines, of Trentham. First Officer Fisher was unusual in that he had seen considerable active service. Before the war he had joined the Volunteer Reserve while working for the Prudential Assurance Company in his home town. As soon as war was declared he had been mobilised and became a Sergeant Pilot, but injuries he sustained led to his being invalided out of the RAF. In 1941, desperate to continue flying, he joined the ATA but died in March of the following year, still aged only twenty-three. At his funeral a contingent of ten officers and members of the ATA formed a guard of honour at St Giles' church and at the graveside in Newcastle cemetery.

Harold Burns, who had survived the crash of his Flying Flea at Meir Aerodrome in 1936, joined the ATA on the outbreak of war and as a Flight

Rita Baines.

Captain flew eighty-two different types of aircraft – from Spitfires to Stirling bombers. Afterwards he returned to work in the motor business formed by his father and became Managing Director of Burns Garages. In 1972 he was elected mayor of Congleton.

Rita Baines began her wartime service by working at the Rootes' aircraft factory at Blythe Bridge before joining the ATA. For two years she then piloted all types of single-seater planes (including the Spitfire), twin-engined aircraft, and even a four-engined bomber. After the war she became an air-line hostess.

With the spring of 1945, the end of hostilities in Europe grew imminent, but it seemed that some were not prepared to wait. In the early hours of 4 March, ten Germans tried to escape from a large PoW camp at Sudbury, near Uttoxeter. The guards shot two dead, wounded another, and quickly recaptured three more. An intensive manhunt then began for the others. The war ended nine weeks later.

Celebrations began in North Staffordshire on 7 May, in expectation of an announcement later that day. Flags, V-signs, and bunting (some of which had been used to mark the end of the First War) appeared in the twinkling of an eye. Suddenly Hanley Town Hall was flying the Union Jack, the Stars and Stripes, and the Red Flag, combinations of which were then seen on all major buildings except the Michelin factory in Stoke, where the Union Jack was joined by the French Tricolour. The top of Trinity Street in Hanley was 'gorgeously beflagged' as were the Queen's Gardens in Newcastle, where flags of the United Nations flew from newly painted standards. In many streets every house displayed its own flag, and suppliers quickly ran out of stock despite the special deliveries of only a few days before. Caution was being thrown to the winds. One Hanley shop put up the notice 'Fish For All – But Bring Your Own Paper'. There was an instant queue.

Yet as the hours passed without an announcement, an element of bewilderment clouded the proceedings. A reporter, out on the streets, was asked by a boy of eight 'what peace was like'. Late in the afternoon a 'Victory' edition of the *Sentinel* went on sale and there was a rush to buy. But it was as darkness fell that the reality began to sink in. Suddenly, astonishingly, there were bright lights everywhere – even bonfires! One of the largest in Trentham Park had been built from logs gathered by German PoWs. With a forgivable touch of rhetoric, it was described as 'the funeral pyre of Nazism'. But still there was no announcement.

The following day began in a subdued manner, partly on account of the overcast sky and heavy morning rain. By midday, however, the weather had improved and streets began to fill with crowds sporting red, white, and blue hats, scarves, sashes, and rosettes. They were deserted again at 3 p.m. when Winston Churchill broadcast to the nation and officially announced the end of the war in Europe. He also sanctioned 'a brief period of rejoicing'. As if on cue the sun appeared, and from then on the weather remained fine. Everyone now took to the streets.

Victory peals rang out from the bells of Stoke parish church, St Giles' in Newcastle, and many other churches across the county. An hour after Churchill's broadcast, short interdenominational services were held in the centre of all six towns, with more formal ones to follow that evening. In the interim, young and old let their hair down in the overwhelming relief and happiness of the moment.

In Burslem, a team of horses drew the 'Victory Coach' of Parkers' Brewery on a mad-cap excursion round the Potteries with members of the armed forces as passengers. In Hanley, GIs poured out of their Red Cross Club on the corner of Tontine Square and danced with their girlfriends on the tops of buses. Sailors of all nationalities linked arms with girls and marched singing through the streets eight abreast, while a gigantic conga was danced the length of Waterloo Road. Everywhere there were impromptu football matches, parties, processions, and parades. At Clayton, seven-year-old Jean Titley, whose father was a prisoner of the Japanese, was crowned 'Victory Queen' and toured the village with an escort from the Home Guard; in Shelton, a fancy-dress procession toured the area led by a girl dressed as Britannia; in Newcastle, the Salvation Army band marched through the borough before giving a concert in the Gardens, where the YMCA canteen served free drinks to over 2,000 servicemen.

In street after street, tables and trestles were set up for children's parties. After years of rationing and shortages, they were laden with sandwiches, home-made cakes, custard, mince pies, fruit, and ice cream! At Milton, tables ran the whole length of New Street and Adams Street. Radios, portable gramophones, even pianos were carried outside to provide the musical accompaniment for singing and dancing. One of the records played over and over that day was 'In the Mood'. Sadly, five-year-old Derek of Stoke was taken ill and missed it all. His playmate Shirley, when told that he had German measles, replied derisively, 'Huh! Why doesn't he have British measles on VE-Day?'

The carnival atmosphere gained momentum as it grew dark. Newcastle was floodlit! At Norton and other collieries, huge V-signs were illuminated on the pithead gear with the Union Jack above them. At the service of thanksgiving in Stoke parish church, a vast congregation (which included the Lord Mayor and other civic dignitaries) sang with real passion the hymns 'Praise, My Soul, the King of Heaven' and 'Now Thank We All Our God'. Theatres, cinemas, and dance halls were crammed, and in licensed premises – which had been granted an extra hour to 11 p.m. – it was impossible to move. By 10 p.m. many had been drunk dry.

On nearly every hillside, and in many open spaces, bonfires were ablaze with effigies of Hitler, Goering or Himmler on top – at Hartshill a spectacular bonfire and torchlight procession could be seen for miles. Everywhere rockets soared into the night sky before bursting into ever more fantastic patterns of light. In Longton, 10,000 people danced the night away in the floodlit square in front of the Town Hall and then, as the finale, sang 'Land of Hope and Glory'. At midnight in Newcastle, hundreds of revellers thronged the Market Place and, accompanied by a GI with an accordion, sang 'Roll Out the Barrel', 'Tipperary', and 'Auld Lang Syne' till 3 a.m. It had been like a glorious pre-war Bank Holiday and a colossal New Year's Eve Party rolled into one.

*

At Meir Airfield, where giant Liberator bombers were starting to arrive in order to be converted to transporters, Eric Clutton did not see any celebrations ('not on Rootes Securities' time!'). However, a crowd did come out of the factory to watch the first plane being taxied up to the flight sheds. These huge hangars were 120 feet apart and the Liberator's wingspan was 110 feet, so the test pilot wisely asked for guides below each wing tip to help him negotiate the gap. Nevertheless, the right wing struck one hangar door and pushed it forcefully along its track until it hit the next one. The massive doors began to thunder down towards the spectators – who scattered at once – before smashing into the opposite end of the hangar with an almighty crash, sending dust and bird droppings billowing into the air. Fortunately, the only real damage was to the wing tip, which was soon replaced.

A surprise arrival a few days later was just as memorable, but for an entirely different reason. A mass of twenty-seven Dakotas and Commandos suddenly appeared overhead. 'We had no radio contact and eventually a Commando landed,' Eric Clutton recalled. 'We were at the top end of the runway waiting for him. The pilot leaned out from his lofty perch (about 20 feet in the air) and said, "Is this Lichfield, Mac?"'

> By that time the second and third aircraft were landing, and eventually we had all twenty-seven big twins parked all over the place. They were full of cheery GIs. We didn't think much of the US system of navigation where they had just a Lead Navigator, and if he got lost everybody got lost! The ramps came down on the aircraft and one guy wheeled out a beautiful gleaming BMW motorbike, while some other had a huge Nazi flag about twelve feet by fifteen feet. All the aircraft were crammed to the roof with kitbags and loot! Cigars, cigarettes, and booze were handed out liberally before we lads were chased off by the older workers, so I'm not sure how it all ended. They were still there when I left for home.

Another arrival at the aerodrome was Peter Berry, who, at seventeen, had just completed his Runway Controller Course at RAF Westcott. Meir was his first assignment. On 11 May, he reported to Squadron Leader Bill Man, DFC, who had been appointed full-time Aerodrome Controller the previous year to cope with the increased traffic. Next day he took up his duties. After VE-Day, the need for fresh supplies of aircraft ceased, and work on the Harvards and Mustangs dwindled. Life was still far from dull, however:

> My first morning Watch began by aligning the landing T into the wind direction, 'opening' the airfield by removing one of the yellow cross-bars on the red signal square, and driving out to the runway caravan at the touchdown end of the runway. Whilst colleague Tom 'Paddy' Boyd plugged cables into the 'tulips' for electrical power and the telephone line to the tower, I busied myself with opening the log book, checking the Aldis signal lamp, and placing a red cartridge in the Very pistol in case of need.
>
> Although the small Meir control tower sported an ageing TR9H/F R/T set, it rarely received messages and it was usual for inbound aircraft to arrive unannounced. Suddenly a 'finger-four' flight of RAF Mustangs, flown by ATA pilots, arrived overhead and broke for a stream landing. As each Mustang turned onto final approach, I checked the wheels were down and gave a 'green' light for landing clearance. Numbers One and Two touched down in turn and cleared to the right, off the runway and across the grass towards the dispersal point. Number Three landed, but instead of turning off the runway, it made a 180-degree turn on the runway and started to backtrack into the landing path of Mustang Number Four.
>
> I grabbed the Very pistol, cocked it, and, with one finger in my ear, squeezed the trigger. A loud bang, and a bright red flare arched into the sky, to be answered by the roar of the Rolls-Royce Merlin engine as Mustang Number Four applied full power for the overshoot. 'Paddy' arrived, breathless, up the steps to greet a new, shaking Airfield Controller after his first 'experience'.

There would be many such 'experiences' to come – but not at Meir, for Berry was re-assigned to the Ministry's airfield at Clifton in Yorkshire two weeks later, where he spent the following six months before joining the RAF.

At the end of May, Labour rejected Churchill's plea to keep the Coalition Government going until Japan was defeated. A general election was therefore called for 5 July. In the campaign that followed, Brigadier Lord Lovat, DSO, MC, the famous commando leader, addressed a packed meeting in Cheadle's Guildhall in support of the Conservatives and in particular his brother, Major the Hon. Hugh Fraser, who was standing at Stone. He spoke of Churchill's great war-leadership and the nation's need for it in peacetime, but the mood of the country had changed and he was heckled throughout. 'Who turned the troops out against the miners?' and 'Would 50 shillings a week keep him in cigars?' were shouts from various sections of the hall.

Even more raucous was a meeting on 19 June at the Broadway Cinema, Meir. The *Sentinel* reported that there were some 'lively exchanges' between Major Fraser and the large crowd, which included many miners. The next speaker, the Home Secretary Sir Donald Somervell, was also subjected to

An aerial shot of the aerodrome on 11 August 1945 shows the concrete runway, the hangars, and a number of planes parked on the airfield just above the flight sheds (bottom left).

heckling on a grand scale, with the chairman having to intervene ('I am going to insist on law and order'). Happily, the meeting ended in an orderly manner with the singing of the National Anthem before everyone repaired to the King's Arms for some necessary refreshment.

Observing from the back had been Jack Kennedy, a twenty-seven-year-old American ex-serviceman, who was staying at Trentham as a guest of the Frasers. He had been commissioned to write a series of articles on the election process by the Hearst newspaper syndicate and, as Mr J. C. Moore, the Conservative agent for the district recalled, 'he took a good look at a British election from the constituency point of view and at the same time made a number of friends in North Staffordshire.' The meeting obviously left an indelible impression on him, for eighteen years later he could recall it effortlessly and still mimic the chairman to perfection. By then he was the 35th President of the United States.

Unusually, the result of polling was delayed to give the armed forces the chance to vote. During the weekend prior to the announcement, 21 and 22 July, the North Staffordshire Area of the Air Training Corps (with the co-operation of Rootes Securities) held a combined flying and gliding rally at Meir Aerodrome. A large assembly of civic dignitaries was present, together with Royal Navy personnel, RAF officers, representatives of the North Staffordshire Gliding School, and ATC officers.

Members of the Corps gave a demonstration in their single-seater gliders, and four medium bombers provided flights for 250 cadets during the event. Wearing his chain of office, the Lord Mayor (Alderman W. H. Kemp) also took to the air in a two-seater glider that was winch-launched. His pilot, Squadron Leader E. J. Furlong, DFC, who represented the London Command Gliding School, rapidly reached 900 feet and then soared over the grandstand so that the mayor could wave to the large assembly below (which included his wife). On landing, he said that he had enjoyed the experience immensely.

A highlight of the rally was the presentation of a Dagling glider to the North Staffordshire Gliding School by Captain C. A. Shaw, CBE, RN. Sir Francis Joseph, president of the Stoke Wing of the ATC, gratefully received the gift and paid a warm tribute to the Royal Navy, to whom the people of Great Britain owed so much. The mayor then acknowledged the fine work of the ATC and hoped that it would continue to flourish. A few days later the election result was declared – Labour had won by a landslide. At the Potsdam Conference then in progress, Clement Atlee replaced Churchill. Within a fortnight, with the bombing of Hiroshima and Nagasaki, the world entered the atomic age and the Second World War ended abruptly.

After the surrender of Japan on 15 August 1945, the Blythe Bridge works began to run down and flying by military types of aircraft virtually ceased at the aerodrome. But the record of the shadow factory was impressive: 978 British aircraft produced, together with their complement of spare parts; 362 British aircraft modified; 2,178 American and Canadian aircraft assembled and modified to RAF requirements – a grand total of 3,518 aircraft test flown and handed over to the Services.

It had been a notable and noble page in the history of Meir, as Sir Stafford Cripps, Minister of Aircraft Production, acknowledged on a visit to the factory in 1944. Commending the resilience and dedication of the workforce – which at its peak had numbered over 5,000 – he said: 'The men and women in this factory have done a really magnificent job and your output has been of the very greatest value to the country's war effort.'

19

Engines Galore!

Postwar, it was all change. The Yanks went home, and GI brides started to follow them. Gladys Hall, of Hanley, married her American boyfriend over the transatlantic telephone! One GI who wished to settle with his Potteries' wife in North Staffordshire was refused permission by the Home Office because of 'shortages of food, clothing, etc'. Bananas made a guest appearance in some shops, much to the amazement of many children who had never seen them before. Demobbed servicemen and prisoners of war began to return, the latter with appalling tales of the brutality and deprivation they had suffered at the hands of the Germans. The Nuremberg War Trials opened, while the Rootes factory closed, its premises taken over by the Tube Investment Group to produce cookers, washers, boilers, and water storage heaters. The airfield, still under government control, was largely unoccupied.

Indeed, there seemed to be more aircraft elsewhere in the city, which in October had embarked on a 'Thanksgiving Week', its fifth campaign in connection with the National Savings movement. Throughout the week there were special services and parades, dances, bonfires, sporting events, and a presentation of the pageant *Forever England* at the Queen's Hall, Burslem. The Military College in Sandon Road also threw open its doors to exhibit its mighty arsenal of war weapons. In Market Square, Hanley, a Fleet Air Arm Barracuda dive-bomber was on display before the £1 million target indicator, while in Tunstall a jet-propelled German plane and V1 flying bomb were on show.

Eric Clutton, who had left the flight sheds at Meir to join the RAF, was astonished to see how deserted it all was on his return in February 1946: 'I went to the airfield and the sheds were abandoned, with no aircraft or any signs there had ever been any. When I left things were beginning to run down – the last Mustang and the last Liberator had been delivered, but there were still plenty of Harvards, so it was a bit of a shock to find it all gone.' In May 1944, there had been 354 aircraft on site; now there appeared to be only the model plane that Eric had taken with him.

The Gliding School at least maintained its presence at weekends and continued to attract distinguished visitors for tours of inspection. On Saturday, 24 November 1945, Flight Lieutenant Nadin welcomed two former pilots of the First World War who had recently held senior positions in the RAF – Air Marshal Sir Leslie Gossage and Air Vice-Marshal W. B. Calloway, who watched the day's proceedings with considerable interest.

So far the school had enjoyed an exemplary safety record, but this was about to change. On Sunday, 21 April 1946, thirty-one-year-old Desmond Daroux of Newcastle, who had just been appointed a civilian gliding instructor at the Meir school, took off for his first flight that day. The Chief Instructor witnessed what happened: 'The glider was winch-launched. Mr Daroux released the cable on reaching a height of about 100 feet. We expected that he would glide gently to the ground, in a straight line, but after a few seconds the glider suddenly started to dive steeply and crashed to the ground.' Spectators rushed to the scene to find Mr Daroux had apparently escaped without any of his limbs being broken, but a sharp piece of plywood from the wrecked glider had pierced his throat. He was unable to speak and was taken at once to Longton Cottage Hospital where he died the next day. At the inquest, the coroner announced that death had in fact been due to a broken neck.

In May, the *Sentinel* published a letter deploring the 'complete lack of activity' at the airfield and pointing out the benefits of a thriving airport to local industry. Its writer also noted that many people had expressed an interest in joining a revived flying club. Referring to the wide publicity given to the Mitchell Memorial Fund, he went on: 'Would it not be a most fitting part of his memorial to create a flying school named after him, where, by means of some form of subsidy from the fund, flying could be brought within the reach of the ordinary man?'

He recognised that the airfield had its detractors, but set out to confound them by meeting them head on:

> To critics of the size and general characteristics of the airport, I would only answer that to my knowledge over 3,000 test flights took place there from 1941 without accident. In addition several thousand delivery flights took place, to say nothing of visiting aircraft, which included Flying Fortresses and Lancasters. The few accidents in that period were in no way due to the airfield.
>
> Its position, moreover, on a main road and near to a railway station makes it more than usually accessible, and being in the centre of England, it lies on many of the internal air routes.
>
> Is it too much to ask that our City Council wake up to the opportunity presented to them at Meir and place Stoke-on-Trent on the air map of the country?

The letter was published under the *nom de plume* 'Air-Minded', but after an inconclusive discussion of the aerodrome's future at a council meeting later that month, the writer tried again, this time identifying himself as E. G. Shults, the war-time test pilot for the Rootes factory. His credentials were impeccable. 'I have flown at Meir for 4½ out of my ten years' flying experience,' he wrote, 'and have made over 2,500 flights from there without accident, even though I had some serious failures on machines in that period.'

He went on to argue that the airfield had much to commend it – it had tripled in size since 1941, the runways could easily be increased, and the buildings were first-class (although the control tower was now out of place and virtually useless). All in all it was 'eminently suitable' for the relatively small aircraft likely to use it and could be made 'a source of pride to the city if properly managed and controlled'. He ended by repeating his suggestion for a flying school, 'so that the ordinary ratepayer could find it in his financial power to taste the unlimited joys of flight.'

Support for his views came from a *Sentinel* editorial and from the Meir and District Chamber of Commerce. At a meeting on 12 June 1946, the Chamber considered a suggestion put forward by Mr J. Davenport that the aerodrome should be converted into a huge sports stadium and showground catering for speedway, greyhound and horse-racing, football, agricultural shows, county cricket, circuses, and all kinds of exhibitions. There was strong disagreement, especially from Mr E. W. Brookhouse, the pilot of the first private plane to land in Stoke-on-Trent since the war, who said that he had been approached by many people wanting flying lessons and charter service work. The meeting rejected the proposal and adopted instead a resolution exhorting the Council to give urgent consideration to the development of an airport on the most modern lines and comparable with other cities in the British Isles.

The Council was not unresponsive to such promptings and may have been all too conscious of the fact that when distinguished guests visited the city there was now no functioning airport ready to receive them. In October 1946, Air Commodore (later Sir) Frank Whittle, the aeronautical engineer and inventor of the jet aircraft engine, gave the first Mitchell Memorial Lecture at the Victoria Hall in Hanley. Among many notable guests was Lord Brabazon, the veteran airman. The irony of such illustrious figures in aviation coming to pay homage to the designer of the Spitfire and having to travel by road and rail was inescapable.

At first the Council seemed determined to revive the airfield, and up to and beyond the date of its derequisitioning (31 March 1949) various strategies and proposals were tried, most of which came to nothing. In 1946, a deputation went to the office of the Ministry of Civil Aviation to discuss the future use of the aerodrome. Representatives also went to a conference at Elmdon Airport, Birmingham, to consider how best to organise scheduled air services to and from the Midlands. The Aerodrome Committee then tried (in vain) to persuade the government to establish a reserve training school there. In the same year, a proposal from Air Schools of Derby to develop and operate charter, club, and training-school flying at Meir was seriously entertained. The proposal hung in the air for a considerable time before vanishing without trace.

Over the years a number of other companies contacted the Council with business propositions. In 1947, Kenning Aviation wanted to operate a charter service, put on sales demonstrations of various types of aircraft, and set up an aircraft servicing organisation. In 1949, Starways Ltd wished to provide charter services, establish a maintenance depot, and organise a flying school; Wright Aviation also applied to operate private charter services. In 1950, both Giro Aviation of Southport and Melba Airways of Manchester asked for permission to provide charter and pleasure flights. In the House of Commons in 1952, John Profumo, the Minister of Civil Aviation, stated that his department had no plans for the future use of Meir Aerodrome. A year later, however, the Air Ministry expressed an interest in using it as a gliding centre for ATC personnel throughout the Midlands – a proposal that was turned down because of the agricultural use being made of the land at that time and the capital expenditure required.

From 1945 on, other concerns had begun to encroach on the airfield. Clifford Aero & Auto had a factory there, which manufactured first washing-machines, then fork-lift trucks. When it closed in June 1949, Keele Street Pottery (later Staffordshire Potteries) took over the tenancy of the hangar and began to expand into an industrial complex, taking over the lease of other land and buildings from Collingwood China in 1956. The Midland Chemical Company had the tenancy of another building on the site, while some of the Bellman hangars were sold for storage units. One of them was in use as a motor mart and a garage for buses. The Education Committee also leased several acres for playing-field purposes. The former Rootes works was meanwhile taken over by Simplex Creda and converted to a factory producing electrical appliances. One employee was Freddie Jones, of Dresden, who later took up acting and went on to enjoy international success on stage and screen.

Ratepayers at Meir, seeing a valuable piece of land being neglected, were becoming impatient, if not a trifle fractious. One resident of Uttoxeter Road wrote to the *Sentinel* that the aerodrome was 'a dead loss' and felt 'a handsome relief from rates could be obtained if it were put to better use'. Another correspondent, who had noted the changes happening to the hangars, asked: 'Surely we are not going to see a pottery factory or a bus depot?' He was not slow in putting forward his own proposals:

> Throughout the summer months it could be used for agricultural shows etc. instead of using our parks; there would be room for all from near and far. Then why cannot we have a horse-racing track for flat and National Hunt meetings? Let us have a 'Potters' Derby and National'. Chester can do it, why not the Five Towns?

Applications for permission to use the land were also coming in thick and fast to the Aerodrome Committee. They included a request from the North Staffordshire Motor Club to use the runway for rally driving tests; an appeal for the construction of a cycling track; a letter from the Chief Constable asking to use the site to train police dogs; an application from the Meir Dancing Troupe to use the airfield for practice; a request from the Stoke Kart Club for track facilities; an application to exercise two racehorses; a plan to establish a golf driving range; and numerous requests to hold carnivals and barbeques. The Meir Central Methodist Mission also wanted to build a church there, while the Stoke-on-Trent Education Committee visited the aerodrome in the quest for a site for new premises for Longton High School, though the school was eventually built in Box Lane.

Above all, for the gangs of children from the adjacent council estates, the aerodrome remained a glorious adventure playground in their own backyard where they could play football to their hearts' content and dream of joining Stoke City like their hero, Stanley Matthews. One of them, Denis Smith, did just that when he signed for the club in 1966. In its service he would become 'the most injured man in football', according to the *Guinness Book of Records*. At least the financial rewards were greater than those once offered to his boyhood idol: thirty years on Smith's basic wage was £12 a week.

*

Thankfully, some aircraft still touched down at Meir. On 12 June 1947, an Anson arrived to take Bill Nadin (recently appointed Gliding Officer for the Midlands) and John Sadler (who had replaced him as CO of the Gliding School) on a fortnight's tour of gliding centres in the British zone of Germany in order to compare equipment and methods of training. A month later, on 11 July, the North Staffordshire Federation of Homing Pigeon Societies chartered a flight to ferry their birds from Meir to Rennes, in France, in time for the next day's race – the principal event in the calendar of homing pigeon fanciers with more than 2,000 birds taking part.

Sunday, 24 August, brought Air Marshal Sir Alan Lees into Meir in his special Anson XIX. In his party were Air Commodore Robert Ragg and Wing Commander Donald Finlay, the champion hurdler who had won the silver medal at the 1936 Olympics in Berlin. More recently he had led Nos 41 and 54 (Spitfire) Squadrons in the Battle of Britain, when he had shot down four enemy aircraft and shared in the destruction of two others. No doubt they would have been discussing the shocking news that Roy Chadwick, designer of the Lancaster bomber, had been killed the previous day on a test flight at Woodford Aerodrome, just north of Macclesfield – another grievous loss to British aviation.

Lined up for their inspection were the winches, motor vehicles, and gliders of No. 45 Gliding School – painted in the RAF training colour of bright primrose. Afterwards there was a march past of the school's staff and thirty ATC cadets from Stafford, Hanley, Newcastle, and Stoke, ten of whom were then presented with their Gliding Proficiency Certificates by Sir Alan. A demonstration followed, with Sir Alan keen not only to see Meir's double-winch method of towing in action, but to try it for himself. Later the visitors chatted to members of the Five Towns' Model Aircraft Club who were on site and who demonstrated some of their power models. The club's secretary, Mr D. Griffin, answered many questions about the aircraft and showed how a fountain-pen filler was used to refuel their tiny engines.

Somewhat larger engines preoccupied the Corporation over the next two years. A popular film of the time *Whisky Galore!* portrayed a war-time incident in which islanders of the Outer Hebrides availed themselves of a cargo of whisky from a stricken ship. Meir's landlocked version might well have been called *Engines Galore!,* for scavengers had started to unearth new, used, and scrap engines from a field adjoining the aerodrome, where they had been dumped in a large hole and covered with debris from demolished air-raid shelters. With metals such as copper, lead, brass, and aluminium at a premium, the site was a veritable gold-mine. The Town Clerk swiftly had a notice erected warning that 'Unauthorised persons removing materials will be rigorously prosecuted.'

Mr F. Oakes, of Harvey Road, Meir, a charge-hand on the site during the dumping operations, told how the engines had arrived at the Rootes factory for storage. 'Many of them had seen service abroad, for in the packing cases we found anything from desert sand to monkey nuts,' he said.

> Most of the engines were nursed like babies at Rootes, in accordance with Government instructions. Then came the time when we had instructions, which, I understand, came from the Ministry of Aircraft Production, to dump them. This was before the end of the war. The last consignment I sent to the dump was 294 Cyclones. The dumping went on over a long period and I estimate about 500 engines went into it.

No sooner had the Corporation's Salvage Department begun work on the site than a second one was pinpointed, on the aerodrome itself. This had once been a huge marl-pit, which, when full, had been covered with soil by a bulldozer. A worker who had been engaged there estimated that it was three times as large as the first site and contained about 1,500 engines besides other components – coolers, spinners, and propellers. For the cash-strapped Council, this was treasure trove. The excavations went on.

When the Council was not digging up the aerodrome, it was harvesting what grew on it. Since 1939 a grass-drying factory had been in operation, which employed a staff of seven and became the city's largest producer of grass meal. Its average yield was about 400 tons a year. During the war, when demand was greatest, the plant worked double shifts and had a seasonal output of between 600 and 700 tons. It proved to be a nice little earner – in one year alone 560 tons of dried grass meal was sold for £11,000. For this reason Meir was one of the very few aerodromes in the country that did not need a subsidy. Mr G. Dale, vice-chairman of the Airport Committee, felt that the Council deserved a pat on the back and duly administered it. 'This is one municipal trading scheme that does show a profit,' he said. 'There is no doubt

A workman climbs among a huge dump of aero engines and components at Meir in 1949.

we are doing a grand service to the country. At other aerodromes the grass is allowed to go to waste.' This emphasis on agriculture rather than aviation led one councillor to ask whether the site should be developed as an airport or 'offered to the Parks and Cemeteries Committee to grow and dry grass'.

However, there were still some people who were grateful for the chance to fly at Meir – and sometimes for the strangest of reasons. In the spring of 1949, five-year-old twin sisters Ann and Susan Mountford, of Bucknall, were racked by whooping cough day and night. Their exhausted father mentioned it to a work colleague, Derek Jones, who had been awarded a DFC in Italy during the war and who still flew as a member of the Cheshire Squadron of the Royal Auxiliary Air Force at Hooton Park. The latter immediately suggested a 'cure-flight', a standard practice at Hooton, which 'never failed'. The desperate father agreed.

On 19 May, Mr Jones flew a three-seater Auster into Meir. As soon as the Mountfords' taxi arrived at the runway, Susan had another attack and it was some time before she could board the plane with her mother and sister. Then the children waved excitedly to their father as the Auster took off – the first flight for all three passengers. After a half-hour's trip, with ten minutes spent at 5,000 feet – the recognised height for a successful outcome – the plane returned. 'Lovely!' exclaimed Mrs Mountford. 'The twins appear to have enjoyed every minute of it.' It also seemed to have done the trick. The twins were smiling and not coughing. That night the whole family slept well.

20

The Last Hurricane

There was a brief glimpse of the aerodrome's former glory on Saturday, 17 June 1950, when the King's Cup Air Race again used Meir as a turning point and brought a vast crowd to the aerodrome one last time. The race – the 19th since it was inaugurated by King George V in 1922 – was a handicap over a closed circuit held at Wolverhampton Aerodrome, whose aero club was promoting the event for the first time. The machines had to race round three laps of a 62-mile circuit, in the course of which they passed over Sandon and Stone on their way to Meir and over Newcastle and Trentham on their way from Meir to Newport (Salop).

Among the thirty-six entrants was local hero and ex-fighter pilot John Ashton, who was then living at Wolstanton. He had competed in the race the previous year, the first time it had been held since 1938, and had been placed third. Now he was flying at Number 7 in a silver Miles Hawk Trainer III – a low-wing monoplane that he had hired – which was handicapped by 50 seconds. Another notable entry was the last Hurricane ever produced, PZ865, which Hawker had immediately purchased back from the Air Ministry and initially mothballed. Now, flying under the civilian registration G-AMAU, it was sponsored by HRH Princess Margaret and flown by the fighter ace Peter Townsend.

The aircraft, which ranged from veteran biplanes to ultra-modern Spitfires, got away in a steady stream, and spectators at Meir had an excellent view as the planes approached from the Abbots Bromley direction to negotiate the black and white pylon erected in the middle of the airfield. The first plane appeared on the horizon at 2.45 p.m., followed a few seconds later by several more, some flying several hundred feet high, others almost hedge-hopping to the pylon. Shortly afterwards nine aircraft – the slower ones – arrived bunched together, but all took the turn safely. A loudspeaker kept the crowd up to speed with the latest developments.

When the planes reappeared on the second circuit, the crowd quickly realised that John Ashton was in the lead and gave him a rousing cheer as he went round. During this second lap, the oldest competitor, Mr W. H. Moss, flying his own machine, a Mosscraft, crashed at Newport, which somewhat marred the event. The winner was eventually Mr Edward Day, of Rochester,

Above and below: Youngsters watch as the planes make their turn at Meir during the King's Cup Air Race in June, 1950, and a section of the spectators in the car enclosure.

who crossed the finishing line 60 yards ahead of Peter Townsend (who was second) and a minute ahead of John Ashton (who finished in sixth place). Years later when he was reading a newspaper cutting of the event, Peter Townsend discovered that he had created a world speed record over a closed circuit.

Such occasions were now very much the exception at Meir. The days of the 'flying circuses' were no more, and the aero club had gone, its clubhouse converted to a canteen before being demolished. Empire Day Air Displays were a thing of the past, along with the Empire itself. The annual 'Open Days' held to commemorate the Battle of Britain were the province of Tern Hill – although Bill Nadin and members of the Meir Gliding School would appear there to put on a show. By now they were much more accomplished as the school had introduced two-seater gliders and the dual system of training, all launches being free flights with the gliders able to circle the aerodrome after casting off the winch cable at a height of about 1,000 feet.

The doyen of such events was naturally Bill Nadin, who in 1948 had achieved the blue riband of gliding, the International Silver 'C' Certificate, only the second ATC officer to hold the qualification. On one occasion his performance was so stunning that he was mobbed like some sporting superstar. 'Birdlike is the only adjective to describe his flying,' recorded the *Sentinel*, 'and it caught the fancy of the many small boys of the audience to such an extent that, when he came in to land, the youthful crowd swarmed over the rope boundaries with the enthusiasm of the spectators at the Oval Test match and surrounded the small red sailplane in an admiring cluster.'

Meir Aerodrome, meanwhile, remained largely unused, serving to provide only the odd footnote to local history. One such moment occurred on 5 September 1952, when Stoke City made club history by using air transport for the first time to sign a player and bring him to the area. That morning the Stoke Manager, Frank Taylor, had flown to Scotland to clinch the transfer of Aberdeen's twenty-two-year-old centre half Kenny Thomson for £22,000, a fee exceeded only by the £25,000 paid to Wolverhampton Wanders for Sammy Smyth the previous season. As soon as the transfer was complete, Mr Taylor flew his new player directly to Meir Aerodrome on a specially chartered plane. 'We had a good journey,' said Thomson on arrival. 'Stoke have spent a lot of money on the transfer and I hope it will be worth it. So far as I am concerned, I shall give all I have to make it so.' The following day he made an impressive debut in Stoke's 1-0 defeat of Middlesborough.

Apart from a few individuals, the main user of the airfield became Staffordshire Potteries Ltd. Pottery companies had first begun to send goods by air in November 1949 when Spode-Copeland dispatched dinner services to Canada and America. The following month 500 Royal Doulton Dickensian figures were taken 'hot out of the kilns at Burslem' and were on sale in New York two days later. The same month the Empire Porcelain Company of Stoke sent a small consignment of dinnerware to Ceylon where it was urgently needed by the Prime Minister. Again it was ironic that with Meir Aerodrome lying idle, the first stage in the journey of such items was by road to Stoke station and then rail to London, before being taken immediately to Heathrow.

To try to exploit the facility on their doorstep, Staffordshire Potteries eventually bought a de Havilland Dragon Rapide, the aircraft being the only one regularly employed in the pottery industry. On one occasion in 1953, it was used to meet an emergency order for a consignment of coffee cups and saucers a few hours before a banquet at a London hotel. Four gross were dispatched aboard the Rapide, which flew from Meir to Elstree Airport in 45 minutes to save the day.

The coronation of Queen Elizabeth II on 2 June 1953 involved a special delivery in the opposite direction. Photographs of the ceremony in Westminster Abbey and the state procession through the capital were flown to Meir and published in later editions of the *Sentinel* that day. The coronation also involved the airfield in what would be its most noteworthy example of air freight. As Princess Elizabeth, the Queen had been the first member of the royal family to visit the area after the war in November 1949, and during her two-day tour she had called at several pottery firms. It seemed eminently fitting therefore for Colonel G. A. Wade, Chairman of the Wade Group of Potteries, to suggest that the British Pottery Manufacturers' Federation should pay tribute to the new monarch.

Subsequently, an exquisite vase, 'one of the most complicated and magnificent pieces of bone china ever created', was designed by Mr John Wadsworth, Art Director and Designer of Mintons, to commemorate the coronation and symbolise the Commonwealth. The vase, surmounted by a crown, was just over two feet high and weighed 29 lb, including the base of Australian black bean wood. Between forty and fifty colours had been used to decorate its ten panels, the front one of which bore the Royal Coat of Arms and the Royal Standard. The remaining panels carried the arms and floral emblems of countries in the United Kingdom and the Commonwealth. Coloured models of the Queen's Beasts appeared in niches at the front of each panel, and the legend – 'To commemorate the coronation of Her Majesty Queen Elizabeth II' – was inscribed in gold around the plinth.

When it was finished, it was packed in special containers and flown from Meir Aerodrome to London by Neal Fagg, a member of staff of the accounts department of Staffordshire Potteries, who was formerly a Flight Lieutenant in the Royal New Zealand Air Force. Accompanying him were representatives of the Federation, headed by its Director, Mr W. F. Wentworth-Sheilds.

From Elstree the vase was taken by Rolls Royce to Buckingham Palace, where it was handed to the Yeoman of the China and Glass Pantry for safekeeping before being presented to the Queen at a private audience on 14 July 1954. Days later, on 20 July, the Duchess of Gloucester attended the Dorchester Hotel to present facsimile vases to the High Commissioners of the seven Commonwealth countries and representatives of the four Mother Countries of the UK. The Lord

The Queen's Vase.

Mayor of Stoke-on-Trent (Mrs A. L. Barker) was present with about 250 pottery operatives from the six firms of the Fine China Association responsible for the manufacture of the vases. The original 'Coronation Vase' or 'Queen's Vase', as it became known, was later placed in Windsor Castle.

*

Shortly before her London trip, the Lord Mayor had visited Meir Aerodrome where No. 1037 ATC Squadron had been provided with a new headquarters by Staffordshire Potteries. Mrs Barker officially opened the accommodation – a hut with lecture rooms for engineering, aircraft recognition, and navigation – on 16 June. Accompanied by Flight Lieutenant T. Mason, the commanding officer, she then inspected a guard of honour before praising the work done by the Air Training Corps.

Equally complimentary was their first guest speaker, Group Captain R. J. Burns, Commanding Officer of Tern Hill, when he addressed cadets on 21 July on the topic 'The Value of the Air Training Corps to the Royal Air Force'. It was apparent to all concerned, however, that numbers had dwindled and were only a fraction of what they had been a few years before. The squadron strength at Meir was then about thirty. Its members were also, as events proved, on borrowed time at the aerodrome.

Mrs Barker made a return visit on 17 April 1955 to perform a similar ceremony for the Gliding School, whose new headquarters (a hut with classrooms, storerooms, and a kitchen) had also been provided by the pottery firm. Afterwards cadets and instructors put on a demonstration, with a loudspeaker giving a running commentary on the aerobatics for the spectators. The highlight was undoubtedly the display given by Bill Nadin, who delighted the crowd with a series of loops, dives, and turns, but sixteen-year-old Barry Crews from Stafford stole some of the limelight by making his first ever solo flight. The Lord Mayor, who had made her own maiden flight earlier that day in the de Havilland Dove then used by the pottery firm, warmly congratulated him on his safe return.

Also present at the opening ceremony was the current chairman of the Airport Committee, Alderman H. Hopwood, who said he looked forward to the day when there would be more flying at Meir. His hope was fulfilled in the following months, albeit still on a modest scale. On 7 May, members of the 1609 unit of the North Staffordshire Women's Junior Air Corps arrived for special training flights over the Potteries, bringing with them their own aircraft, the Grey Dove, and their own pilot, Miss Freydis Leaf. The latter was aviation adviser to the Corps and a distinguished flyer who had served as an ATA ferry pilot during the war. She had logged over 1,600 flying hours and in 1954 had been the only female entrant in the King's Cup Air Race, coming third. In 1955 she had just won the Grosvenor Cup. Bill Nadin was on hand to assist, and added a little spice to the occasion by taking some of the girls up in his Auster for a session of 'mild aerobatics'.

Meir was still a convenient landing-strip for those in a hurry, and on 14 June 1955 Mr L. W. Joynson-Hicks, Parliamentary Secretary to the Ministry of Fuel and Power, arrived to confer with Coal Board officials on facilities available for the transport of coal during the nationwide rail strike. In the same year, there was a belated attempt to reintroduce scheduled passenger services when the Liverpool-based Dragon Airways was allowed to operate an experimental summer service from Meir to the Isle of Man and the Channel Islands. The first passengers were the Lord Mayor and Lady Mayoress, who flew to Jersey on Saturday, 21 May, as guests of the company in their new de Havilland Heron. They returned that evening, calling at Birmingham for customs' clearance. The actual service was inaugurated on Whit Saturday, but again it was very limited and was discontinued about a year later because of the condition of the runway, which the Corporation refused to repair.

Perhaps the Council felt that the future of the airport lay elsewhere. Its members had already discussed the possibility of its being used as a helicopter station, and civic officials were given a taster of this mode of transport later that year. Selected parties from Stoke-on-Trent, Staffordshire, Shropshire, and Burton-on-Trent gathered at the aerodrome and were deafened as a Westland S/55 loomed out of the mist and touched down. It had been hired by the

AIR SERVICES FROM MEIR AIRPORT

Weekly air-services from Meir Airport, Stoke-on-Trent, to the Isle of Man and the Channel Islands will be operated from Whitsuntide, subject to final approval of all authorities. Charter flights will be undertaken as necessary. Fares to the Isle of Man from Stoke-on-Trent will be £7. 5. 0d. return (single £4), and to the Channel Islands £14. 14. 0d. (single £7. 17. 0d.), It is anticipated that these services will be of great value to holiday-makers from a very wide area, for whom the faster travel will mean longer effective holidays.

The type of aircraft used by the operating company (Dragon Airways Ltd.) will be a de Havilland Heron liner, seating 14-17 passengers. The Heron has a cruising speed of 183 m.p.h. and is powered by four Gipsy Queen engines.

The service would normally continue until late in September.

Air services are briefly reinstated at Meir.

Home Office and was touring the country to provide air experience for local authorities to allow them to assess its potential.

The original intention had been to fly the various parties over their own territories, but flights had to be confined to the airfield owing to the poor visibility. The Stoke party went up first, and for ten minutes the helicopter demonstrated its manoeuvrability and speed, flying low, banking, turning, hovering, and then climbing steeply. On its return Mr G. P. Shearing, a Civil Defence Officer, was convinced of its usefulness, especially for reconnaissance. Mr W. Watson, the Chief Constable, was also impressed, as was Mr W. Smith, the Chief Fire Officer, who thought the helicopter would be invaluable in fire fighting. The most appreciative audience, though, was probably the clutch of schoolchildren who had clambered up the aerodrome fence to catch a glimpse of this whirling dervish of the skies.

*

Two years later, on Monday, 28 October 1957, the project inaugurated in 1943 to honour R. J. Mitchell finally came to fruition with the opening of the Mitchell Memorial Youth Centre in Broad Street, Hanley. The centre, which had cost £50,000, was floodlit for the occasion, with searchlights from the Cobridge-based anti-aircraft unit forming a cone of light over the building.

Dr Gordon Mitchell, R. J.'s son, and other members of the Mitchell family were present, together with test pilots of the Spitfire and probably the most famous participant in the Battle of Britain, Group Captain Douglas Bader, whose story had recently been filmed in *Reach for the Sky*.

Outside the building the architect, Mr Harold Goldstraw, handed him a golden key with which to open the door of the centre. Despite repeated attempts, in which the key was bent, the door remained obstinately locked until a quick-witted official waiting inside forced it open. Their famous guest joked that, as a former prisoner in Colditz, the door would not have held him up for long! Everyone then entered the theatre, where Group Captain Bader was enthusiastically acclaimed by the audience, which included members of the City Youth Council.

In a short informal speech, he said that it was an honour to be there because the name of R. J. Mitchell meant so much to people of his own generation and he hoped that the centre would help make Mitchell's name better known to future generations. He praised those who had had the vision to erect a youth centre as a memorial – better by far, he said, than those 'statues of chaps sitting on horses, which used to be favourite forms of memorials in the past'. He then paid tribute to the test pilots in the audience who had flown the Spitfire in the mid-1930s so that 'ham-fisted pilots like myself could later fly the plane without endangering our lives'. He concluded by declaring the centre open and hoped that young people would derive tremendous pleasure, fun, and education from it.

Douglas Bader (right) attends the opening of the Mitchell Memorial Youth Centre.

After further presentations, the film *The First of the Few* was shown to round off a truly memorable occasion.

*

Since the war royal visitors to the area had invariably arrived by train or car, but in 1958 the Duke of Edinburgh's whirlwind tour of the country to see his recently established award scheme in action meant – literally – flying visits.

On the morning of 21 May he was in Monmouthshire, and then flew himself in a helicopter straight to Meir where he was due to land at 3.30 p.m. He was ten minutes early. 'The wind was with us,' he said as he emerged, hatless and wearing a grey suit, accompanied by Sir John Hunt, leader of the victorious Everest expedition of 1953 and now secretary of the award scheme.

Waiting to greet them was the Lord Lieutenant, Mr H. Wallace-Copeland, who presented the Reverend Perry, Mr Harry Taylor (the Town Clerk), and Mr H. Dibden (the Chief Education Officer). Also present in the welcoming party were Squadron Leader Nadin and Sergeant Egerton VC, now a lodgeman at the pottery factory on the airport.

Prince Philip then travelled by car to Barlaston, where sixty-seven boys from four city schools and youth clubs were spending a training week at the Wedgwood Memorial College. He dropped in on a first-aid class and a pot-holing class, and then observed one group studying mobile camp craft and another group undergoing fitness training. His final stop was at the canal side to chat to boys who were returning from a two-day expedition by canoe. 'It was all first-class,' was his verdict on what he had seen.

After tea the trainees gathered on the lawn, while on the terrace above the Prince presented gold awards and certificates to three boys who had successfully completed the course – Norman Hoskins of Chell Youth Club and twins John and Derek Cliffe of Harpfields Youth Club. He told Norman, who was first up, that he was only the second boy in the country to whom he had presented the award. He was then cheered on his way as he left for the airfield, where he took off at once for the north to continue his tour. The whole visit, which had been strikingly informal, had lasted less than two hours.

The ease and convenience of the Duke's visit seemed to convince the Council that Meir should become a heliport, thus eliminating the need for costly repairs to the runway (estimated at £20,000). The Town Clerk was particularly enthusiastic and saw the aerodrome as a vital link in an inter-city helicopter service. 'There is no question at all of Meir's being used for any other purpose than an airport,' said Mr Taylor. 'It is scheduled on the town map as an airport, and it is the Corporation's intention that it shall remain as such.' In ten years' time, he predicted, it would be an active airways centre.

21

On a Wing and a Prayer

Through thick and thin, No. 45 (later renumbered 632) Gliding School continued to thrive at the aerodrome, in 1954 breaking the all-England record by making 106 launchings in one day. By then it was one of the best equipped units in the country, with five two-seater gliders (three tandem, two side-by-side), three launching winches, and three towing vehicles.

Since its inception about 12,000 cadets had undergone glider training at Meir, and there were now seventeen instructors and assistants, some of whom were ex-ATC cadets like John Ash and Mike Ruttle. John Sadler, one of the original officers when the school was formed, had retired and been presented with the Cadet Forces Medal; his replacement as Commanding Officer was Flight Lieutenant Bill Hutchinson, DFC, from Stafford.

'Hutch' had been a Lancaster bomber pilot and had taken part in thirty-four raids over Germany. Afterwards he became a flight commander at the RAF College, Cranwell, and had been Chief Flying Instructor at Meir since 1949. His second-in-command was Flying Officer Charles Webb, who had served in Sunderland flying boats during the war. Together they ran a strong team, which on 21 October 1956 was presented with an award for outstanding achievement by Air Commodore J. B. Wallis, OBE. If anything the pace quickened thereafter, with the school hoping to exceed 3,000 flights annually, and provide training for every North Staffordshire cadet over sixteen and joyrides for many of the under-sixteens.

Besides members of the ATC, pilots included sixth-formers from local grammar schools and colleges, who could take advantage of the free flying lessons on offer by virtue of belonging to their school's cadet force. In the summer of 1959, Tony Chadwick and the author decided to apply. We were then attending Longton High School (now Sandon High), which possessed a rough and ready glider of its own. The school had applied to the Aerodrome Committee for permission to fly it at the airfield, but it is unclear if this was ever granted. However, it did occasionally take to the air, as Nicholas Cartlidge, an old boy of the school and the author of two books on Meir, recalled:

It was launched by the entire first XV rugby team and an enormous piece of elastic. Saw it lift off once – never forget the expression on the pilot's face of sheer terror as the craft flew over Rhead's quarry in Lightwood Road, which lay hundreds of feet below behind the top hockey pitch behind the school. Wonder where that glider went? Imagine that today and Health and Safety!

We decided that the gliding school was the safer option and duly turned up on the first Sunday, in uniform and clutching a packed lunch, to meet our instructors, who looked and acted just like the fighter and bomber pilots we were then seeing in films. Our first task was to clear up the small untidy kitchen with its litter of unwashed plates and cups. This proved difficult as the tap produced no water whatsoever.

The next task was to push the Sedbergh and Kirby Cadet gliders from their hangers, and by mid-morning the more experienced pilots were in full flight. Those not flying helped recover the gliders after they landed. Strapped into the seats on the back of a jeep, we bounced along over the uneven grass to hook the nose of the glider to the vehicle's hitch. Then we had to hold on to the leading edge of the wing to stop the tip digging into the ground while the glider was hauled back to the launch point. We also helped with the next take-off by steadying the wing and running alongside for as long as possible as the glider picked up speed and was then miraculously winched into the startlingly blue sky. No one wore a parachute. 'These gliders are expensive,' said one instructor. 'We want you to bring them back, not jump out of them.'

Out of the hangar.

Tony Chadwick.

A glider is winch-launched...

... and then soars over Meir.

At long last it was my turn and, strapped into the open cockpit, I experienced for the first time the gut-wrenching thrill of being winched at speed over the grass and then tugged abruptly into the boisterous air, faster and faster until mercifully the release handle was pulled – then, at once, as if in a dream, floating in pure silence, a stillness so perfect that I'd experienced nothing like it before. I had a bird's-eye view of Meir, way below, which looked like a radio with its back off.

The first lessons, naturally enough, were spent learning how to take off and land, and the open cockpit could prove problematic. One day storm clouds lowered and it was obvious we were in for a downpour. 'Just time to get off,' said my instructor imperturbably. And off we went, the heavens opening on cue as we were leaving the ground. As we hurtled upwards, the rain hurtled down, sharp as grit, and I could see nothing. What a relief when we were free of the cable, and I was able to clean my spectacles and gather my wits. I was completely drenched.

With a good headwind it was possible to reach 850 feet on launch, but without a strong thermal to give lift there was only enough time to glide down two legs before turning to land. My first couple of landings were on the heavy side, and it was as well the shock absorbers lived up to their name. On the third occasion I was determined to land so smoothly that we would caress the ground instead of jolting into it. I was fully focussed, but my instructor's mind was elsewhere. As I was making my final approach, I heard a sudden yell from behind of '*Mushrooms!*' and as soon as we banged down he was off, returning with a veritable harvest.

Over the weeks we progressed to more advanced training and also learned to keep an eye open for low-flying Dakotas, Bill Nadin's Auster, and other gliders. In preparation for my first solo, the instructor said he would show me how to get out of a dive so that I would be prepared if this happened when I was on my own. We found a thermal and rapidly gained height. 'Make sure you're well strapped in,' he shouted. I barely had time to check before he thrust the nose steeply downwards and I was staring in horror at the ground rushing towards us at an incredible rate as if we had plunged headlong over a precipice. Dextrously he brought us out of the dive, but my stomach had been left several hundred feet above, and when we landed my legs were still shaking. 'Nothing to it,' he said nonchalantly.

Each Sunday more students would fly solo and usually it all passed without event. But one gloriously sunny afternoon, a group of us were lazing on the sweet-scented grass while the latest flight was in progress, the cadet's instructor keeping a desultory eye on him. After a while, he said: 'He's a bit low.' Shortly afterwards he was sitting up: 'He's coming in too low.' Suddenly we were all standing. '*He's going to land in the main road!*' We had visions of a beached glider blocking Uttoxeter Road, but as we watched helplessly the glider skirted the houses, floated gently over the road and landed just on the outer edge of the field. There was an audible sigh of relief. Unbeknown to us, it was almost a case of history repeating itself, for in May 1941 a trainee had crashed his aircraft in the road at the same spot while trying to land.

The following week it was our turn. Tony went first:

The day I did my solo flights, it was sunny and warm. The first flight was uneventful, with a reasonable launch and a good landing. I even managed to keep the glider balanced on its wheel for a while before allowing it gently to fall to one side. On the second flight I got a really good launch. The second leg took me over the main road to Derby, and about half way down I got a huge lift from a thermal, so that instead of turning for the third leg, I had to double back to lose height. When I came in to land, the short-tempered officer shouted at me for missing the opportunity to stay aloft (no-one had mentioned that as a possibility) and then explained to me that if I stayed up for 15 minutes I would get my 'C' licence as well as the 'A' and 'B'. Technically, one was supposed to stay above 5000 ft for 5 minutes for the 'C' licence, but Meir did not have the equipment to measure that. Needless to say, my third flight was straightforward – average launch, no thermal – and I ended up with an ordinary licence and dreams of what might have been.

During the six weeks of Sunday training, I developed a strong desire to fly powered aircraft, and even wondered about joining the RAF. However, my eye-sight was not good enough for that (no contact lenses allowed) so I dropped the idea. My dream did get a boost, however, from the visit of an Old Longtonian who had been in the sixth form when we arrived at Longton High School. He had joined the RAF, gone to Cranwell (where he got the Silver Sword), and was something of a legend having got his pilot's licence in a week. I heard that after his feat a new regulation was brought in that required a minimum of a month's flying before a licence was awarded. He showed up one afternoon at Meir driving this wonderful sports car (can't remember the make, but it was a large two-seater). He took me out for a spin along the Derby road (which was laid over part of a Roman road). On the way back he decided to 'open her up' and as we approached 95 mph, everything seemed to rattle, at which point he pressed a button on the dash to engage a second fuel pump and the engine smoothed out and took us over the ton. Talk about hero worship!

As soon as we had flown solo three times, we had completed the course and had to make way for novice pilots. We also gained a small metal badge for our uniforms and a pilot's licence that looked like a miniature green passport. Unfortunately, we were never to use it, for with A Levels and university on the horizon our thoughts turned elsewhere. Neither of us ever went gliding again. In 1963, Longton High School disbanded its Combined Cadet Force, and shortly afterwards the Gliding School relocated to Tern Hill.

No. 1037 Squadron of the ATC was also nearing the end of its time at the aerodrome. The accommodation provided for them had turned out to be less than perfect and the years had taken their toll. Nicholas Cartlidge recalled conditions and activities while he was a civilian instructor there for three years:

The CO was Flight Lieutenant J. F. D. Davies, the adjutant Flying Officer John Carter, and there was a Flying Officer John Cooke, who was ultimately promoted to Flight Lieutenant when he was made CO of the unit. The squadron met in old wartime huts on Meir Aerodrome, which in the 1960s were at the end of their useful life. The rain poured through the roof when the weather was inclement.

The squadron met twice a week for two hours and again, I think, on Sunday morning when we had .22 rifle range practice at the T.A. Centre, Meir, which had a miniature rifle range within its walls. Like the Longton High School equivalent, the ATC offered cadets and staff flying experience: I had a couple of flights from Shawbury in a Provost and Chipmunk in the 60s. Cadets attended courses on various aspects of flying; some obtained gliding qualifications as well. I did a course on meteorology. We'd planned to have a met. station at Meir, but vandals wrecked it and it was finally removed. I attended two annual camps at RAF Bassingbourn, Cambridgeshire, and RAF Kinloss in Scotland in 1966. I typed and printed the magazine *The Albatross* as well.

A new ATC hut was eventually built within the curtilage of the TA Centre, but with the coming of the new A50, it had to be demolished and the squadron moved to Anchor Road, Adderley Green. Sadly, the connection of Meir with all things aeronautical ceased with its move. Very sad indeed.

22

Opportunity Knocks?

By 1960 prospects for the aerodrome looked bleak. The Lord Mayor, Alderman Harold Clowes, stated that he saw no future at all for Meir as an airport and that his preference was for a helicopter base nearer the city centre, in one of the parks or other suitable open spaces. The North Staffordshire Chamber of Commerce agreed, declaring that Stoke-on-Trent was unlikely ever to need an international air terminal, for which in any case Meir would be inadequate. Its secretary, Jim Glover, also felt that an inter-city helicopter service would be quite sufficient.

Several visits to the area at that time might have helped reinforce their convictions. On 18 May, the Duke of Devonshire flew by helicopter from London to open the Jubilee Industrial Exhibition that was being staged in Hanley Park. Billed as the biggest tented exhibition ever held in this country (apart from the Chelsea Flower Show), it was designed to showcase local industry to the world and at the same time provide an enjoyable day out for the ordinary man and his family.

In total there were seventy-nine exhibitions, fifty of which were in the main marquee that covered an area of 250,000 square feet. A restaurant, bank, Labour Exchange, and replica of an old English inn were also on site. 'We have built a small village in the heart of Stoke-on-Trent,' said Jim Glover. Added attractions were performances by the band of the Grenadier Guards, film shows, competitions, and the arrival of the Duke himself, who was to fly direct to the park and thus become the first man to land in the middle of the city.

As it turned out, the flight was not a success. Bad weather delayed the departure from London by an hour, and then strong wind and low cloud forced the helicopter down at Elmdon Airport in Birmingham. When it finally arrived – 2½ hours late – the pilot thought the designated landing area 'too tight' and came down 200 yards away on the football pitch. The Duke, experiencing his first flight by helicopter, said: 'We were very unlucky all through.'

More fortunate was the Secretary of State for War, Mr Christopher Soames, who landed in the park the following month. Accompanied by General Sir Hugh Stockwell, who had been in command of ground forces during the Suez operations of 1956, he had flown from Chester in an Alouette helicopter as part of his tour of Army Information Centres in the Midlands. He was met by civic officials and senior officers of Western Command before he made a 20-minute visit to the Army Centre in Kingsway, Stoke. On the same day Princess Margaret, President of the then University College of North Staffordshire, was conferring degrees at Keele. She had flown in to Tern Hill that morning. Meir Airport, it seemed, was now all but redundant.

Such activity as there was at the airfield followed a familiar pattern. On 20 June, cadets of the North Staffordshire Unit of the Women's Junior Air Corps sampled 'first-flight' experience in an aircraft piloted by Mrs Elizabeth Overbury. In August, the airport was so quiet that the gliding school could put on an intensive week-long course, at the end of which sixteen complete beginners from all parts of the country had gained their 'wings' by flying solo. On 4 November, Santa Claus again arrived by air to make his traditional tour of the Potteries.

*

In 1961, with Yuri Gagarin, the world's first spaceman, being mobbed in Manchester during his tour of the country, Meir's aeronautical ambitions seemed to be going from bad to worse. 'What is the future of Stoke-on-Trent City Airport?' asked the *Sentinel* that September (almost echoing the words of an editorial of 1934!). It referred to the fact that the helicopter service had not materialised, and that the idea of transforming the area into a 'garden city' seemed to be flavour of the month with the Council. A correspondent to its letters' page expressed the commonplace view that the airport was too small for modern aircraft and too large and too distant from the city for a helicopter site. He suggested replacing it with a municipal golf course, restaurant, putting and bowling greens, and tennis courts.

As ever, the opinions of people who actually flew were radically different. Following a long line of pilots who had found little fault with the aerodrome, Captain John Beard of Derby Airways (whose own back garden overlooked the airfield at Meir) castigated the Council's latest proposal and its handling of the airport in general. 'Meir is a relatively good airfield, which needs attention,' he wrote to the *Sentinel*.

> Given attention, air lines would operate through Stoke-on-Trent. The attitude of the Council is to close it altogether because it is not being used. This is like closing a shop because no one is buying due to the fact that no goods are on sale.

Drawing on his own wide experience, he went on:

> Northampton, Carlisle, Leeds, Cheltenham, and Cardiff all have regular services to various points in Europe, and with the exception of Cardiff they are not as good as Meir is now. Derby Airport, a small grass field half the size of Meir, has

no runway at all, but aircraft are arriving and leaving every hour or so during the week, and every 15 minutes at week-ends. From there one can travel anywhere on the Continent and as far as the Canary Islands during the winter.

North Staffordshire, he stated, had a far larger population than any of these places and a vast industry to boot. All that Meir required was a fire-tender and a radio operator, and later, a better runway and lighting for night operations. Once the airfield was declared open, he was certain that aircraft would soon be operating through Stoke-on-Trent.

Eric Clutton then weighed in, deploring the 'appalling lack of imagination on the part of our civic leaders who seem entirely unable to appreciate modern developments in air transport' and for whom 'the revenue from the grass is apparently more important than the development of an air terminal for Stoke-on-Trent.' When a contracting firm offered to take up the runway without charge for hard core, it was the turn of Newcastle businessman Charles Strasser to denounce the proposal: 'It is my opinion that Meir should be developed for all classes of users, to include feeder-line services, business and executive users, flying clubs and gliding, and in the interests of all these it would be a retrograde step for the existing facility of a quite usable runway capable of development to be removed.'

After this backlash, the Council underwent one of its periodic changes of heart and decided to keep the airport. After all its members had seen how the recent return of Stanley Matthews from Blackpool to Stoke City had transformed the club's fortunes. (In the 1962/63 season, he again helped Stoke win the Second Division Championship – after a gap of thirty years.) Might not a revived aerodrome do the same for local industry? The *Sentinel* thought so and praised this 'wise decision', declaring that it was 'almost unthinkable' for Stoke-on-Trent to be without some form of air travel. Readers agreed, pointing to the Common Market then being formed in Europe and stressing how important an airfield might be for exports. The Airport Committee at once adopted a more positive attitude, stating that it would meet several organisations in the near future to determine how best the airport might be used.

It first considered a proposal to form a flying club from Mr T. Jervis Madew, an architect and surveyor of Newcastle who was acting on behalf of a group of professionals and businessmen. It was not long, however, before the committee took fright at the financial and technical implications involved and in March 1962 shelved the proposal for the time being. Mr Madew was not to be deterred so easily and a few days later presided over a meeting at the airfield. The guest speaker was Captain Beard, who reiterated many of the points he had made in his earlier letter to the *Sentinel*. He spoke of the site's enormous potential and compared it favourably in size and condition to the Burnaston Airfield in Derby, from which his employers ran thirteen medium-sized planes to all parts of the world. He added that Meir had a runway that was better than many of those he landed on which were in regular commercial use.

With a nod in the direction of the cost-conscious Stoke-on-Trent Corporation, he contended that Meir could be opened immediately as a local 'feeder' airfield without any expensive outlay. Burnaston had no extensive facilities whatsoever: it had a wooden control tower and a jeep with buckets of water to act as a fire-tender. Indeed, he stated that the Corporation could make a handsome profit from renting the airfield and from the fees for take-off and landing – ten guineas a time in each case. He also dismissed the idea that a heliport should be established somewhere in the city centre by observing that a helicopter was five times more expensive to run than the average passenger plane.

His words were enthusiastically endorsed by several businessmen, who spoke of their irritation at having to drive to Ringway, and by members of the North Staffordshire Flying Club, which was officially formed at the meeting. They said that the club already had 500 potential members and were convinced that once the airfield was open, many local executives would use it for private and business trips. Indeed, fifteen letters had already been received from local firms supporting the reopening of the airport. The account of the meeting in the *Sentinel* ended with the question 'Can Stoke-on-Trent afford to throw away its opportunity?'

The Council was at least able to look sympathetically on applications from organisations and individuals that did not involve it in any outlay. In 1963, the Staffordshire Gliding Club was given permission to begin operations at Meir. Eric Clutton, the club's Technical Officer, also kept alive the tradition of the 'Flying Flea' enthusiasts by being allowed to use Meir to test fly his self-designed and homebuilt aircraft FRED (which stood for 'Flying Runabout Experimental Design' or, as it was sometimes suggested, 'Flipping Wreck Expecting Disaster').

Once when he was working on it, a charter plane landed carrying the Beatles manager, Brian Epstein. While he took a taxi to a meeting, Eric took the pilot to a local chip shop. When the plane left several hours later it was dark, and Eric had to shine his headlights down the runway to light a path for its take-off. On 11 October 1963, the Fab Four themselves performed at Trentham Gardens and received a tumultuous reception, the like of which had never been seen before by the staff there or by the Beatles, who described it as 'the most enthusiastic welcome we have ever received'. It was soon to be called 'Beatlemania'.

During that winter there was regular flying practice over Meir, but only by the model aircraft of the Five Towns Club, which (after more than a decade of trying) had finally been given permission to use part of the airfield for meetings and demonstrations. Meanwhile, with Meir station earmarked for closure under the Beeching axe, the Airport Committee agreed to reconsider Mr Madew's proposal when the group of enthusiasts he represented came forward with an offer of financial help towards the cost of restoring the airfield. The following year the committee was hopeful that a licence for club flying might be granted, and the possibility of the airport's being used again for limited commercial services was explored.

Eric Clutton and FRED.

It was at this juncture that the Council became involved in a proposal advanced initially by Stafford Rural Council – that Seighford Airfield, a wartime bomber base near Stafford, should be developed by a number of local authorities into a new airport serving the whole of the West Midlands. The airfield had a 2,000 yard runway – recently resurfaced – and a fully-equipped control tower with radar and radio. After the war, it had been leased by Boulton Paul Airways of Wolverhampton, which still carried out some work on military aircraft on the site for the Ministry of Defence. Executive planes were also landing there, carrying businessmen who then took advantage of the nearby M6 to get to factories all over the Midlands.

A practical demonstration of its potential was provided on 9 April 1964 when a Viscount airliner carrying thirty-seven test pilots and staff from the Empire Test Pilots' School in Farnborough flew into Seighford. Any doubts that the airfield was unsuitable for modern machines were swept aside. Boulton Paul's Chief Test Pilot, Ben Gunn, saw its future as a 'bus-stop' airport handling passengers, executives, and freight aircraft, but nothing too big or too noisy. 'We could make this a civil airport tomorrow,' he said. 'We are quite ready and have the best landing devices. We could bring a plane down in practically any weather.' He did warn, though, that action was needed at once, while everything was in working order and costs would be minimal: 'It is no good waiting five years and then spending millions of pounds to renovate it.' Despite his warning, it would take seven years to resolve the issue.

23

The Seighford Controversy

That autumn, for the first time, the *Sentinel* despaired of the airfield's ever being developed into a modern airport. Apart from the site's much-discussed 'problems', it also detected in the interest shown in the Seighford proposal a hint that Meir had no future. The newspaper now favoured a helicopter station in some central location.

The following month, to everyone's surprise, the City Council sanctioned an 'all-out drive' to get the airport back on the flying map, with a series of advertisements and invitations aimed at airlines and other organisations. 'At the moment, Meir is not in the air manuals as an airport,' said the Town Clerk. 'A lot of these people are not aware that it exists.' An Independent member of the Council congratulated the committee on its new-found sense of commitment after having 'flirted' with the notion for years. Public reaction was mixed. One correspondent to the *Sentinel* declared that 'the idea of putting Meir Airport back on the flying map is long overdue – so long overdue, in fact, that the idea is now quite useless.' Another urged the Council to 'get the airport fully operational for the holiday traffic of 1965 and 1975', and pointed out that short runway landings and take-offs were now possible and well within the capacity of Meir.

As ever, nothing was straightforward where the airfield was concerned. Negotiations with the Ministry of Transport regarding a licence became protracted and continued through and beyond 1965 until it was refused on safety grounds. By then it was clear that the response to the advertisements had been disappointing, especially from commercial organisations. Ind Coupe and the National Coal Board were said to be interested in flying from Meir, although the Michelin Tyre Company, mindful of the cost that was likely to be involved in bringing the airport up to scratch, was more dubious. The 'all-out drive' stalled, to the annoyance of local residents. Always in the background was the tantalising prospect of Seighford.

The Chairman of Staffordshire County Council, Mr George Newman, had been appointed head of a special sub-committee to investigate that proposal. At first he seemed to favour the scheme and, although sixty years old, was thinking of applying for a flying licence himself. When he explored the financial implications of the proposal, however, he rapidly changed his mind. The committee deliberated for more than eight months – most of 1965 – and supporters of the idea urged them to make progress. Claim and counter-claim followed in bewildering succession, making it difficult to credit at times that the same airfield was being described. The president of Stafford Chamber of Trade declared that they could have an airport for £6 10s – the cost of a civil airport licence. Stafford's mayor replied that it would take £1 million to make Seighford a going concern, a figure later revised downwards to £250,000 by the committee. On top were the running costs, which would be 'colossal' according to Mr Newman and could be kept under £10,000 a year according to Charles Strasser.

The current notion that the airfield would be instantly usable was also derided by Mr Newman: 'There is nothing there except a large runway. There is not one sound building. All are badly deteriorated – if you were on a farm, the health authority would stop you keeping pigs in them.' Charles Strasser flew over to see for himself and found 'a long, fully operational runway, a sound air traffic control building, a sound fire station, and three sound hangars'. Finally Mr Newman contended that there was no demand for an airport, a claim that flew in the face of Stafford's own Chamber of Trade's wholehearted support for the scheme.

On 18 January 1966, a meeting of Staffordshire County Council decided not to proceed further with the proposal. Yet so great had been the criticism expressed at and after the meeting, especially by the Chairman Elect, Alderman John Amery, that the decision had to be ratified at a later meeting on 12 March. Within a few months, Southampton Airport expressed an interest in operating the airfield. Seighford was obviously not such a 'lame duck' as it had been portrayed, said Mr Amery, also noting the continuing interest of Wolverhampton and Stoke-on-Trent. For the moment, however, the whole business was shelved.

*

Yet again the *Sentinel* questioned the future of Meir Aerodrome: 'Will it ever become an airport in fact as well as in fancy? The prospect recedes annually. There is about as much chance of it happening as there is of Staffordshire County Council getting airborne at Seighford.' Some correspondents argued that a proposed new town destined for Swynnerton should go to the aerodrome with a new international airport being built there instead.

If Meir seemed doomed, it was determined to go out with a bang. On 8 June, a series of small explosions was heard coming from a building where the Midland Chemical Company manufactured house paint and cellulose. Five fire engines rushed to the aerodrome and were met by a mighty explosion that ripped through the plant, blowing off its doors and cracking the concrete walls. It was then engulfed in flames. When the blaze was eventually extinguished, the owner, Mr Witold Horbik, had to wear a gas mask to inspect what was left of his factory.

Out of the blue Meir became operational again in September when Charles Strasser tried to administer the kiss-of-life to the ailing airport. He had learnt to fly in connection with his photography business, Photopia, and had bought first an Auster, then a Piper Tripacer, before deciding to upgrade to a Cessna Skymaster. The TV quiz personality and pilot Hughie Green had one for sale – a Skymaster 336 – and he flew to Meir to demonstrate it to his potential buyer. However, the latter finally settled on the latest model that had just come onto the market and bought a Skymaster 337, G-ATNY, which he later made available as an air taxi to any airport in Britain or elsewhere within a 2,000 mile range.

Two professional pilots operated the service, and in the first two months there were charters to Stuttgart, Cologne, Paris, Oslo, Stockholm, and Frankfurt. But again it was short-lived. 'We offered it for about six months,' wrote Charles Strasser, 'but we were ahead of our time as we had very few takers.' In November, on the same day that the *Sentinel* reported on its progress, it also published the Council's decision to use the airfield for 'residential development, public open spaces, and industry', subject to approval from the Minister of Housing. The ground had effectively been cut from under the wings of Meir's last remaining flyers.

Public reaction was at first muted, perhaps because (it was said) the plan would make Meir a 'boom town'. Roger Lycett-Smith, who one day would write a notable book on the airfield, was one of the few to criticise the decision. He was also less than enthusiastic about the proposed alternative of Seighford, which he felt would be too large, too costly to maintain, and too distant from the Potteries.

Nevertheless, the Council's aeronautical ambitions now centred on Seighford. A survey of potential users was ordered, an inspection of the airfield was carried out in April 1967, and the plan was vigorously backed by the Lord Mayor Elect, Alderman Edwin Holloway and by Charles Strasser. Then at a City Council meeting in July came two revelations that were, according to the *Sentinel*, 'as disturbing for ratepayers as a couple of sonic booms'. The first was that the West Midlands Civil Aviation Committee had advised against turning Seighford into a civil airport; the second was that – despite this advice

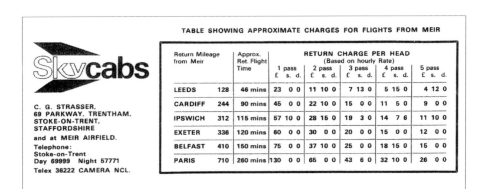

Charles Strasser's Skycab brochure details destinations and costs.

– the Council was to commission a survey of the airfield's potential at a cost of nearly £5,000. The implication – that the city might be prepared to 'go it alone' – caused some consternation to the newspaper. 'There is no point in inviting bankruptcy,' it warned, 'for the sake of belatedly entering the air age.'

*

In November 1967, a local inquiry was held at Stoke Town Hall into the city's development plans for Meir. The Ministry Inspector, Mr A. J. Hunt, heard both sides of the argument, visited the aerodrome, and then left to write his report. It would be seven months before the Minister of Housing reached what would be a highly unusual decision.

Meanwhile, in January 1968, the survey commissioned by the Council, entitled *Airport Facilities in the North of the West Midlands Region*, was submitted by Alan Stratford and Associates, Consultants in Aviation Transport. It recommended Seighford as 'the most suitable of the sites inspected' for private, club, and business flying, although it acknowledged that scheduled air services were unlikely to operate there for some years. The report also gave a last description of the aerodrome at Meir, which is as dispassionate as a death certificate:

> This is a field which is at present used by a very small number of private aircraft and has not been licensed for some years by the Board of Trade (Civil Aviation Department). [...] The runway is in very poor condition and is, in our view, dangerous; the grass surface is particularly uneven. No traffic control or landing aids are available and it is necessary for a pilot to land at his own risk. Although we find from the records that 360 acres of land are available within the airfield boundary, the site is closely built up on the north and west sides, so that the total effective area is less than the acreage would indicate. We understand that during the last 12 months only 16 movements took place at this airfield apart from those of the two light aircraft owner/operators who made constant use of the field.
>
> This airfield is not suitable for investment as a major city airport with a new runway and terminal facilities such as might attract airline operators, and its closure will not affect to any extent the future air transport facilities in the region.

The City Council convened a conference of local authorities in the catchment area and other interested parties to consider the report, and in April a 'full and frank meeting' took place. If the Council was hoping that others would be willing to share the estimated £300,000 cost of developing the airfield at Seighford, it was to be sadly disappointed. Staffordshire County Council – which had leaked the report to the press in advance of the meeting – saw no reason to change its mind; other authorities were lukewarm. The Chairman of the West Midlands Advisory Committee for Civil Aviation said publicly that it would be 'unwise to spend ratepayers' money' on the proposal.

Even the businessmen who flew from Meir were having second thoughts about Seighford and now favoured Hixon, another former RAF airfield near Stafford. Their spokesman, Mr C. E. Edwards, reasoned: 'Hixon is better situated for weather, it has three usable runways compared with Seighford's one, and it would be more economical to develop.' With the motto of 'Keep the Potteries airborne', a consortium of nine companies was prepared to make use of Hixon privately or as part of an authority scheme. Stoke's Town Clerk promised that the Council would keep an open mind on the subject.

At the end of May, the Corporation was jubilant at the news that the Housing Minister, Mr Anthony Greenwood, had approved their development scheme for Meir Aerodrome. Astonishingly, the Minister had disregarded the recommendations of his own expert, Mr Hunt, who had presided over the local inquiry. The latter had concluded that the scheme should be rejected because 'the long term future of this large and important site merits further consideration'. He was dubious about mixing industry with high-class housing on the same site, and supported local businessmen in their assertion that an airport was a necessity.

'All the evidence is that Seighford would be a preferable alternative if available,' he concluded. 'If it is not then Meir could be developed as a landing ground for the lighter type of aircraft likely to be used for business purposes without undue difficulty or excessive expenditure.' In overruling him, the Minister said that he had in mind 'the very grave problems which face the council – especially the need for suitable land for the expansion of existing industries and for attractive housing to halt the decline in population.' The *Sentinel* thought that the decision would give 'general satisfaction'. This was premature; the controversy was only just beginning.

First of all the Hixon proposal came to grief when it aroused considerable local opposition and was blocked by the County Council. But this was a mere dress rehearsal for the events that were to follow at Seighford. In July, the Home Office approached Staffordshire County Council about the possibility of using part of that aerodrome as a maximum security prison, a proposal which generated headlines such as 'Prison or planes – it will be a village of fear'. A hornet's nest of opposition was being stirred up.

Stoke-on-Trent Corporation, now in direct competition with the Home Office, decided to 'go it alone' and enter into negotiations with the Ministry of Technology for the sale or lease of the airfield, to the dismay of some Tory councillors. Mr J. S. Heath described the idea as 'throwing money away', and suggested instead a heliport on the top of Stoke station. The consortium of businessmen had no option left but to back the scheme and offered the Council £72,000 for limited use of the airfield. However, with the Ministry of Technology not prepared to make a decision on Stoke's application until the Home Office issue was settled, the affair dragged on month after month.

Even worse, the Council's intentions for Meir now came under sustained attack from parish councils and local residents alike. After several stormy public meetings in October, the Meir Aerodrome Development Committee was formed, to urge the Council to abandon plans to extend the existing industrial site and instead to enlarge the provision of playing fields. Particular anger was directed at the siting of a colour works with a proposed 100-foot-high chimney. (Perhaps the recent explosions were still fresh in people's minds.) The Council responded that such protests were now 'too late', although it did agree to look at Meir's own plan for the old airport. But as far as the colour factory was concerned, the Corporation had sold the land for £90,000, the contract was signed, and Harrison Mayer could proceed as soon as it wished.

On 14 October, more than forty pupils of Holden Lane Junior High School experienced the thrill of an airborne geography lesson when they took part in a shuttle service between Meir Aerodrome and Manchester. However, such trips were now much rarer as the airfield had become something of an obstacle course, with the fly-tipping of household rubbish, including old bedsteads. Courting couples lying in the grass, children playing cricket, and cars parked on the runway were also common hazards, while one pilot had a close encounter with a man racing whippets.

A warning was issued that the airport was still in use and that trespassers might be prosecuted – or decapitated. Pilots were also warned that they used the airfield at their own risk. Mr C. E. Edwards relocated to Manchester, as Meir was 'virtually unusable', while Charles Strasser made arrangements to move his aircraft to Castle Donington. Other local executives, who had all but given up on the Seighford project, were threatening to move their businesses out of the city because of the lack of airfield facilities. Fred Holdcroft, head of Holdcroft Electrical Contractors Ltd of Etruria Vale, was one. 'At the public inquiry, the Seighford project was dangled in front of the Ministry as a carrot,' he said. 'Now Meir is being abandoned without any alternative facilities being provided for the growing number of businessmen who rely on their aircraft to bring orders and employment into the city.'

Another such businessman was Toby Harding, an ex-RAF fighter pilot and Chairman of Vanroy Ltd of Burslem, manufacturers of pump and chemical plant. In January 1969, the company bought a new aircraft, but their application for hangarage at Meir was refused by the Airport Committee. 'We are expanding like mad,' said a frustrated Mr Harding, 'and exporting a lot more to Europe. The airport is a necessity. If Cheltenham and Gloucester, with half the population of the Potteries, can operate an airport – surely Stoke-on-Trent can.' As a last resort he and other executives intended to write to the Minister of Housing with a request to reverse the decision on the aerodrome. They might well have agreed with councillor Stanley Heath who declared that 'what has happened at Meir over the past 30 years is really quite tragic. Meir Airport is a chapter of mistakes from beginning to end.'

24

Broken Wings

In October 1969, the RAF returned to the city with a huge static display, including a Bloodhound Mark II missile on its launch pad, a Gnat, a Hawker Hunter F6, and cockpits of Lightning and Vulcan aircraft. Pilots and technicians attended to answer visitors' questions and demonstrate the equipment. It was reminiscent of the pre-war Empire Day displays at Meir Aerodrome – but this was held on the forecourt of Tom Byatt Ltd in Victoria Road, Fenton.

At least the RAF still came. When a Skyvan STOL (short take-off and landing) aircraft made a tour of twenty-one British cities to demonstrate a possible 'commuter' service for executives, Stoke was not on the list. 'We just do not have the facilities,' lamented the *Sentinel*, 'and will not have them until the powers that be stop dithering on the Seighford Airport proposal.' Adding insult to injury, the Rank Organisation announced that its much heralded film *The Battle of Britain* would have a royal première on 15 September – Battle of Britain Day – with special showings in ten provincial cities. Despite its association with Reginald Mitchell, Stoke-on-Trent was not one of them.

There had, however, been better news that June when the Home Office confirmed that it was no longer interested in the Seighford site. The following month the Corporation was offered a seven-year lease with an option to buy – on condition that the necessary permission for flying to continue there could be obtained from Staffordshire County Council. A formal application was therefore made, despite a bid by some Tory councillors to scrap the whole project and a broadside from the chairman of the Aviation Advisory Committee, who stated that Stoke would be 'committing suicide' if it went ahead. Alderman Sir Albert Bennett, the Labour leader, appealed to his fellow councillors to 'look to the future'.

Also looking to the future – with anxiety – were the residents of Seighford and a number of neighbouring parish councils. The outcome was an invitation to the City Council to explain its intentions at a public meeting on 19 September at Great Bridgeford. Sir Albert Bennett and several members of the Airport Committee represented Stoke-on-Trent, with three businessmen who flew regularly from Meir in support. It was not a comfortable experience. Noise, traffic volume, finance, and plans for future development were the prime topics raised in a question-and-answer session, and although Sir Albert did his best to calm their fears, stating that there would be no flying club and no commercial traffic, the residents remained unconvinced. At the end of the meeting, the 120 residents present voted unanimously for a public inquiry into the affair.

Relations between the County Council and City Council had been less than cordial for some time and on the subject of airports they were barely on speaking terms. In 1970, things went from bad to worse as the city's application regarding flying at Seighford seemed to be getting nowhere, with the County accused of 'putting obstacles in the city's way'. 'Stafford County Council are definitely against us,' said the chairman of the Airport Committee, 'although they have no use for Seighford themselves. I think it is a matter of jealousy.' The *Sentinel* likened the elaborate process of move and counter-move to a 'continuing game of airport chess'.

Predictably, on 6 April, the application was turned down, a refusal variously described as 'short-sighted', 'misguided', and 'prejudiced'. The City Council immediately said that it would consider an appeal. For the moment, however, it was in check.

*

Beset with problems both external and internal in its efforts to secure Seighford Airfield, the City Council now tried to placate the residents of Meir by revising the allocation of the land available for public spaces. It also assured residents that the industrial section would be effectively screened, thereby eliminating any possible nuisance.

Its case had not been helped by another explosion on the site a few months earlier, when a kiln at Staffordshire Potteries blew up just after it had been fired by teenager Terry Roberts, who was extremely lucky to escape with his life. Much worse was to follow on 16 July 1970 at the same plant. Minutes before the 1,200 staff were due to finish work, a fire suddenly erupted in the large export warehouse that had been built only the year before at a cost of £36,000. The alarm sent staff scurrying for the exits and attracted the attention of forty-eight-year-old Mrs Marjorie Edge, a clerk in the building who happened to be working elsewhere. She returned at once and went inside to retrieve her handbag. She died in the fire as did David Dikta, a sixteen-year-old who had started work at the factory only a week before. Throughout that night, forty City and County firemen fought the blaze, enduring intense heat and smoke, with asbestos sheeting crackling around them. Eric Clutton flew over the conflagration in FRED – 'it was quite a sight looking down inside the inferno', he recalled. Next day the gutted warehouse had to be demolished on safety grounds.

At a council meeting ten days after the fire, a joint Labour and Independent vote saw off the Tory opposition to approve an appeal against Stafford's rejection of their Seighford application. The Council was given a boost by support from various quarters. Mr J. W. Mole, an ex-RAF officer and the owner of Enstone Airport in Oxford, volunteered to speak for the proposal at any inquiry. 'It would be criminal not to use Seighford,' he said. 'It is excellently sited to make a first-class airport, not only for executive flying but for charter flights. I could put it into operation reasonably cheaply.' A Stoke-on-Trent businessman, Mr Digby Rofe, boss of Nimrod Heating Ltd of Hanley and himself a qualified pilot, began a petition in support of the scheme. Not only had he been sent more than thirty letters from other executives, but he had received backing from the former owner of a Birmingham flying club, who said that his members would be keen to form a club there. Finally, with a public inquiry now in the offing, the powerful Telford New Town Development Corporation gave the proposal its blessing.

The year that it took to set up the public inquiry gave the opposition ample time to marshal its own forces, which eventually included parish councils, women's institutes, village hall committees, civic societies, NFU representatives, the Road Survey Committee, and the Owner Occupiers' Association. Resistance groups were formed, campaigns coordinated, and preliminary skirmishes fought in cold print in the local press. Car stickers reading *Say No to Seighford Airport* were everywhere. Any residents who argued that the airport would bring much-needed jobs to the area were drowned in a rising tide of near hysteria. If scare stories of crops being polluted and property being damaged by vibration were not enough, the spectre of 'another Luton' on their doorstep usually did the trick. Stone MP Hugh Fraser spoke at one protest meeting and denounced the proposal as 'absurd'; the chairman of the West Midlands Civil Aviation Committee described it as 'the biggest white elephant of all time'.

With solicitors, barristers and acoustic experts retained, the inquiry opened on 27 July 1971 in the packed village hall at Great Bridgeford. More than 200 protestors paraded outside – some from Stoke-on-Trent's Ratepayers' Association – with placards reading *Sink Seighford*, and a 5,000 signature petition was handed to the Ministry Inspector, Mr A. D. Owen. During the six days of the proceedings more than twenty-five witnesses spoke, and an aerial inspection of Seighford – ironically from Meir Airport – was organised for Mr Owen and the Aeronautical Assessor, Group Captain G. F. K. Donaldson. One of the most dramatic revelations came on the second day when Stoke's Town Clerk said that the Corporation was prepared to budget a 'substantial' sum of money annually on top of the initial £100,000 payment for the airfield. The Corporation was going for broke – it was now Seighford or nothing.

The inquiry ended on 4 August. In summing up, Mr Stephen Brown, QC, on behalf of the Corporation maintained that the objections were 'emotional ones' and that the airfield was a 'necessity' for Stoke-on-Trent. However, according to Mr Michael Gregory of the Country Landowners' Association, the appeal was 'civic pride running ahead of necessity'. In a scathing attack, he continued: 'If Stoke-on-Trent were given permission to operate Seighford Airfield it could turn out to be a Fred Karno affair run by Dad's Army.' With that evening's *Sentinel* also sceptical, the appeal seemed doomed.

*

If Meir Airport was in its death throes, it was not yet dead. Three aeroplanes were still based there and flown for sport, recreation, and educational purposes. Fred Holdcroft was now the sole businessman on the site, but he put the airfield to good use, especially during the first national postal strike in 1971 when he transformed himself into a 'flying postman' to provide an 'air-mail' service for his company. On 6 February he flew to Southend, saying that with 300 air bases available to him he could distribute mail almost anywhere in the country – with same day delivery guaranteed.

Besides flying FRED, Eric Clutton belonged to a twelve-strong syndicate (the Staffordshire Light Plane Group) that flew a two-seater Jodel 117 from Meir. Members generously gave free flights to anyone who turned up at the aerodrome and even allowed passengers a turn at the controls. Colin Pepper, another member, recalled how on one occasion a number of the syndicate decided to paint the undercarriage and stood the aircraft on its nose. Within minutes piercing sirens heralded the arrival of the emergency services, which had been told that a plane had nosedived into the ground.

The most regular user of the airfield, however, continued to be the Staffordshire Gliding Club, which had gradually become more firmly established, with its own clubhouse and workshop on the airfield. It had been formed on 19 December 1962 with fifty founder members, but had not begun operations until 13 April 1963 when their first (and only) glider, a T-31, was launched into the steady drizzle falling over Meir. Bertie Aranyos, a beginner, accompanied by Chief Instructor Bill Hutchinson, were the first men into the air and both survived what was indeed a baptism.

During its first year, 1,100 launches were made, twelve pilots reached solo standard, and Dr Peter Bradwell gained the first Silver 'C' awarded to the club. With thirty-five of its members quite new to gliding, there was inevitably a high degree of wear and tear on the equipment. Fortunately, there were many engineers in the club, and a well-organised technical committee led by Ray Johnson overcame many snags and even got the winch off the danger list. With the donation of an old car for use as a retrieve vehicle and the purchase of a single-seater Tutor, the club was able to open its waiting list, and among those admitted was their first lady member, Gillian Wilkinson.

Besides flying every weekend throughout the year, the club also put on periodical training courses (known to members as the 'the art of coarse flying'). One such course ran from 1 to 5 June 1964, with ten members and two instructors taking part, and the Coventry Club had lent its Tiger Moth and a Ka-2B two-seater glider for the occasion. Despite the atrocious weather, which allowed flying on only 2½ days, 140 launches were made and nearly 17 hours of flying logged. A *Sentinel* reporter and photographer turned up to sample the delights on offer and were met by John Kaye, one of the instructors, who handed them a parachute and an indemnity form and said: 'Just put your names here and sign your lives away.'

The account published by the reporter, Peter Harrison, allows us to share the various stages of the experience. First the take-off, towed by the plane:

> The rudders begin to move restlessly in front of your feet as the pilot flexes them from behind. The Tiger Moth, 50 feet in front at the end of the cable, is purring like an eager bee. And then you are rolling forward through the grass and it is wrong to be moving so swiftly through the grass. 'We'll be airborne before the Tiger. Watch!' And then you are soaring upwards on outstretched wings, as ardently as any angel, to your rendezvous in the sky. One thousand feet and the glider is pitching. You feel the absurd need for something to hold on to. You open the Perspex window to the uproar of the wind. Staffordshire, green and carefully arranged, turns below you. You are beginning to catch 'gliding fever'.

With the release of the cable, 'you are alone at 2,000 feet, and intruding. Not with the confidence of powered flight but diffidently, in a begging-your-pardon way. And all the time the wind fingers the craft in curiosity, like a boy with a wild bird.' After a sublime period, during which time seemed to stand still, they came back to earth:

> There is a bump. A dash through the grass. The glider is still for a moment before leaning wearily over on its side. The pilot says that once you have glided you are never the same again. You look back into the sky and you believe him.

*

So favourable had been the comments on aero-towing that the club bought its own Tiger Moth, G-AHUE, in December 1964, when it also acquired a two-drum diesel winch of such formidable size that it was christened 'Winchosaurus'. A recruiting drive brought in more *ab initios*, including their second lady member, Jacqueline Hurst, and their first Gold holder, Hugh Browning, who was quickly enlisted as an instructor.

By 1966 there were five club gliders (a T-31, Capstan, Swallow, Tutor and Olympia), two winches, the Tiger Moth tug, three vehicles and trailers, and eight instructors, not to mention one or two private gliders. Membership had soared to a hundred, with ages ranging from twelve to sixty-five. The club also began to set aside Wednesday evenings as youth nights, when cut-price flights

Eric Clutton pilots the gliding club's Tiger Moth.

were on offer to schools and youth organisations of North Staffordshire. The club's chairman said that gliding was more popular than ever and was not just 'a rich man's sport'. 'We have an excellent cross-section of the community,' he explained, 'with whole families joining the club. There is also an active social side.' As a mark of its growing success and reputation, the club was invited to become a full member of the British Gliding Association, thus enabling it to have a representative on the governing body for gliding in the British Isles.

Cross-country flying had now become possible for more advanced members, although some distance flights did not always go according to plan. Laurie Birch, who had been the first person to complete his Silver C award entirely at Meir, once landed the Olympia in Longton Park and had to take the bus back to Meir, an incongruous figure carrying his parachute and a barograph. The park-keeper had been most put out when he could not find any by-laws about planes landing in his park, but had been somewhat mollified by the promise of a free flight. He was obviously completely unaware of the flying activities that had taken place there fifty years before.

Alistair Wright, who progressed from *ab initio* to instructor at Meir, achieving both Silver C and Gold distance awards, also had to make 'land-outs' on occasion. Once he ran out of sky near Uttoxeter and came down in a paddock behind the house of Mr J. C. Bamford. 'It was a very hot summer's day,' he remembered, 'and Mrs Bamford, who had been sunbathing, leaned over her garden fence and invited me in for tea.' On another occasion he landed heavily in a field in North Yorkshire and was invited to a 21st party going on in the house nearest the field. 'The hospitality was so generous,' he recalled, 'that I was feeling no pain at all by the time the retrieve arrived.'

Not everyone showed such composure when descending gliders came into view. In May 1969, residents were so alarmed when they saw one landing on Trentham Park golf course that they telephoned the police, the fire-brigade, and the ambulance service. 'It was a fabulous turn-out,' said the pilot, Frank Hemmings, a Basford newsagent who had been a member of the gliding club for four years.

> I took off from Meir Airfield and headed for a storm cloud to give me more height. However, on the other side there was a severe down-draught, so I landed perfectly on the golf course. There was no one playing at the time. I must say the various emergency services arrived very quickly. I was just getting out of the glider when the first fire engine came speeding across the course.

By now the end was in sight for the club at Meir, for its existing agreement with the City Council ended on 31 August 1969, and from then on it was permitted to continue flying only on a monthly basis. Some residents gave the impression that they would be only too glad to see the back of it, complaining of the 'intolerable' noise of the Tiger Moth and of interference to their television reception. Others worried about possible mishaps. 'While there has not been an accident,' wrote one, 'there is all too often a first time.'

Tragically, the words turned out to be prophetic, for at lunchtime on Sunday, 5 April 1970, the club suffered its first real misfortune since its formation – and two of its most experienced pilots were involved. Somehow there was a mid-air collision between the Tiger Moth and a privately owned Olympia 463. The Moth, in a descending turn, suddenly hit the fuselage of the Olympia with its wing. The glider pilot, Dr Bradwell, baled out immediately and survived, though he lacerated an artery in his arm. He landed in a tree only yards from where the Moth had plunged into playing fields belonging to the North Staffordshire Polytechnic. The pilot, fifty-year-old Ken Sherriff, was killed instantly and later had to be identified by his fingerprints. The aircraft had missed a housing estate by less than 150 yards.

It was the beginning of the end of the club's time there, for although its secretary, Norman Bartlett, publicly stated that 'it would be "business as usual" that Saturday – using winches', the days of gliding at Meir were numbered. The Council finally imposed a deadline of 31 December 1972 for all flights to end. By then the Staffordshire Gliding Club had migrated to a moorland site at Leek, and in 1992 it moved to Seighford where it remains to this day.

*

Five months after the public inquiry, on 17 January 1972, the Secretary of State for the Environment, Peter Walker, dismissed Stoke's appeal and accepted the recommendation of the Ministry Inspector that the Seighford site should be restored to agricultural use. The principal reason was the major change in character that the proposed development would bring to a remote rural area. The inspector, Mr Owen, also felt that the need for an airport had not been established. 'The support from local business firms and flying associations does not add up to evidence of a public need which is not being met or which cannot be met elsewhere,' he stated. He added that existing airfields were 'reasonable alternatives' for city people.

The Chairman of the County Council was 'delighted', as was the Chairman of the Staffordshire branch of the Council for the Protection of Rural England, who called the decision 'a victory for common sense'. It was all over bar the shouting of frustrated city businessmen, who lambasted the verdict – one described it as 'a national scandal'. Equally disappointed was the Town Clerk, Mr L. K. Robinson, who said: 'I saw this as one of the last opportunities for Staffordshire as a whole, and North Staffordshire in particular, to find an airport to serve its industry.' It was left to the *Sentinel* to write the epitaph of the whole sorry saga: 'Stoke-on-Trent City Council are obliged to beat a retreat from the air age. Future generations will judge whether the decision was for good or ill.'

In February, almost by way of consolation, the city did achieve another of its ambitions – a Spitfire for permanent display – when a Mark XVI version presented by the Ministry of Defence in 1969 finally arrived – by road. There had been much discussion beforehand about possible sites for the plane, and locations near the Mitchell Memorial Centre and in Hanley Park had been considered. Once Spitfires had graced the skies above Meir and the aerodrome would have been the perfect place, but with its closure imminent this was now impossible. The plane was therefore erected on a site in Bethesda Street, Hanley, and encased in a transparent 'hangar' as protection against the elements and vandals. (In 1985, it was moved to its present location in the Museum and Art Gallery.) Local hero John Ashton, who as chairman of the Appeal Fund had been instrumental in securing the Spitfire, said: 'There can be no more appropriate memorial to Mitchell's genius.'

The same month the Council sanctioned the beginning of the development project at Meir Airport. City councillors were elated when they discovered that the sale of the land was likely to bring in an astonishing profit of up to £1½ million – the 'white elephant' had become, in the words of the leader of the Council, 'a little gold mine'. The initial phase, to begin that August, was the construction of the first fifty-seven of the 2,000 top-flight houses to be built there, each with a price tag of about £10,000. With large areas of open spaces, it was envisaged that the estate would have a 'garden city' image. Meanwhile Major Richard Eld, the former owner of the Seighford site from whom it had been compulsorily purchased years before, was expecting confirmation from the Department of the Environment that he could buy back the airfield and reclaim it for farming.

Meir Airport was officially closed on 1 January 1973. By that time most of its users had already departed for pastures new. With industrial and residential development already beginning to encroach, air activities had become dangerous, and the site was largely given up to model-aircraft aficionados, dog-walkers, golfers practising their swing, and learner-drivers trundling down the litter-strewn remnants of the runway (which was taken up in 1979). In the meantime Staffordshire Potteries had acquired a helicopter pad.

Fred Holdcroft clung on to the bitter end because 'for the last eight years, it's been like having my own private airstrip'. His family doubtless had the longest connection with the airfield, since the first delivery of goods by air – a consignment of Marconi sets – had arrived there in November 1933 for Messrs. W. A. Holdcroft Ltd. Forty years on, after an ultimatum from the Council, it fell to Fred Holdcroft to make what is regarded as the last official flight from Meir when he flew his Piper Tripacer to Ringway on 16 August 1973. 'So that's it,' he declared. 'Instead of being ideally placed for reaching anywhere in the UK rapidly, Stoke no longer has airstrip facilities, and there is a huge gap between Birmingham and Manchester. Make no mistake about it, this is a very sad day.'

However, because he was able to fold and tow his homebuilt plane, Eric Clutton continued to use Meir for a year or two after the official closure, until a brush with the local constabulary convinced him that the last flight from Meir really had taken place.

Fred Holdcroft makes the last official flight from Meir Aerodrome on 16 August 1973.

25

From Meir to Eternity (Afterword)

Dolly Shepherd continued her parachute jumping until 1912. Then she was ascending in a balloon when she heard a voice warning her not to go up again or she would be killed. She immediately ended her career at the age of twenty-five. During the First World War, she became a WAAC driver-mechanic and served in France. One of her passengers was a Captain Sedgwick, whom she later married. In the Second World War, she was active as a Fire Service Volunteer and then as Shelter Staff Officer in London. She died in 1983, two months short of her ninety-seventh birthday. A tree planted on the spot of her famous landing at Fields Farm is still called 'Dolly's Ash'.

The parachutist Edith Maud Cook (also known as Viola Spencer) later took up flying and became the first British woman to make a solo plane flight. She was killed in 1910 after making a balloon jump over Coventry as a stand-in for Dolly Shepherd. She was buried in an unmarked grave, but in 2010, as a result of the efforts of aviation enthusiasts, a headstone was erected and a dedication service held to commemorate her brief life.

Harold Hales survived not only his aerial pursuits, but also service in the First World War and numerous other adventures. In 1929, he founded the Hales Brothers' Shipping House and later presented a Blue Riband trophy, the Hales Trophy (made by Pidducks of Hanley), for the fastest ship crossing the Atlantic. From 1931 to 1935, he also served as a Conservative MP. He drowned in a boating accident on the Thames in November 1942, aged seventy-four.

Of the pilots who gave the earliest flying exhibitions in the area, Sydney Pickles went on to serve with the Royal Naval Air Service during the First World War and later worked as a test pilot and flying instructor. He died in 1975. Lord Carbery also flew with the RNAS during the war. He later renounced his title and as John Evans Carbery settled in Kenya until his death in 1970. He was one of the group of ex-pats featured in the film *White Mischief*. Frank Goodden became a test pilot on the outbreak of the war and was swiftly promoted to the rank of major in the Royal Flying Corps. In January 1917, while he was flying a prototype of the SE-5 (the fighter he had co-designed), his plane plunged into Farnborough Common, killing him on impact. 'Professor' Lowe-Wylde, who gave the first gliding displays in the Potteries, later crashed to his death in a glider of his own construction.

Prince George was killed in a plane crash in 1942 at Caithness in Scotland, while on active service. His brother Edward was never allowed to return to live in the country where he had once been king. He died in France in 1972.

Captain Fielden, the Prince of Wales' pilot, became the first Captain of the King's Flight, a position he retained after the abdication. During the war, he took charge of RAF Tempsford, where he directed the operations of No. 138 (Special Duties) Squadron in support of SOE and the Resistance in Europe. He then returned to royal service, first with King George VI, and then with Queen Elizabeth II, until his retirement in 1969. Air Vice-Marshal Sir Edward Hedley Fielden died in 1976, aged seventy-two.

Sir Alan Cobham maintained his interest in aviation throughout his life, first setting up a small airline, then establishing Flight Refuelling Ltd, a company dedicated to introducing air-to-air refuelling. He died in 1973, aged seventy-nine. His autobiography is called *A Time to Fly*.

Lady Bailey died in 1960, aged seventy. Her story is told by Jane Falloon in *Throttle Full Open*. After touring with the British Hospitals' Air Pageant, the Hon. Mrs Victor Bruce formed a company called Air Dispatch Ltd, which carried passengers and freight and also operated as an early air ambulance. She died in 1990 aged ninety-five. Her autobiography is entitled *Nine Lives Plus: Record Breaking on Land, Sea and in the Air*.

As the titles of these books suggest, the early pilots belonged to a breed that tended to 'live fast – die young'. That the three above survived to old age was pure chance, as all of them had many narrow escapes. Other pilots featured here were not so lucky, though ironically their deaths were sometimes nothing to do with flying or took place in relatively safe situations compared to their normally hazardous lives. Tom Campbell Black was killed in a freak accident in 1936 as he was taxiing to take off at Speke Aerodrome, Liverpool. He was thirty-six. Charles Scott, his co-pilot on their victorious flight to Australia, was apparently unable to come to terms with his loss of celebrity and shot himself in 1946, aged forty-two.

After commanding the women's section of the ATA, Pauline Gower joined the Board of BOAC, the first woman to achieve such a position in any national airline. In 1945 she married Wing Commander William Fahie, but died of a heart attack two years later, having just given birth to twins. Her friend and business partner, Dorothy Spicer, married Flight-Lieutenant Richard Pearce. In 1946 they were travelling (as passengers) to Rio de Janeiro when their plane flew into a mountainside, killing everyone on board. Jean Batten was unable to find a flying job during the war and devoted herself to fund-raising activities. After the war, she abandoned flying and became a recluse, dying in obscurity in Palma, Majorca, in 1982, where she was buried in a communal paupers' grave.

Harry Ward somehow managed to survive two years as 'Britain's First Birdman'. When war began, he rejoined the RAF and helped establish a parachute training school at Ringway for airborne forces and SOE agents. In 1942 he was awarded an Air Force Cross and ended the war as a Squadron Leader. He finally dropped off the perch in 2000, aged ninety-seven.

From 1940 onwards, Alex Henshaw was Chief Test Pilot at Castle Bromwich, the story of which he chronicled in *Sigh for a Merlin: Testing the Spitfire*. In March 2006, aged ninety-three, he flew in a two-seater Spitfire to commemorate the 70th anniversary of the first flight of the plane. He died in 2007, one of the most revered airmen of his generation.

Members of Meir's Volunteer Reserve distinguished themselves in many theatres of war. In March 1941, John Ashton was awarded a DFC, his citation crediting him with the destruction of at least five enemy aircraft, four of them in France. He was then appointed a flight commander with No. 64 Squadron and flew Spitfires in the defence of London and Coventry. In January 1942, he was posted to Egypt and promoted to Squadron Leader. The same year he took part in the Battle of Malta and also commanded the Malta air-sea rescue squadron. In 1944, as commander of No. 73 Squadron, he led sorties over Italy, Yugoslavia, and Austria until he was made Wing Commander. At the end of the war he had flown forty-eight different types of aircraft (including British, American, and German) and had made more than 500 operational sorties. He died in 1988, aged seventy-three, and is buried in Whitmore churchyard.

After serving as a night fighter pilot on the outbreak of war, Don Edwards was posted as a Squadron Leader to South-East Asia where he was killed in October 1944, aged twenty-four. He was buried in Gauhati war cemetery, India. According to the Roll of Honour Board at Haywood High School, he served with No. 45 Squadron.

Cedric Moores went on to join Nos 234 and 152 Squadrons. He was killed on 18 February 1941 at No. 56 OTU at Sutton Bridge in Lincolnshire, while test flying Hurricane N-2557 in poor weather conditions. He was twenty-two, the first Audley casualty of the war.

Dennis Armitage rejoined the battle in October 1940 when his squadron flew most of its operations as part of Douglas Bader's controversial 'Big Wing'. In June 1941, he was given his own squadron – No. 129 – and received a DFC from the King. On 21 September 1941, during a fighter sweep over France, he was forced to bale out and was taken prisoner. After numerous escape attempts, he was finally sent to Colditz, where he remained until he was liberated. After the war, he returned to Macclesfield and his former career as an electrical engineer in the Staffordshire coal mines. He also became chairman of the Lancashire Aero Club (where he had first begun in 1936) until he gave up flying in 1953. He subsequently moved to Petersfield, Hampshire, where he lived until his death in 2004.

Eric Bann was one of eighteen pilots lost by No. 238 Squadron during the Battle of Britain. His body was recovered and laid to rest in Macclesfield cemetery. Eric Lock has no known grave, but his name lives on in 'Eric Lock Road' in his birthplace near Shrewsbury and in the 'Eric Lock Bar' at the Shropshire Aero Club. Despite the fact that he died four years before the end of the war, his final tally of twenty-six confirmed 'kills' (and a further eight probables) makes him one of the outstanding aces of the conflict.

Ken Bishop, who was killed during a training flight on 4 August 1940, six weeks after enlisting, was buried in Leek cemetery. John Waite, the clerk whose interest in aviation he fostered and who later won the George Medal, returned to the Hanley Economic after the war and eventually became its General Manager. After demobilisation in 1950, Vic Reynolds took an active role in the training programmes of the ATC and also learned to glide at Meir. He retired in 1981 with the rank of Flight Lieutenant (Training Branch) and then continued as a civilian instructor, receiving a commendation from the Lord Lieutenant of Staffordshire for his many years of service in 2009. He died the following year, aged eighty-nine.

Of those who trained at Meir's No. 1 FPU, Maurice Mounsdon recovered from his severe wounds in the Battle of Britain and spent most of the remainder of the war as an instructor. He left the service in 1946 as a Flight Lieutenant and eventually retired to live in Spain. Geoffrey Page ended the war as a Wing Commander and worked firstly as a test pilot and then as a sales executive for Vickers Armstrong. He later became the driving force behind the creation of the Battle of Britain memorial that is situated on the cliffs near Dover. He was appointed OBE in 1995 and died in 2000, aged eighty.

Bill Hodgson was buried in Saffron Walden military cemetery in Essex. In June 1986, while a Hurricane flew low over the area, a commemorative plaque was unveiled by his former commanding officer, Peter Townsend, near the site where he had crash-landed during the Battle of Britain. A road – Hodgson Way – was also named in his honour. Of his fellow New Zealanders who passed through No. 1 FPU at Meir, fourteen were killed during the war. Profiles of the pilots are given in Errol Martyn's *For Your Tomorrow*, vol. 3 (Christchurch, 2008).

The four who took part in the Great Escape were liberated in 1945, three of them having survived the terrible forced march from Sagan as the Russians approached. After the war, Keith Ogilvie transferred to the Royal Canadian Air Force and flew various aircraft, including Vampire and Sabre 6 jets, until his retirement in 1962. He died in Ottawa in 1998, aged eighty-three.

Clive Saxelby returned to England and joined No. 617 (The Dam Busters) Squadron, first as a Flight Commander and then, still aged only twenty-four, as its Commanding Officer. Subsequently, he was posted to the Empire Test Pilots' School for three years, but resigned his commission in 1969 and was then employed by Handley Page. Group Captain Saxelby, CBE, DFC, AFC (and Bar), died in 1999, aged seventy-eight.

After leaving the RAF, Desmond Plunkett travelled widely and later lived in India and Rhodesia [Zimbabwe] where he was involved in instructing and aerial surveys. He then returned to England to live in West Sussex where he died in 2002, aged eighty-six.

Ken Rees rejoined the RAF after the war and trained as a flying instructor at Little Rissington before being posted to Tern Hill. He also returned to first-class rugby and from 1948-51 he played wing-forward for Cheshire, captained London Welsh, and trialled for Wales. He retired in 1968 with the rank of Wing Commander, having served in Cyprus and Singapore. He now lives on Anglesey.

Edward Sniders finally managed to escape in the last days of the conflict and returned to Oxford to complete his degree. In 1946 he was made a Member of the Order of the British Empire (MBE) for his war service. He then joined the Foreign Service and served in Berlin, Vienna, and Geneva. He died in 2003, aged eighty-two.

Colin Cole Jerromes joined BOAC and flew first from Hurn Airport in Hampshire and then from Heathrow until his retirement in 1976.

On 3 July 1947, the *Evening Sentinel* published the names of North Staffordshire airmen of Home Commands of the RAF who fell during the Battle of Britain (several of whom had trained at Meir). Their names had been inscribed on the Roll of Honour to be unveiled by the King in the Battle of Britain Chapel in Westminster Abbey later that month. They were as follows (with birthplace in parenthesis):

Coastal Command (pilots and other aircrew): A.C.1 L. C. Caunter (Stoke-on-Trent); A.C.2 E. Sneyd (Stoke-on-Trent); Sergeant P. W. Swinson (Stoke-on-Trent).

Bomber Command (pilots and other aircrew): Sergeant G. C. Ankers (Newcastle-under-Lyme); Sergeant G. E. Bloor (Stoke-on-Trent); Sergeant H. Day (Leek); Sergeant W. E. Elliott (Stafford); Sergeant P. K. Garvey (Stoke-on-Trent); Sergeant H. Haggett (Stafford); Sergeant M. E. Sambrook (Stoke-on-Trent); Pilot Officer M. R. Tagg (Newcastle); Pilot Officer W. Walker (Cheadle).

Army Co-operation Command: Pilot Officer R. W. Harris (Stone).

In 1949, Bill Nadin was awarded an MBE (Military Division) in recognition of his services to the ATC. When he retired in 1959, a farewell dinner in his honour was held at Federation House, Stoke, when he was presented with a silver tankard inscribed 'The first, the best, and the last of the district gliding officers.'

Reg Bott, who was introduced to flying through the ATC Gliding School at Meir, went on to join the Fleet Air Arm in 1943 and did 70 hours flying Boeing N2S Stearman aircraft from US Navy fields in 1944, before being returned to the UK. He then became Squadron Staff Officer of a Barracuda squadron in Scotland until the end of the war. He now lives in Christchurch, New Zealand.

Neil Wheeler, the youngster watching the 1929 Schneider Trophy Race, entered Cranwell in 1935 and later flew Spitfires on sorties over occupied Europe as part of the RAF's Photographic Reconnaissance Unit. As Air Chief Marshal Sir Neil Wheeler, KCB, CBE, DSO, DFC (and Bar), AFC, he was guest of honour at the presentation of Spitfire RW388 to the City of Stoke-on-Trent on 28 June 1972.

Eric Clutton and FRED emigrated to America in 1983 and now live in 'aviation heaven' in Tullahoma, Tennessee. The aircraft is still flying. Peter Berry served forty years in air traffic control before retiring in 1987. He now lives in Ayr and has written numerous articles and books, the latest of which is *Prestwick Airport & Scottish Aviation*. Charles Strasser went to live on Jersey where he produced *Skylog* (computerised log books) and became chairman of the Aircraft & Pilots' Association for the Channel Islands' region. In 2000 he was awarded an OBE for services to Staffordshire and Jersey. Professor Tony Chadwick lives in Newfoundland where he recently retired from his post at the Memorial University. He is a frequent flyer (as a passenger) though a more recent passion is sailing, and he recently completed a month's voyage to Antigua. Nicholas Cartlidge was born at Meir in 1942 and lived most of his life there, working as a chemist. He also published two books on the area, *A Meir Half Century* and *Meir Today, Gone Tomorrow*. He died in 2007.

*

Janette Tyreman (née Sankey) grew up knowing little about her father, who had been killed, aged thirty-three, while serving as an RAF instructor at Meir in 1940 (see chapter 14). Her parents had divorced just before the war, and both subsequently remarried. When her father died, Janette was at a boarding school in Kent and so learned none of the details. Since 1957 she has lived in Canada, but in 2003 began the search for information about the father she had lost almost 60 years before. This is her account of that search and the pilgrimage that followed:

> My first letter was written to the RAF Records Office in Gloucestershire, and while waiting for a reply I started looking for leads on the Internet. During the next few months, I made numerous new acquaintances and reconnected with family members. Gradually I saw the pieces of the jigsaw falling into place as I painstakingly delved into the recesses of my father's past.
>
> I received a reply from the Air Historical Branch (RAF) at Bentley Priory enclosing a log sheet about my father's accident and details of where he was buried. The following is an excerpt:

Reginald Sankey.

Thank you for your letter dated 11 December 2002 seeking the circumstances surrounding the death of your father, 77473 Pilot Officer Reginald Charles Sankey, who sadly lost his life whilst serving with the Royal Air Force during the Second World War.

The information from the Casualty File states that your father was employed as a flying instructor attached to No. 5 Elementary Flying Training School, based at RAF Meir, Stoke-on-Trent, Staffordshire. He was taking part in a dual-instrument training flight with 742573 Sergeant Dennis Arthur Green as his pupil. They were flying Magister N3852 on 2 July 1940 when it hit some high-tension cables which run across a small valley, crashing at approximately 1405 hours at Beechcliff, Trentham, near Stoke. Your father's aircraft was seen to be diving and climbing before the tip of the left wing struck the overhead cables, sending the aircraft into a spin. Sadly both he and Sergeant Green lost their lives in the accident. They are both buried in Longton cemetery.

I started contacting sources in Stoke-on-Trent where my father had been stationed for a short while. It was now becoming clear that a trip to England would be the next step in the search, and that Staffordshire would be the place to start.

Stoke-on-Trent

The pilgrimage began in Stoke-on-Trent. Accompanied by Peter, an old family friend who also lives in Canada, I travelled to the Midlands by train and booked into the North Stafford Hotel. We met and dined with our friends Betty and Stanley Joseph, who had generously driven up from Sussex especially to see us and to drive us to our intended points of interest. Peter and Stanley were both in the RAF during the Second World War – Peter received his training in England, and Stanley received his at Goderich, on Lake Huron, here in Canada – and thus were obliquely interested in my quest.

Beechcliff, Trentham – Site of Accident

We asked at least four people in the approximate neighbourhood if they knew where Beechcliff was located. We had so many conflicting leads that in the end we decided to investigate each and every possibility for ourselves.

After we had back-tracked up and down many, many turnings, we found a range of high hills and a valley criss-crossed by electricity pylons. As the same features had been described in the letter from the Ministry of Defence, plus a nudge from my female intuition, I decided to take photographs of the area, hoping that I had been led to the correct site. At the end of the day a resident in the town surmised that the hill we described to him was probably Beechcliff.

[*Author's note*: In 2006, with the help of senior residents of Tittensor, I was able to discover an eye-witness to the accident who identified the exact field where the plane came down. The crash site is in Beechdale Lane at the point where the lane reaches a bridge over the M6. The motorway now runs through the outer edge of the field.]

Meir Aerodrome in 2003

After wandering around Meir and finding nothing resembling a runway or control tower, we asked a passer-by if she knew where the old wartime aerodrome had been located, and she replied: 'You are standing on part of it.' We found a few barely recognizable relics of the hangers, which were in the process of being bulldozed to make room for new housing. If we had visited Meir a few weeks or maybe days later, even this evidence would have been erased from memory and I would never have seen proof of its existence. I was surprised, to say the least, that there was absolutely no indication that an RAF airfield had ever existed in the town – we were unable to discover even a small plaque commemorating its active past.

[*Author's note*: There has been a small plaque since 2002 in the entrance to the B & Q Warehouse, which replaced Staffordshire Potteries Ltd. It reads: 'This B & Q Warehouse has been built on the site of Meir Airfield which was used during the Second World War. This plaque was unveiled by George Stevenson MP on 15 February 2002 and commemorates those servicemen and women who sacrificed their lives for this country.' A more substantial memorial is long overdue.]

Longton Cemetery

When we arrived at the huge cemetery it was starting to rain, and the grass and flowers were sparkling with moisture and the air was fresh. Fortunately, we found my father's grave relatively easily, thanks to an elderly gentleman and his niece who happened to be walking in the cemetery that day. After we introduced ourselves, they graciously led us to a shaded enclosure where the War Graves section lies.

The area is enclosed by a thick, waist-high hedge and is slightly removed from the other burial sites. My father's was one of seven graves, all of which had been well tended, and several had fresh flowers placed upon them. Although the headstones were reminiscent of the many which we had previously seen in European War Cemeteries, these understandably were even more poignant. Carol and Fred, our angels in disguise, led us to a

The war graves section at Longton Cemetery. Pilot Officer Sankey's grave is the first left, front row.

nearby florist who gave me water and towels to clean the headstone before I placed my offering of flowers on the grave. Before our parting, they said that in future, during their frequent walks in the cemetery, they would visit my father's grave in memory of their meeting with us.

As I placed a deep red rose at the head of my father's grave, I expected that emotions would come to the surface but was surprised to find how strong the emotions actually were. We took several photographs when the sun came out for a little while, and I left feeling peaceful and happy that I had discovered where my father had been laid to rest so many years ago.

*

Meir Today, Gone Tomorrow was the title Nicholas Cartlidge gave to his last book, and certainly much of the village we knew has gone, especially since the controversial A50 was driven through its heart. The promised 'boom town' did not materialise – indeed, if anything, there is an air of dilapidation about the place. The Broadway Cinema closed in 1971, its last film being *Hallo, Goodbye*. Described as the 'grandest picture palace in the Potteries', it was later demolished and the site is now a rather forlorn-looking parking lot.

The Drill Hall with its miniature rifle-range also vanished, as did the ATC hut. Staffordshire Potteries, which once produced more than three million earthenware mugs a month at Meir, was taken over by Coloroll in 1986, which itself went into receivership in 1990. After a management buyout, the ceramics division continued to trade as Staffordshire Tableware Ltd, but this too went into receivership in 1999. The former Longton High School in Sandon Road has been razed to the ground and replaced. The wartime 'shadow factory' at Blythe Bridge – latterly the Indesit cooker plant – closed in 2007. The King's Arms at the crossroads is the latest – and nearly the last – of Meir's fine old buildings to be demolished after attempts to have it listed failed. Once, with its oak-carved panelling, fireplaces, and the full-size bowling green at the back, it played host to pilots, US servicemen, and on one occasion to John F. Kennedy; it was also a useful landmark for pilots flying in to the airfield. Now the site has been developed as a 'state of the art health centre', much to the chagrin of local residents. Of the once busy airfield there are few reminders: a small weathervane shaped like an aircraft on top of Tesco, the plaque in B&Q, and a number of road names that commemorate magnificent men (and women) and their flying machines – Cobham Place, Batten Close, Lysander Road.

But the old ghosts seem reluctant to depart. Although some residents on the Meir Park Estate are unaware that an airfield lies beneath their feet, others are only too conscious of the fact, for at times they see young men in uniform whom they believe to be the spirits of pilots killed there. When Mrs Carolyn Wood and her family moved into their house, her daughter Victoria 'saw figures in uniform in the house and garden from an early age.' Other weird happenings were experienced by the whole family – in particular the draughts:

> You don't really expect new houses to be cold and draughty, but sometimes we'd be sitting in the living room, reading or watching telly, when suddenly there'd be a huge draught come right over us, an icy blast, like 'Whooooosh!'
>
> It sounded like a plane taking off!
>
> It wasn't coming from the window because the window was in front of us. This was coming from behind us. It came straight through the wall and over our heads, and then no sooner had it come than everything was calm again. It unnerved us; we didn't know what it was.
>
> There'd been other strange goings-on too; dark shadows and objects flashing by and I'd sometimes feel there was someone standing next to me when there was nobody there. But it can't have been a ghost. It was a new house and ghosts don't create draughts like the ones we'd been getting.
>
> We got our explanation when my daughter was doing a project about the local area. After borrowing some 1950s Ordnance Survey maps, we discovered that our house was built right in the middle of what used to be the runway of the Meir Aerodrome.
>
> Our draught was not just a draught any more. It was a plane taking off from or landing on that runway. It was an echo of the past.

Selected Bibliography

George Barber, *From Workhouse to Lord Mayor* (privately printed, 1937)

Graham Bebbington, *Trentham at War* (Leek, 1995) and *Trentham Reflections* (Leek, 2005)

Alec Brew, *Staffordshire and Black Country Airfields* (Chalford, 1997)

Nicholas Cartlidge, *Meir Today, Gone Tomorrow* (Leek, 2004)

Martin Chorlton, *Staffordshire Airfields in the Second World War* (Berkshire, 2007)

Eric Clutton, *An Aeroplane Called FRED* (privately printed, 2003)

Len Deighton, *Battle of Britain* (London, 1980)

Ken Delve, *The Military Airfields of Britain: Wales and the West Midlands* (Wiltshire, 2007)

Michael Fahie, *A Harvest of Memories: The Life of Pauline Gower, MBE* (Peterborough, 1995)

Anton Gill, *The Great Escape* (London, 2002)

Midge Gillies, *Amy Johnson: Queen of the Air* (London, 2003)

John Godwin, *Early Aeronautics in Staffordshire* (1986)

Harold Hales, *The Autobiography of The Card* (London, no date)

Alex Henshaw, *The Flight of the Mew Gull* (London, 1980)

Gary Jenkins, *'Colonel' Cody and the Flying Cathedral* (London, 1999)

Judy Lomax, *Women of the Air* (New York, 1987)

Lord Longford, *John Fitzgerald Kennedy* (London, 1976)

Roger Lycett-Smith, *Airfield Focus: 34(Meir)* (Peterborough, 1998)

Ian Mackersey, *Jean Batten: the Garbo of the Skies* (London, 1991)

C. A. Miller, *Rootes Securities Ltd: Aircraft Division (A History of the Stoke Factories 1940-45)* (privately printed)

Gordon Mitchell, *R. J. Mitchell* (Buckinghamshire, 1986)

Geoffrey Page, *Shot Down in Flames* (London, 1999)

Desmond Plunkett (and the Revd R. Pletts), *The Man Who Would Not Die* (Durham, 2000)

Ken Rees (with Karen Arrandale), *Lie in the Dark and Listen* (London, 2004)

Peter Reese, *The Flying Cowboy* (Stroud, 2008)

Dolly Shepherd (with Molly Sedgwick and Peter Hearn), *When the 'Chute*

Went Up: the Adventures of an Edwardian Lady Parachutist (London, 1984)

Christopher Shores and Clive Williams, *Aces High* (London, 1994)

Christopher Shores, *Those Other Eagles* (London, 2004)

David J. Smith, *Military Airfields of Wales and the North West*, vol.3 (Cambridge, 1981)

Richard C. Smith, *Hornchurch Eagles* (London, 2002)

Edward Sniders, *Flying In, Walking Out* (South Yorkshire, 1999)

Charles Strasser, *From Refugee to OBE* (Florida, 2007)

Harry Ward (with Peter Hearn), *The Yorkshire Birdman* (London, 1990)

Giles Whitell, *Spitfire Women of World War II* (London, 2007)

Kenneth G. Wynn, *Men of the Battle of Britain* (Norfolk, 1989)

Newspapers: *City Times, Evening Sentinel, Newcastle Times, Staffordshire Advertiser, Staffordshire Sentinel*, and the *Weekly Sentinel*.

Quotations from the letters of Eric Bann and the war memoir of Dennis Armitage are from *Eric* (1988) and *Squadron Leader Dennis Armitage, DFC*, (1989), two pamphlets issued by the Macclesfield Historical Aviation Society.

Unpublished material:

The National Archives hold the combat reports of Eric Lock (Air 27/428) and Trevor Oldfield (Air 27/748) quoted in the text.

The log books of Amy Johnson, Bill Hodgson, R. J. Mitchell, and Jim Mollison were consulted on my behalf by relatives or the museums that now hold them.

Index